SCOTLAND'S RURAL LAND USE AGENCIES

The history and effectiveness in Scotland of
the Forestry Commission
Nature Conservancy Council and
Countryside Commission for Scotland

SCOTLAND'S RURAL LAND USE AGENCIES

The history and effectiveness in Scotland of
the Forestry Commission
Nature Conservancy Council and
Countryside Commission for Scotland

Donald Mackay

SCOTTISH CULTURAL PRESS

First published 1995
by
Scottish Cultural Press
PO Box 106
Aberdeen AB9 8ZE, Scotland
Tel: 01224 583777
Fax: 01224 575337

British Library Cataloguing in Publication Data
A catalogue record for this book is available
from the British Library

ISBN: 1 898218 31 5

The author acknowledges with thanks a grant from
the Carnegie Trust for the Universities of Scotland
towards the publication of this volume

Printed by Redwood Books, Trowbridge, Wiltshire

CONTENTS

LIST OF FIGURES AND TABLES

AUTHOR'S NOTE

As it could have a bearing on the interpretation of events and even on the selection of material, it is necessary at this point in the book to refer to the author's own background. His entire working life was spent in the British Civil Service, and almost wholly in the Scottish Office. From 1975 to 1978, and again from 1986 to 1988, he was in that part of the Scottish Development Department responsible for planning and land use, involving *inter alia* sponsorship of the CCS and liaison with the NCC and FC. The intervening period (1978 to 1986) was spent in the Department of Agriculture and Fisheries for Scotland (DAFS) – now renamed Scottish Office Agriculture and Fisheries Department (SOAFD) – first as head of the Land Use division, with responsibilities towards forestry and nature conservation, and second as under–secretary responsible for the commodity and land use divisions.

On the positive side, this first–hand involvement with land use in general and the agencies in particular gave the author something of the character of a privileged observer, if not an 'inside actor'. It has certainly assisted in sifting through the agencies' papers, and in conducting interviews with people connected with the agencies, whose help is gratefully acknowledged.

On the other hand, this 'inside track' position has conferred some disadvantages. The fact that the author is subject to the Official Secrets Acts has not affected the study directly; however, it made it difficult for him to take DAFS/SOAFD into consideration along with the land use agencies. This was a course urged upon him initially, and one which had much to commend it in principle – because the agriculture Department has been by common consent the biggest single influence upon Scottish land use during this century. It is, however, in no sense an agency: and it is on the agency concept that the present investigation is focused. Moreover, a study widened to embrace DAFS/SOAFD could not in practical terms have been handled by a single individual; or, to put it another way, the inquiry into the organs responsible for land use would have had to be redesigned and pursued in less depth.

More serious, perhaps, is the possibility of observer bias because of prejudices retained from the author's Scottish Office career. The conclusions reached must, of course, remain his sole responsibility; however, independent critics were shown drafts of the analytical chapters for initial comment.

Some unevenness might be noted in the treatment of personalities in the agencies. This may be partly accounted for, in the case of recent office–holders, by the author's own involvement with the individuals concerned, which makes it difficult to express a view on their personal input or effectiveness. In any case, it is arguable that personalities have been less significant in the performance of the agencies than structural factors.

Every effort has been made to identify sources not merely of data but also of informed opinions and judgments, and to make the appropriate attributions. Where an opinion concerning a recent event or decision is recorded without a reference, it can be attributed to the author's personal judgment or recollection.

ACKNOWLEDGMENTS

This book could not have been written without unstinted help received from a variety of sources.

The author would wish to thank first the 'agencies' themselves for providing facilities for study, papers, copying services, etc. Mention should especially be made of Alwyn Coupe, Dr Rod Fairley, Helen Forster and Freda Ross (all now of Scottish Natural Heritage), and of Ros Bull, Peter Edwards and Tim Rollinson (Forestry Commission). Their cooperation and personal kindness has been much appreciated.

The author had formative discussions with a number of individuals in the early stages of the work, and he would like to acknowledge their help most warmly. They include Dr Morton Boyd, Roger Bradley, Duncan Campbell, Professor Terry Coppock, Ronnie Cramond, Dr Rod Fairley, Dr John Francis, Professor Bill Heal, Sir Alan Hume, Alastair Scott, and Professor Michael Usher.

Various people were kind enough to read parts of the text and to offer helpful comments. Among these were Dr Bob Aitken, Lord Arbuthnott, Dr Jean Balfour, Dr Morton Boyd, Peter Clarke, John Compton, Bill Gauld, Tim Hornsby, John Mackay, Dr Bill Mutch, Tim Rollinson, Professor Chris Smout and Alexander Trotter. Naturally none of these can be held responsible for the accuracy of the statements or the nature or validity of the views expressed. Nevertheless, each has made a contribution for which the author is grateful.

The author would wish to record his appreciation of the guidance and help given to him by the Department of Geography in Aberdeen University. He acknowledges in particular the support given by Dr Sandy Mather, and the stimulus offered by his colleagues – among whom mention should be made of Professor Frank Lyall and Dr Jeff Stone.

Finally, the author feels deeply thankful to his wife Elizabeth, who has borne with patience and good humour a fair degree of neglect during the research for and writing up of the book, and has repaid good for evil by making helpful suggestions at various stages.

ACRONYMS AND ABBREVIATIONS

The practice generally followed is to cite the entity concerned at its first occurrence in a chapter or Part by its full title, with the abbreviation immediately following in brackets, eg Forestry Commission (FC).

AGLV	Area of Great Landscape Value	NCCS	Nature Conservancy Council for Scotland
AR	Annual Report		
ASPC	Area of Special Planning Control	NCGB	Nature Conservation in Great Britain
CAP	Common Agricultural Policy	NCR	Nature Conservation Review
CAS	Centre for Agricultural Strategy	NDPB	non-departmental public body
CCEW	Countryside Commission	NERC	Natural Environment Research Council
CCS	Countryside Commission for Scotland		
		NFU	National Farmers Union
CEED	UK Centre for Economic and Environmental Development	NGO	non-governmental organisation
		NNR	National Nature Reserve
COSLA	Convention of Scottish Local Authorities	NPDA	National Park Direction Area
		NRA	nature reserve agreement
CSD	Chief Scientist Directorate	NSA	National Scenic Area
CTT	Capital Transfer Tax	NTS	National Trust for Scotland
DAFS	Department of Agriculture and Fisheries for Scotland	PAC	Public Accounts Committee
		PDO	potentially damaging operation
DOAS	Department of Agriculture for Scotland	PWFP	Post-War Forestry Policy
		RAC	Regional Advisory Committee
EC	European Community	RDC	Red Deer Commission
EU	European Union	RSAS	Royal Scottish Arboricultural Society
FC	Forestry Commission	RSFS	Royal Scottish Forestry Society
FICGB	Forestry Industry Committee of Great Britain	RSPB	Royal Society for the Protection of Birds
FWH	forest workers holding	SAC	Scottish Advisory Committee
GB	Great Britain	SDD	Scottish Development Department
ha	hectare	SF	Scottish Forestry
HC	House of Commons	SLF	Scottish Landowners Federation
HFRO	Hill Farming Research Organisation	SNH	Scottish Natural Heritage
HGTAC	Home Grown Timber Advisory Committee	SOAFD	Scottish Office Agriculture and Fisheries Department
HIDB	Highlands and Islands Development Board	SOEnD	Scottish Office Environment Department
HIE	Highlands and Islands Enterprise	SSSI	Site of Special Scientific Interest
HL	House of Lords	STB	Scottish Tourist Board
ITE	Institute of Terrestrial Ecology	SWOA	Scottish Woodland Owners Association
JNCC	Joint Nature Conservation Committee		
MLURI	Macaulay Land Use Research Institute	SWT	Scottish Wildlife Trust
		TGO	Timber Growers Organisation
NAO	National Audit Office	TGUK	Timber Growers UK
NC	Nature Conservancy	WPO	Wood Production Outlook
NCC	Nature Conservancy Council		

I

SCOPE

AND

METHODOLOGY

Glen Doll - blanket planting

1

INTRODUCTION

This book assesses the effectiveness in Scotland of three Government–appointed agencies concerned with rural land use: the Forestry Commission (FC), the Nature Conservancy/Nature Conservancy Council (NC/NCC), and the Countryside Commission for Scotland (CCS). Not only have these bodies individually had major impacts on land use, but through their coverage of three key sectors of the rural environment – woodland, wildlife and landscape – they have also had the opportunity jointly to bring about, or to influence, significant changes in the face of Scotland.

There is a special reason for undertaking a review at this particular time.

In April 1992 the three agencies were radically reconstructed. The FC was divided into two functional arms – the Forestry Authority, responsible for regulation of forestry, and Forest Enterprise for the management of the publicly-owned forestry estate built up by the Commission mainly since the Second World War. The NCC was split geographically – into separate units for England, Scotland and Wales – and the Scottish unit was combined with CCS to form a new agency, Scottish Natural Heritage (SNH).

The changes were described as having been made in response to criticism – not least in Scotland – of the structure and performance of the pre–1992 agencies. It therefore seems timely to assess the record and effectiveness of the three agencies in relation to Scotland, where both afforestation and nature conservation have been particularly active and controversial, and have had significant effects on land use. So far as is known, no such project has been attempted hitherto, either for Scotland or for England and Wales.

Before investigating the detailed evidence bearing upon the performance of the three agencies, it is necessary to answer some basic questions:

a. To what extent, and why, do governments feel obliged to control or influence rural land use?
b. Why should they choose to do so (as they do to quite a marked extent) through appointed agencies rather than directly?
c. What are the characteristics which appointed agencies possess, or acquire, and how do the agencies relate to central government?
d. How far can they be held responsible for their own success, or the lack of it?
e. In what ways does Scotland commend itself as a proving ground for the performance of rural land-use agencies?

A different group of questions concerns methodology and approach. What sort of background information should be obtained against which to appraise the performance of each agency? How can their effectiveness be measured, and by what criteria is it legitimate to reach a 'verdict'? What degree of robustness can be attached to the conclusions reached?

State intervention in rural land use

In Scotland, as elsewhere in the developed world, the pattern of rural land use is mainly the result of a series of decisions taken by individual land owners or occupiers. 'Decisions' is a somewhat grandiose term for what in many cases will be a constrained response to market pressures, or an unthinking habit of continuing what has always been done in the past, or a failure to do anything very much at all. But the choice whether and how to act will be generally attributed to the person (or – increasingly – the corporate body) in occupation of the land (Lowe et al. 1992). That picture has however to be qualified.

Progressively in the Western world during this century, the freedom of the individual to make whatever use he chooses of his land has been narrowed by 'state' action. The factors influencing the state to intervene vary widely, but broadly speaking they hinge on a recognition, or a belief, that the unfettered play of market forces is acting somehow against – or not sufficiently in – the public interest. Of course much depends on the view which the state takes of its own role: whether as the defender of a particular interest or class of society, as arbiter among different groups in society, or as exercising a stewardship responsibility. This last attitude, which is becoming more prevalent in the western world, reflects the deeply held belief that land is not merely a commodity but also a kind of heritage of which the occupier *pro tempore* is a trustee (Mather 1986, Cloke 1989).

State intervention may take any of a number of forms. Cloke (1989) conveniently summarises these under the headings *statutory regulation* (whether of land use or of land occupancy), *fiscal or monetary constraints* or inducements, and taking land into *public ownership.* Such measures may be introduced on their own or in combination. As an example, during and subsequent to the Second World War, when food production in the United Kingdom (UK) was a national priority, a failure in crop husbandry became a statutory offence and could result in the removal of the occupier. At the same time, production was encouraged by substantial grants of both a capital and a recurrent nature, and by subsidies on farm produce. An elaborate network of agricultural executive committees was created to administer grants and enforce compliance (Symon 1959).

The intensity of state pressure on land use comes and goes, depending on the strength of public opinion and the ideological standpoint of the party in power, as well as on objective factors. It has had a general tendency to increase. The history of governmental assistance to farming in Western Europe throughout the twentieth century provides a good illustration of the prevailing trend – ranging from rigid free-trade policies at the start of the century, through total support and protectionism in mid–century, to an uneasy synthesis of subsidy, quota and set–aside at present (Tracy 1989).

Alongside the farm policies of the period there have to be set the concerns to make agricultural land available for forestry on the one hand, and for urban uses on the other. The combination of all these policy trends makes it difficult to trace, on the ground, how effective they have been in directing land use – though there is no reason to doubt that each has had a significant influence.

Agriculture became the focus of attention for Western European governments in the mid–twentieth century because it met a human need which was believed to be vulnerable to world political or economic forces. At about the same time, in the UK in particular, rural land began to be perceived as a resource in its own right, requiring positive planning and indeed protection against certain kinds of development. Thus it was that in the UK three massive statutes (with their Scottish counterparts), which still form the pillars of rural policy today, came to be enacted within a three year period – the Agriculture Act 1947, the Town and Country Planning Act 1947 and the National Parks and Access to the Countryside Act 1949.

The role of governments and agencies[1]

A study of these three Acts is instructive in showing how government in the UK tends to approach the control of land use. The statutes, long and involved as they are, do not concern themselves to any extent with particular uses of land. Rather they are devoted to defining *concepts* – whether of good husbandry, or of change of use, or of areas of scientific interest – around which control measures can be formulated, and to establishing *machinery, outside government itself,* for the enforcement of control.

Why is it that governments which are thoroughly interventionist in spirit seem nevertheless reluctant to take upon themselves the execution of the policies they are anxious to see implemented? This is not a characteristic confined to the UK, or indeed to policies relating to land use. Hood (1982) finds what he calls 'the growth of government at the margins' during the second half of the twentieth century somewhat mystifying, flying as it does in the face of a philosophy which holds that the normal form of administrative organ is a ministerial Department. The only justification he proposes for the creation of extra–governmental machinery is that formal independence from Whitehall of a particular body will enable it to act dynamically and without red tape to tackle some important task. [2]

The growth of agencies to carry out significant functions ought, however, to be perceived as neither monstrous nor mysterious. Government Departments or Ministers facing new and detailed responsibilities do not rush to take upon themselves the burden either of defining or enforcing them (Wilding 1982). Their first reaction is to cast around for some existing machinery (local government being the obvious first target) upon which the duty of implementation can be devolved. If none is deemed suitable, the next option is to create such a body. Ministers and Parliament have to be satisfied that there is sufficient answerability both for the execution of functions and for the expenditure of monies provided. If that hurdle can be surmounted (and it is in practice a very easy one to surmount) the Department can heave a sigh of relief, for the problems of establishing and 'sponsoring' an agency seem much less than those of carrying out a function 'in–house'. Such considerations have ruled in the UK for long enough, since the founding of the Navy Board in 1662, through the creation of the Boards of Health, Education and Agriculture in the late nineteenth century, to the enormous growth of 'quangos' at the present. Only where a function is seen to be getting much too important for an agency to handle – as happened during the Second World War – will government step in to reclaim it to its bosom.

It is understandable, however, that recent commentators have expressed alarm at the increase of 'intermediate government' in Britain today. The point is that the creation of agencies, in itself eminently defensible as a means of getting things done, has been so random and *ad hoc* – uncontrolled both as to form and as to the means of answerability prescribed for each. No one knows how many agencies there are, let alone exercises any effective monitoring function over them (Hood 1982). Each sponsoring Department has done what has seemed right in its own eyes, and no amount of quango–hunting appears to have had more than the slightest effect (Holland and Fallon 1978, Pliatzky 1980, Barker 1982). When the Conservative party claimed, in its 1983 election manifesto, that the Thatcher government had slain hundreds of agencies since 1979, the reality was that the net 'body-count' had actually increased (Hood and Schuppert 1988). In the late 1980s and 1990s things have taken a new turn, with a proliferation of bodies concerned with the promotion of industrial growth, housing or health but purporting to have some of the character of a commercial enterprise.[3] Agencies are certainly topical, and the notion of assessing their effectiveness is equally in fashion, with the emphasis of the current Government on evaluation and monitoring of performance, not merely in economic but also in environmental terms (UK Government 1993).

The situation in other Western countries is somewhat different[4] for, though agencies exist, there are few with the precise character of the typical UK agency. The distinguishing features of the UK, which have made the agency phenomenon so striking, are the absence of a written constitution and the practical dominance of central government over the legislature (Johnson 1982).

Although UK agencies come in all shapes and sizes, there are family likenesses among the major agencies handling executive functions. This may owe something to the rationalising efforts of Pliatzky and the Treasury, but it is due mainly to the simple fact that a civil servant designing a new agency does not start from scratch but reaches out for a handy precedent to follow. The features which are more or less common among major agencies include the following:

> Appointment and term of office of chairman and members
> Appointment and tenure of chief officers
> Executive and advisory powers and duties
> Powers of Ministerial direction and dismissal
> Means of provision of Exchequer finance
> Accountability for receipts
> Requirement to submit annual report.

These tell us next to nothing about the working relationship between an agency and its sponsor Department. This depends to some extent on the nature of the statutory functions conferred on the agency, some of which may be absolute and not subject to review: in others the Department may be able to 'second–guess' the agency constantly. More important is the degree of trust placed by Ministers and civil servants in the chairman and chief executive. But an agency will rarely be coerced into effectiveness by pressure from a Minister, or by the day–to–day interference of his Department. If a Minister wants to see a change in the direction of an agency's policy or effort, he will rarely resort to the use of his power of direction: more likely he will talk to the chairman – or, in extremity, replace him.

The survival capacity of UK agencies, through widely different political regimes, is remarkable but has not attracted much academic analysis. Until recently most agencies have arisen under Labour administrations, in circumstances where it is safe to say that a Conservative government would not have felt the same urge to legislate. Rarely, however, has an agency, once created, come under serious threat from a successor government of a different political hue. This is certainly true of environmental agencies, which come to be seen as doing a useful job and to some extent absorbing criticism which would otherwise focus on the Minister (O'Riordan 1982). After a period the origins of a particular agency will become dimmed in the eyes of politicians, and the agency may find that it cannot count on the unqualified support of the party that set it up, especially when that party is in government. This is a factor which, in the eyes of some, has influenced land use agencies, perhaps unconsciously, towards adopting 'safe' policies which would not be assailed from either side of the ideological divide. It is, at any rate, the case that the agencies which form the object of this study have not come under sustained party political attack as regards the main thrust of their functions. The upheavals to which they have been subjected – dramatic as they have been in recent years – stem from other factors.

A government tends to view an agency as a means of achieving its own ends. But – notwithstanding the constitutional dominance of the Minister and his Department – an agency once established invariably takes on a life of its own. It struggles to justify its existence; it seeks to extend its influence; and it establishes networks in the 'outside' world which the government may neither foresee nor approve. This is particularly true of 'single–issue' agencies. Thus arises the secondary phenomenon of the 'client group' – a penumbra of private bodies or associations which cluster around the agency, all with a particular interest in its agenda. In time these may even become more closely involved by way of being regularly consulted by the agency, or even receiving assistance from it (the ramifications in relation to private industry are explored in Barker [1982], and in relation to US environmental groups in Hays [1988]). Finally there is what might be called the tertiary emergence of relationships among agencies themselves (Barker 1982).

The fact that agencies develop their own style and relationships should not cause surprise. Volumes have been written about the 'personality' of organisations, even within a monolithic public service (eg Simon 1956, Scott 1967, Hood and Dunsire 1981, Cyert and March 1992). The very act of deliberately externalising the administration of a function by creating an agency is in effect an invitation to it to assume a personality and to exercise it. But there is a unique feature of UK agencies, unmatched in its prevalence anywhere in the world, which enhances their sense of autonomy. A huge army – Holland (1979) estimated their number at over 40,000 – of private citizens occupy agency appointments in the gift of Ministers. Of these, around 75 per cent are unpaid, while of those who are paid only a tiny fraction receive more than a nominal fee (Davies 1982).

Thus the prevailing ethos in agencies is one of voluntary service, in the same tradition as that of the host of voluntary bodies which provide so much of the back–up for the social services of the UK. If the board of a public agency thinks of itself as doing good works out of a sense of public duty, it will not be disposed to be too servile. The commitment of time and energy to the business of the agency will not have been made without any thought of reward: there will be the satisfaction of worthwhile and perhaps creative activity, the sense of having been entrusted with public responsibility – even with state secrets – the personal prestige, and maybe a fleeting hope of recognition through the Honours system. A kind of unspoken bargain has been struck. The Department knows that in return for an input of voluntary effort and wisdom it must be prepared to grant the agency a measure of self–determination.

If the 'Board members' of an agency are entitled to feel and exercise a degree of freedom in determining policy, it is unlikely that the chief officers will feel the same sense of exhilaration in carrying out their duties. The role of a chief officer is not, in present circumstances, an enviable one. This is essentially because of the financial and management disciplines which have become ever more stringent in the public service since 1979. The stated object is to achieve 'value for money', a concept which will be referred to repeatedly in this volume. These disciplines impinge upon agencies with a double force: first, chief officers are required, at least annually, to produce financial plans and so–called 'corporate strategies' in as much detail as any part of the Civil Service; second, the sponsoring Department will tend to give the agency's management documents a particularly thorough scrutiny, since they will become part of the Department's own financial statements. It is worth stressing that all this paper planning will not necessarily result in the agency being held on a tighter policy rein or being required to make do on a smaller budget. What it does invariably mean is that the senior staff have to spend a higher proportion of their time 'managing', whether in connection with the annual budgeting exercise, or in justification of specific projects, or in staffing. An indirect result is that there is now much more written material for Parliamentary select committees and the like to get their teeth into when they feel the urge to examine the work of agencies – a tendency which is greatly on the increase. How things have changed regarding agencies since a senior civil servant wrote over a decade ago:

> The effort involved in seeking to control their expenditure is likely to be so great, if one tries to do it in detail, that we shouldn't have the means to do it even if we were right to try (Wilding 1982)[5].

Rural land use agencies in Scotland

Scotland has had more than its quota of academic attention so far as agencies are concerned. Partly this is due to the fact that a number of specialists in the field (eg Hogwood, Keating and Hood) have had their base, temporarily at least, in Scotland. Hogwood (1982) argues that Scotland serves as a particularly useful test bed because of the focus it provides on a limited geographical area, with its own central government administration and its own political institutions. However true this may be in overall terms, it is certainly so as regards rural land use, where the number and variety of distinctive agencies with a finger in the pie is remarkable. Those unique to Scotland include Highlands and Islands Enterprise (HIE), Scottish Enterprise, the Red Deer Commission (RDC), the Crofters Commission, the Scottish Agricultural College and the Macaulay Land Use Research Institute. A further group of agencies which over the years either have operated on both sides of the Border or have close counterparts south of the Border includes the Forestry Commission, the Nature Conservancy Council and the Countryside Commission for Scotland.

Why then light upon this latter group only for a study of land use agencies[6] in Scotland? Principally, because of the peculiar significance of these bodies for Scottish rural land use. Of all the agencies, these are the ones which have had the greatest responsibility, and the greatest potential, for effecting (or resisting) land use change. This is not to ignore the contribution of the other agencies mentioned above, but simply to make the distinction that some of them – eg HIE/Scottish Enterprise – have their focus elsewhere than in land use, while others – eg RDC/Crofter Commission – have a geographically limited land use focus. Over the past two decades at any rate, the FC, NCC and CCS have been the big three agencies in Scottish rural land use (Select Committee on Scottish Affairs, 1972 HC 51–xix, A.2172), and land use has been their primary field.[7]

A second reason for choosing these agencies for consideration is that two of them – FC and NCC – have had an even wider scope, namely the whole of Great Britain. It is a rewarding field of inquiry to examine how this type of agency has discharged its functions over a distinctive part of its territory, how far it has adapted its style and organisation to 'regional' requirements, and how its image and reputation have fared in the region concerned. It is relevant that the largest landholdings of both bodies occur in Scotland, and that the FC's headquarters is in Edinburgh. Also that the agencies have recently been radically reorganised – and for reasons which have much to do with Scotland.

No claim is made here that the agencies in question have the overriding say in rural land use in Scotland. The biggest single regulator of land use has been and will continue to be the Scottish Office, operating through its Environment Department (the sponsor for planning and conservation), its Industry Department (sponsor for the Enterprise organisations and tourism) and, above all, the Agriculture Department, which sponsors the farming industry and the grant support system, now virtually a subspecies of the EU Common Agricultural Policy. The contribution of local authorities, too, should not be underrated, through their structure planning powers and, in particular, their ability to prepare indicative strategies for forestry and conservation. Of course, there are all the other agencies previously noted. A helpful diagram showing the relationship among all these organs of government, as they existed in 1988, was drawn up by Fladmark and is reproduced as Fig. 1.

So the agencies under review are operating not on an empty stage but on a very full one, where they are actors rather than directors. Yet theirs is not a minor or supporting role. Each of their remits is clear and far–reaching; each has been equipped with significant statutory powers, finance and manpower; each has had the potential to leave its mark on the Scottish rural scene, for good or ill. These agencies have a status, and a record, which it is both possible and rewarding to analyse and evaluate.

Figure 1: Government and Organisational Relationships in Scotland

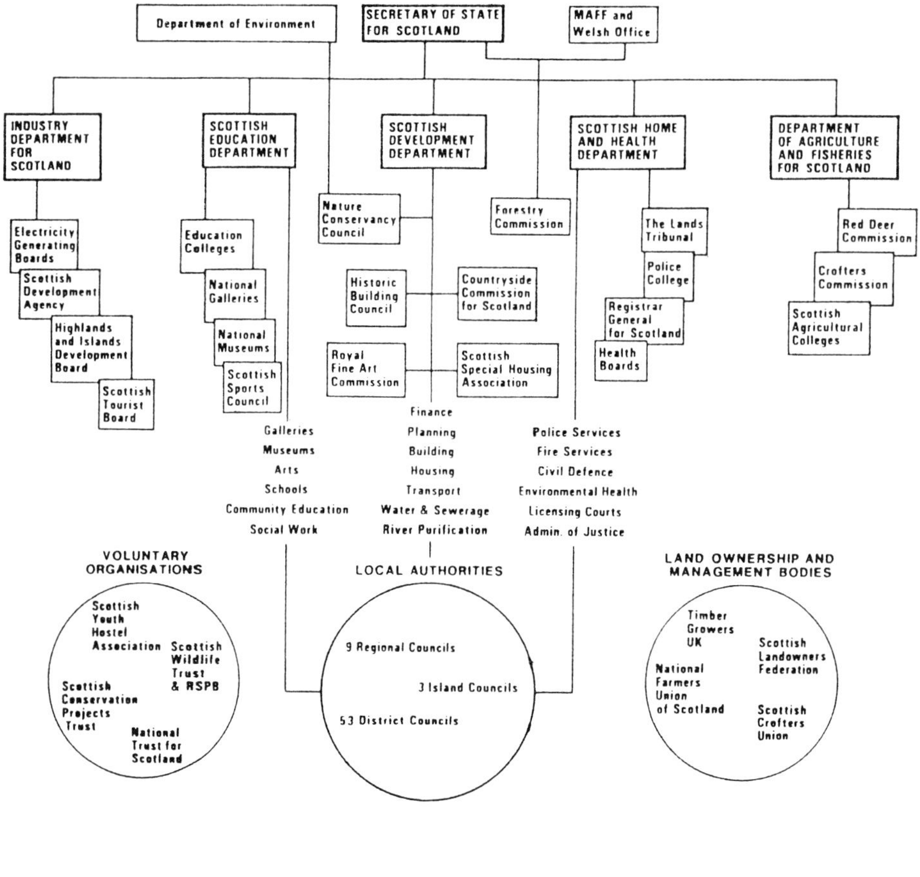

Source: Countryside planning and practice : the Scottish experience (ed. Selman) (1988) p 51

Analysis

Parts II, III and IV of this volume are concerned with how each agency has been constituted; how it has organised itself; how it has sought over the years to influence Scottish rural land use; how it has responded to pressures and external appraisal; and where it stands now. Each agency has been examined so far as possible on a common pattern, to facilitate comparisons at a later stage.

In the descriptive/historical chapters which constitute the bulk of the analysis, extensive use has been made of documents originating with the agencies. In the case of NC/NCC and CCS, these include internal papers made available by SNH. For the FC the main source has been official documents. In each case the viewpoint is, so far as possible, that of the agency itself. The object is not to achieve a conspectus of the land–use situation at any point in time, or to analyse the political or economic forces bearing upon the agencies, or to understand what moved Ministers to appoint particular people or types of people to the governing boards of the agencies throughout their lives. All these are broad, speculative enterprises, whereas the aim here is to establish as objective a database as can be attained, founded on documentary evidence. Obviously selection has been necessary, and the focus is on decisions and developments affecting Scotland in particular.

Evaluation

Part V of this study evaluates the contribution of each agency under investigation; their interactions with each other, and with outside interests; and the lessons which emerge for the practice of 'government-by-agency' in the field of land use.

Evaluation is a tricky concept, especially where it is not sensible, or even feasible, to put a cash value on the end–product. That however is only the start of the problem.

In seeking to appraise the performance of organisations which cannot be tested against a commercial measuring rod, it is helpful to identify some kind of control with which comparisons can be made. Such a control, in the environmental field, might be supplied by land–use agencies in a country where conditions approximated to those of Great Britain. However, although much can be learned from comparisons with other Western countries – and systematic comparison has been made in, for example, Cloke (1989), Hummel and Hilmi (1989) and Mather (1993) – each of the British agencies under review has features which are not paralleled elsewhere.[8] The FC is unique in being both a Government department and an agency; NCC and CCS are unusual in the sharp distinction of their remits, found hardly anywhere else in the Western world, between nature and landscape conservation (Boyd 1983). These features have conditioned the scope and methods of working of the agencies in a way which makes it difficult to compare them closely with institutions abroad, and even more difficult to evaluate comparative performance.

The study therefore proceeds within a looser framework, seeking to identify objectives chosen within the given field by the agency itself, by its departmental sponsor, or by society at large, and seeing how the agency has matched up to these objectives. This presents its own problems. Objectives are often stated with insufficient precision, or they may be inherently 'fuzzy'. They may change gradually, or the background against which they were stated may change, for example in terms of development pressures, economic circumstances, or increased public awareness. Moreover, the agency's success in achieving objectives may be similarly constrained by external factors, such as arbitrary limitations to its budget, its statutory powers, or its staffing. These are considerations which need to be identified and given appropriate weight as evaluation proceeds.

Efficiency

Each agency reports to Government and derives funds from the Exchequer. It is therefore not surprising that each has been subject during its life to a series of financial and management reviews, most of which will have been at the instance of the sponsor Department or the Treasury or the Comptroller and Auditor

General, but some initiated within the agency itself. Their purpose is to establish how well resources have been used in pursuit of the agency's objectives. The measure of success is outputs as against inputs, the elements under review being mainly costs, personnel and units of 'production'. The aim of such reviews is to detect and eliminate 'friction' in the internal working of the agency, and between the agency and its sponsor. Because audits of this type have been carried out rigorously and frequently, it is not necessary to do much more than review their findings.

Effectiveness

Here one gets beyond the mere nuts and bolts of the organisation and crude measures of output, and begins to look critically at its objectives, and the way in which the organisation has set out to attain them. The first problem is to sort out how far objectives have been imposed on agencies, whether by statute or by government policy, and how far they have been chosen by the agency itself.

In practice this is not quite such a fundamental distinction as it sounds. From what has been said already, it will be apparent that agencies are not regarded as blocks of stone. They are accorded a good deal of freedom by Ministers and are indeed expected to make their mark. So even if they are given strong hints by Ministers their duty is to react to them, not just accept them. If they find their statutory powers constricting or inadequate they are expected to press for statutory change. An agency is the custodian of its own conscience, and often of its own destiny.

The most straightforward way of looking at these questions is through the eyes of those with an interest in each agency's field, that is its paymasters (the sponsor Department, the Treasury, Parliament or Parliamentary select committee); its client group; and the wider public (as represented by other professional bodies or agencies, the press, and any indicators of public opinion that may be available). This is essentially analytical work and therefore falls within the earlier sections of the investigation.

An adverse or even a favourable opinion from any or all of these sources need not of course be decisive. One cannot avoid at least raising the further questions of how far the impact of each agency is to be judged 'objectively' beneficial; and whether comparable benefits could have been achieved in some other way.

The drive towards placing objective value on environmental choice and achievement has made progress in recent years (Ahmad et al. 1983–84, Dixon et al. 1986, Pearce et al. 1989, Barde and Pearce 1991). By and large it proceeds by way of surrogate market techniques of assessing aesthetic worth, by manipulating the discounting of market value to give greater weight to more distant futures, and by playing various 'What if?' games to arrive at the public's estimation of how much it would be prepared to forgo in order to safeguard some environmental value or to pay in order to secure one. This sort of calculus forms the stock-in-trade of the environmental manager, whom O'Riordan and Turner (1983) see as an emerging force in the conservation/development debate. But techniques of this kind scarcely get beyond the appraisal of specific *projects*: they have, so far, had little relevance to *policies*. Usher (1986) has attempted to formalise criteria used in the scientific appraisal of nature conservation sites and site selection policies, but his conclusions about achieving objectivity in such criteria are pessimistic. Similarly landscape can be analysed and assessed and placed on a numerical scale of values (Dunn 1974, Brown 1985): but it is note-worthy that in its 1978 appraisal of National Scenic Areas the CCS used a largely intuitive technique instead. It seems that we are some way off from de-vising meaningful quantitative tests for the effectiveness of an organisation whose business is land use.

There may be more fundamental reasons for doubting whether the desirable end–product of a land use agency's work could ever be clear-cut or universally agreed. One of these is that perceptions as to what is desirable in the environ-mental field change over time. Samuel Hays (1988) has charted the develop-ment, first, of the US conservation movement (with its stress on efficient use of material resources, such as water, forests and soils), and then that of the envi-ronmental movement (seeing rivers, forests, wetlands etc as valuable in their own right) which has gradually supplanted it. A similar sequence has been ob-served in Great Britain (Sheail 1976), though on a different time-scale. An agency may and should have a larger perspective and longer–term aims than those of its generation, but it does not stand, nor can it be judged, in abstraction from its generation.

Another reason for caution is that the land–use situation in any country is likely to be the product of a number of conflicting pressures, in which the agency is (as already noted) only one influence out of many. It should be possi-ble to disentangle the agency's part as regards most issues, but a verdict on its overall performance and achievement will always be to some extent a matter of judgment.

It seems, therefore, that a verdict has to await the total review of the agency's record. This will have taken account of such factors as its achievements on the ground, its relations with other interests, its openness to legitimate criticism and its ability to sense and adjust to future trends. It may then be possible to reach some sort of a judgment as to whether the recent organisational changes hold out the prospect of a better distribution of functions and a better resolution of land use issues in Scotland.

Philosophical framework

'Verdict' is perhaps too strong a term for the kind of conclusion which this in-vestigation will arrive at. It has more to do with understanding and explanation than with passing judgment on the agencies' performance. But the concept of explanation itself requires unpacking. As Sayer (1984) has pointed out, social science explanations operate in the area of open systems, not the idealised closed systems with which the physical sciences are concerned, where rigorous proof and repeatability may be looked for. In open systems, patterns of events are not predictable but, in Sayer's view, may be fruitfully analysed and causes hypothesised, for example by demonstrating the existence of relevant mecha-nisms or structures.

O'Riordan, whose interests are in the environmental field, is more sceptical. He concludes that 'the interaction of politics, economics, administration and the law make it all but impossible to disentangle all the relevant factors bearing on a decision or leading to a particular policy' (1982). He particularly draws attention to the equivocal position in which environmental agencies are placed:

... quangos are creatures of the system and exploited by the system... They may not have sufficient information or be expert enough to pronounce definitely on a matter where they feel that action should be taken. Or they may choose to adopt a stance only to find that it is unacceptable to either the government in power or particular pressure groups who may have enough clout to cause political trouble. In neither case, however, are they individually or collectively accountable which, naturally, renders them the focus of attention of any major lobby, environmental or otherwise, when their recommendations are controversial.

In these circumstances how is progress to be made? O'Riordan's prescription is, first, to be aware of the basic principles underlying the institutional process in the country concerned (in this case the UK) and, second, to proceed by way of 'case studies, preferably from the perspective of an inside actor'. This is the method employed here. The institutional framework has been outlined above. In Parts II, III and IV the record of each of the three land use agencies is analysed by way of individual case studies. The 'inside actor' perspective is secured by letting each agency speak for itself.

Even within such a programme there is still room for a variety of emphases. One can approach the work of the agency through the avenue of the personalities involved, whether at board member or official level. Or one can regard the agency's stance on the various issues that confront it as a manifestation of, or a reaction to, hidden but identifiable forces whether of class, sectional interest, or political ideology (Dahl 1961, Lipset 1969). These are meaningful categories, which will be drawn upon from time to time. But the emphasis which has been found most fruitful is that of institutional structure, that is seeking to understand how far the behaviour of each agency is explained by its constitutional status, its place in the scheme of UK public administration, its functional remit, its geographical concentration or decentralisation, the nature of its professional cadre, and its relationship with the client group (Manion and Flowerdew 1982).

Time–frame

It is necessary to go back beyond the dates when the agencies began to operate, as some prior understanding is needed of the pressures leading up to their establishment, the political circumstances which shaped the relevant legislation, and the personalities involved at the start. But, since the focus is on the agencies themselves (FC, NC/NCC and CCS) rather than on their spheres of interest, it is not necessary to survey the whole course of movements and events which gave them birth.

During a period when so much is changing in the world of the land use agencies, it is also necessary to apply a cut-off point to the investigation. Fortunately, this need not be arbitrarily chosen. The first of April 1992 was the date on which CCS and NCCS (Nature Conservancy Council for Scotland) went out of existence and SNH took over. It was also the date on which the management reorganisation of the FC took effect, breaking up the historic unity of the Commission and constituting a distinct Forestry Authority and Forest Enterprise. Since this study is essentially retrospective, it is both appropriate and convenient to treat 31 March 1992 as the terminal date so far as the records of the agencies are concerned. A measure of flexibility will be observed in commenting on later events, or publications, which may have cast their shadow backwards into the time-frame.

NOTES

1. The term 'agency' in this study is used non–technically, with a connotative rather than a denotative function. The object is to get away from the abominable word 'quango' – itself quite incapable of exact definition (Barker 1981). There is another, more precise, option to hand, namely the term 'non–departmental public body' (NDPB) – much used in Government circles. However, because of its clumsiness, it is invariably employed in its acronymic form, which is almost worse than quango, since it cannot be spoken but must always be spelled out. And, in the context of this investigation, there is the even more telling objection that the FC, at least since 1945, has to be regarded as in some sense a government Department and is therefore not a NDPB.

2. The analysis of extra–governmental machinery is taken a good deal further in Hood and Schuppert (1988), which claims to be the first book comparing 'para–government organizations' (PGOs) in western Europe. Unfortunately, PGOs are defined so inclusively as to be of little use for the purposes of this investigation. In terms of scale of jurisdiction, they comprise everything from a transnational body (like a bridge authority spanning a frontier between two countries) to a local bus enterprise. In terms of legal or constitutional type, they include both public agencies (of the kind being considered here) and private or independent concerns like the Red Cross, the RSPB, or a local housing association.

3. Recent work done by Gay (1993) highlights the significance of this new trend. For one thing, because training and enterprise councils are not counted as NDPBs, and health service bodies are counted separately, they do not feature in the Government statistics which purport to show that the number of quangos diminished by 800 between 1979 and 1992. Accountability in these new bodies tends to be to the 'market' rather than to the public. Patronage is exercised in a more overtly political way: a Government Minister is quoted as saying: 'Well, of course you don't put people in who are in conflict with what you're trying to achieve'. Gay concludes that 'in general the hope of academics in the early 1980s that the decade would see a more rigorous treatment of NDPBs has not been realised'.

4. It is not easy to summarise the agency situation even in countries with a predominantly Western culture. The US boasts a number of very powerful Federal agencies, including several concerned with land use – the Bureau of Land Management, the Fishery and Wildlife Service, the Forest Service and the National Park Service. While functionally these have something in common with UK agencies, they differ in being much more clearly organs of government, each with an immense tract of land to administer and statutory powers and duties which are being continually reinterpreted by the Federal legislature and the courts (Hays 1987). In Germany the federal structure and the predisposition towards legislative rather than administrative process has led to land use functions being directly conferred on the Länder, rather than being carried out through appointed agencies (Woodruffe 1989). Even where publicly–funded agencies have been established, they are typically within the private sector (Schuppert 1988). In France, though agencies abound, they are generally of an enabling variety, especially with the provision of finance, rather than the executors of policy. As in Germany, executive functions tend to rest upon the lower echelons of elected government (Aitchison 1989).

5. The issue of control of agencies is addressed at some length in Hood and Schuppert (1988). They note that in Western countries the tendency has been to be seek to bring agencies to account by making them subject to the oversight normally applied to organs of central government – Parliamentary questioning, audit, common procedural rules etc. This type of accountability – Hood dubs it 'comptrol' – is seen as counter–productive as applied to agencies. Instead, the authors propose a range of miscellaneous but consciously introduced controls – through such mechanisms as built–in client group representation, peer group evaluation, market discipline, and competition among agencies. It is clear that controls of this kind would have a limited application to land use agencies in Scotland.

6. The term 'land use agencies' is used with reluctance, in default of a more precise umbrella term. The trouble is that though all three bodies have been intimately concerned with land use, the extent to which they have been responsible for land use is unclear – indeed this is one of themes taken up at length in Part V. 'Environmental agencies' would not have been an improvement, as it would have given a misleading picture of the roles of the FC and CCS, which include a promotional element.

7. Not however an exclusive field. The FC also has the job of controlling imports of alien species, and of regulating the timber market. As the legatee of NCC and CCS, SNH (*qua* nature conservation) also has responsibilities with regard to alien species, and the protection of species; and (*qua* countryside) for the design of countryside facilities, and for publicity and education.

8. A comparison could, of course, be made between the CCS and the Countryside Commission (CCEW). The two Commissions had many statutory functions in common, and not too great a disparity in staffing (see Table 3). One difficulty would be in assessing the importance of the CCEW's responsibility for the National Parks (ie its inheritance of the functions of the National Parks Commission). This is a factor which was not paralleled in the CCS's remit.

II

FORESTRY

Aonach Mor, Glen Spean, Lochaber – Sitka spruce planting

2

THE FORESTRY COMMISSION

The story of forestry in Great Britain is essentially the story of forest establishment by the Forestry Commission in the twentieth century. Not that there does not exist in Britain semi–natural forest, or estate planting which has its own history and owes nothing to the Commission. But the influence of the FC has been so dominant and pervasive as to have left its mark throughout the whole island, as well as on the entire production scene.

More specifically, the story of forestry in Scotland is also the story of the FC. Because of the monolithic character of the Commission – with its emphasis on national needs and priorities and its lack of a Scottish sub–structure – it is virtually impossible to disentangle the story of twentieth century Scottish forestry from that of Great Britain as a whole. Anderson (1967) has tried to do so – as has James (1981) for England – but neither has succeeded in bringing out the dynamic realities.

Further problems confront the researcher seeking to penetrate the workings of the FC, whether in relation to overall policy or specifically in relation to Scotland. The Commission – anomalous as it must seem in relation to a body with its own independent Chairman and board of directors – has the status of a government Department (Scottish Office 1981)[1] and is thus subject to the Official Secrets Acts. It has not been possible, therefore, within the operation of the 30-year rule, to gain access to the proceedings of the Commission or indeed to any significant number of FC papers other than those which it has chosen to publish.

During its early years the Commission set a high standard of openness towards the private sector and the general public, in terms of the content of its published documents. But as time has gone on, and particularly from 1965 onwards, FC has been sucked more and more into the vortex of Government secrecy: and it appears also to have developed a protective carapace of its own – no doubt in response to the criticism which it has increasingly faced, both from within Government and from outside.

The approach in this chapter is conditioned by these difficulties. An attempt is made to trace the origins and evolution of the FC in its corporate identity, but always with an eye to the implications for Scotland. This is not a parochial approach, because the impact on Scotland has been far greater than on any other part of Great Britain.

Origins

The creation of the FC is one of the more fascinating episodes in the annals of British administration. Unlike most British institutions it did not evolve from anything that went before, but sprang new-minted according to the model projected by its inventors. Nevertheless, behind its emergence lies a considerable history.

As in much of the temperate zone of the world, trees form the natural cover of Great Britain (Miles 1987). The reasons why it does not now have this cover are similar to those for other developed countries, and have been fully documented elsewhere (eg Simmons 1981; Peterken 1985). They were summed up succinctly as long ago as 1808 by Dr J Robertson: 'Men are a foe to woods, in proportion as their numbers increase' (Anderson 1967). In Britain the initial phase of exploitation of the natural forest (up to the end of the seventeenth century) was succeeded by systematic agricultural development lasting throughout the eighteenth century, which obliterated all but patchy residues of forest on the low ground, some of it worked as coppice. In the uplands pastoral agriculture had similar devastating effects: and the nineteenth century passion for grouse moors and deer forests gave the natural vegetation little chance of returning.

Recent forestry in Britain (in the sense of managed tree growth) has been largely confined to the establishment of new woodland. This was taken up with some enthusiasm by the new generation of eighteenth-century landlords, using largely exotic conifers and decorative broadleaves to beautify their estates, and to provide a degree of shelter. Only in the late eighteenth and early nineteenth centuries was there a serious attempt at commercial afforestation – initially prompted by maritime needs for hardwood timber (Acland 1918, Anderson 1967). For this the market declined steadily after the Napoleonic Wars, and from 1850 onwards plantations were increasingly dominated by the quicker-growing conifers – larch and Scots pine. But the overall rate of planting dwindled, as did the standard of silviculture, during what Anderson characterises as a period of 'inaction and a policy of laissez-faire'.

Overall, by the early years of the twentieth century, the wooded area of Britain had shrunk to 1.1m hectares (ha), of which 0.35m ha were in Scotland. This represented less than five per cent of the land area of the country – as against a coverage of upwards of twenty per cent in most of continental Europe. Moreover the product per unit area of British woodland – almost all in private hands, as opposed to the massive State holdings on the Continent – was about half of the German average, and a quarter or less of that obtained from the German state forests (Acland 1918).

The poor state of British forestry did not pass unnoticed in the early years of the century. On the contrary, it was a constant nag on the national conscience. It gave rise to one Government committee of enquiry after another in the years up to the First World War – each coming up with ambitious recommendations for afforestation which were, with equal regularity, put on the shelf.

It is generally believed that the Government's change of heart, and decisive action to promote forestry in Britain, can be attributed simply and solely to the First World War, and to the timber crisis to which it gave rise. This does less than justice to the vision and persistence of an unlikely pressure group which mounted its campaign well before the war clouds came on the horizon.[2]

The Scottish Arboricultural Society was founded in 1854 and acquired the title 'Royal' in 1887. It began as a modest and embattled group: but by 1913, when it celebrated its diamond jubilee, it had attracted a large and varied membership of 1400, including a number from England as well as a range of foreign correspondents. Anderson (1967) by implication characterises the Society as 'a small coterie of Scottish landowners': but this is unfair to the practising foresters at all levels, as well as interested members of the public, who formed an active element in the counsels of the Society, and moreover constituted a majority on its governing council until the First World War.

The Royal Scottish Arboricultural Society (RSAS), as a campaigning body, did not go in for the kind of unreal planting targets which had been the stock-in-trade of most of the Departmental committees in the years from 1885 onwards. Instead, it focused on three simple demands: the establishment of a Board of Forestry for Scotland (parallel to the Board of Agriculture which had recently been set up); the acquisition of areas for practical demonstration of forestry; and a survey of afforestable land in Scotland. These demands were first lodged with the Secretary for Scotland in 1909, and renewed each year thereafter: as it is expressed in the *Transactions* for 1915, 'The Society must continue wearying the Government until they declare a definite policy (on national afforestation)'. But the Society did not rest content with words: it carried out at its own hand a sample survey of the Great Glen to establish its suitability for afforestation.

By 1913 the RSAS had so far wearied the Secretary for Scotland (T M'Kinnon Wood) that he consented to receive a deputation. The Society used blunt language:

'To sum up the situation in a word, the attachment between the Board of Agriculture and forestry is a platonic one, nothing comes of it'.

'Are you suggesting that the Government should buy land [for afforestation]?' asked Wood.

'Yes', replied the deputation, and went on to show that large tracts of suitable land existed in Scotland, at reasonable prices; that forestry represented the only hope for the repopulation of the Highlands; and that experienced men were available. Wood, evidently impressed, nevertheless was able to ease out of personal responsibility by pointing out that the only source of new funds was the Development Commission: once it had made up its mind on helping forestry, that would be the time to create a Forestry Board.

The Society now mounted pressure on the Development Commissioners: but they replied that the Treasury 'were not disposed to find money for the purchase of land for afforestation'; and that a leasing scheme was not acceptable to the landowners. The Society responded with a revised scheme which, it was convinced, would be both fair and acceptable to landowners (*Transactions* for 1915).

By 1916 the RSAS was exulting in the fact that the Government – prompted by the alarming timber deficit created by the war – had at last responded by appointing a special committee (the Acland Committee) to look at post–war forestry development for the UK. But the Society did not relax the pressure. A deputation was sent to Westminster, to enforce upon Scottish MPs not only the importance of afforestation in general, but especially the necessity for a separate Department for forestry (*Transactions* for 1916).

Hitherto the Society's concern had been with Scottish forestry alone. Now it was forced to clarify its policy in a UK context. The RSAS Council was emphatic that the best course was to create a separate forestry agency for the whole of the UK: but it faced spirited opposition from the rank and file. At a special meeting in March 1917 it was strongly argued from the floor that a single central authority would be in effect an English authority, and that Scotland could not be guaranteed its proper share of resources. In any case, Scotland had its own climate, its own preferred species, its different land tenure and the peculiarity of

the crofting system. The Council's reply was scornful. Would it be wise, economical or efficient to divide this small area [UK] into three or four? Look at the
Scottish Board of Agriculture, with its puny resources in staffing, expertise and
research capability compared with the English Board. It would be no more sensible to have a Scottish Post Office. In any case, administration would be fully
devolved to each country: and Scotsmen, being so prominent in forestry, could
be relied upon to rise to the top in a bigger organisation. These arguments
prevailed by a large majority, and the resolution in favour of a single UK agency
was conveyed to the Secretary for Scotland and to the Acland Committee.

The attention given to the work of a small and sectional pressure group may
seem disproportionate, but it seems to be a fact that the Scottish Society was a
prime mover in the creation of a national forest authority. Its contribution may
be contrasted with that of the corresponding English body, the Royal English
Arboricultural Society, which played a negligible – almost negative – role in
these developments.

The Acland Report

By 1916 the coalition Government's mind was strongly exercised over post– war
problems, and a 'Reconstruction Committee' was set up with various sub-committees, one of which was on forestry. Its chairman was the Parliamentary Secretary to the Department of Agriculture, the Rt Hon Francis Acland. How the
members were chosen is shrouded in mystery, but it is clear that the balance was
very strongly pro-forestry. Among the active members none was more influential than Lord Lovat, a remarkable character who had made his mark in fields as
far apart as raising the Lovat Scouts in the Boer War and undertaking the Great
Glen Survey on behalf of the RSAS. Lovat's biographer (Lindley 1935) ascribes
to him the overall plan and direction of the sub-committee's report: if this is correct, it was a master-stroke on Lovat's part to have distanced himself from the
report by a reservation which, in effect, did nothing but hammer home its main
principles.[3]

The report (1918 Cd 8881) was an impressive piece of sustained argument, as
well as of opportunism. Starting with a careful analysis of the poor state of pre-
war forestry in the UK, it went on to detail the long series of enquiries and Departmental committees set up to remedy the situation – all full of noble intentions, but foundering on the lack of an effective mechanism for putting their
findings into practice. The report next looked at the depredations on existing
forests necessitated by the war, and the immense effort – and additional cost –
that had to be put into securing timber from foreign sources. It argued that a
'famine of coniferous timber' was a scenario inevitable not only in a future war
but in a time of peace, because of the manifestly escalating demand for wood
and wood products, and the shrinking supply. The case for a change in policy
was rounded off with an eloquent exposition of the social and economic benefits
of afforestation, in particular the provision of diversified employment for
struggling upland farmers and new smallholders, and the potential for increasing
the national wealth, and the economic usefulness of hitherto 'waste' land.

The next section of the Report set out to quantify the requirements for new
forest development and the extent of available land. The minimum need, said the
Committee, was for a national reserve sufficient to supply three years' wartime
consumption (ie 715,000 ha of conifers and 40,000 ha of hardwoods), in addi-

tion to the restocking of the 1m or more ha existing woodland. The total area of afforestable land in the UK was reckoned at between 1.6m and 2m ha, between two and three times as much as required.

A key piece of argumentation dealt with the machinery for carrying the afforestation plan into effect. Here the Acland Committee drew heavily on the representations of the RSAS, in bringing out the error of relying on existing organs of Government, with different orientations and priorities, to promote forestry. There had to be, in Acland's words, 'single responsibility and centralisation of inspiration, direction and control'. Independence was also important, as afforestation policy must be as far as possible apolitical and maintained for generations.

The only way of giving substance to these recommendations, said the Committee, was through a Forestry Commission responsible to no existing government Department or Minister, but only to Parliament. There should be at least three full-time paid Commissioners, backed by part-time unpaid Commissioners with relevant knowledge and experience. Assistant Commissioners for each of the four countries, with appropriate supporting staff, would form the executive structure of the Commission. Broadly-based consultative committees would likewise be constituted for each of the four countries. Finance would be provided through a Forestry Fund, replenished as necessary by Parliamentary vote and accounted for annually, but disbursed at the Commission's discretion in the light of operational needs.

A tailpiece to the main body of the report illustrates the degree of resistance felt within Government to the idea of a separate Commission. The Acland Committee accepted, with reluctance, the suggestion that a Commission might not be needed if certain changes within the machinery of government went ahead, involving apparently the combination of the three agriculture Departments of Great Britain and the Development Commission into some kind of Ministry of Rural Affairs. The Treasury representative on the Committee went further and questioned the need for any new machinery at all, other than a joint committee formed within the three Departments.

Perhaps it was these signs of weakness that prompted Lovat to register his own fierce note of reservation.

The Commission established

The momentum generated by Acland and his supporters within and outside Parliament was sustained. The Government accepted the sub-committee's report and implemented it almost to the letter. Even before the necessary legislative authority had been obtained, an Interim Forest Authority was set up in November 1918, with Acland as Chairman. One of his first actions was to meet the RSAS in Edinburgh in order to take the Society's advice on the best methods of setting about the task of afforestation. Doubts about centralisation were met with the assurance that the Scottish end would be run from Edinburgh, under the control of Scottish officers; and with the comment from Sir John Stirling-Maxwell that, with an Authority composed 50 per cent of Scotsmen, it was the English who should be worrying about their autonomy.

The Forestry Bill was rushed through Parliament in the summer of 1919, receiving Royal Assent on 19 August. Under the Act the Forestry Commission was to consist of eight appointed members, not less than two of whom were to have special knowledge and experience of forestry in Scotland. The Commission was given wide powers to acquire and sell land, to afforest at its own hand or to provide grants or loans for so doing, and to manage woods and forests. Ancillary powers related to forestry statistics, research and education. Assistant Commissioners for each country, and consultative committees, were provided as in the Acland Report.

The Commission came into being in November 1919. According to Lindley (1935), Acland willingly stood aside in favour of Lovat as Chairman. There were two other Scottish Commissioners, Sir John Stirling-Maxwell and Mr Steuart-Fothringham: and the other members and chief officers were in very direct continuity from the personnel of the Acland Committee.

The Scottish emphasis in the early days of the Commission was not entirely appreciated, as shown by the following bizarre incident. Lovat had taken farewell of his fellow-Commissioners a day or two after the Act came into force, announcing as he boarded the night train that he planned to plant the first Forestry Commission trees next morning at Monaughty in Morayshire. This was too much for Lord Clinton, who felt that English trees were every bit as good as Scottish trees. So he boarded the night train for Exeter, arranged for a planting ceremony next morning at Eggesford near his own estate, and despatched a telegram to Lovat informing him that the first trees had already been planted. This was not all: the message was rubbed in by a plaque affixed to the first tree, and by a ceremony in 1970 to mark the planting of the millionth tree – also at Eggesford – and carried out by HM The Queen (Ryle 1969, James 1981).

1919 – 1939

The first years of the Commission were characterised by economic and political turbulence. It was indeed a near-miracle both that the Commission had got itself established in the brief window of opportunity following the First World War, and that it survived the Geddes 'axe' of 1922, which was very determinedly laid at the root of forestry. Lindley asserts that it was Lovat's backstairs work with Cabinet members that rescued the Commission, though at the cost of severe retrenchment. The existence of a statutory Forestry Fund, with its guaranteed capital of £3.5m for the first ten years, did not spare the Commission from Treasury cutbacks on annual expenditure, which made a nonsense of the early land acquisition and planting programme. The advent of a Labour government in 1924 once more threatened the continuance of the Commission, Ramsay Macdonald reportedly being inclined to hive off the Scottish operation: but Lovat and the Technical Commissioner Robinson met the relevant Cabinet committee and again saved the day (Lindley 1935, Ryle 1969).

More seriously in the long run, the Acland Committee's good intentions with regard to private forestry were subverted from the start. Nothing at all had been done to meet the Arboricultural Societies' constant grouse about the impact on landowners of 'Imperial and local taxation' – principally death duties. Moreover the terms on which advances of grant could be made under the 1919 Act to private landowners were impossibly tight. As a result, no planting at all would have been done by the private sector, but for the anomaly that from 1921 separate funds were provided for this purpose in order to relieve unemployment (a post–war measure, paralleled by other land settlement schemes of the period, that grew into the Forest Workers Holdings initiative in which the FC invested a good deal of energy in the early years). As it was, only 20,000 ha had been planted by private owners and local authorities by 1925, including restocking. What is more, the Commission's report for the year ending September 1926, quoting from the results of a forestry census, paints a gloomy picture of felling proceeding at a rate greatly in excess of restocking. Anderson (1969) records evidence of a grave lack of landlord confidence in the Commission, not assisted by a comment by Robinson in 1927 to the effect that the future contribution of private owners could be written off and that the State would have to take over more and more. Robinson's attitude was understandable with a Commission which had the creation of a large national reserve at the head of its agenda. In retrospect, however, it was a grave error, in terms of both the quantity and the quality of the British timber resource, not to have pushed ahead with a dual thrust of public and private sector planting.

Nevertheless, it would be uncharitable not to acknowledge the achievement of the FC in its fledgling years. Ryle has chronicled, from a position of inside knowledge, the intense dedication of the small band of enthusiasts who formed the Commission, struggling against political machinations without and constrained resources within. He details the administrative staff in the early days as numbering 52: five in the London HQ, nineteen to cover England and Wales, nineteen for Scotland, and eight for Ireland – as well as Lovat himself, who gave virtually his whole time to the job. Even ten years later, the staff had grown only to 55. The Scottish end functioned with a good measure of independence, from its Edinburgh HQ in Drumsheugh Gardens – according to Ryle, snapped up as a bargain by Sutherland (the Scottish Assistant Commissioner) without the Commission's authority. However, this independence did not extend to policy or planting objectives. The FC had committed itself to the task of building up a national timber reserve, and the only regional variations contemplated were those of pragmatism in achieving that overall aim. In 1918 Acland, as Chairman of the Interim Forest Authority, had told the RSAS that 'the great bulk of the work should be done in Scotland by a purely Scottish executive, manned by Scottish officers, and the Central Forest Authority should only supervise in order to be certain that the same lines of policy are being carried out in the different parts of the United Kingdom' (*Proceedings* 1918). The letter of that undertaking was still being honoured, but the spirit was becoming more and more diluted.

By 1927, when Lovat retired from the Commission, about 100,000 ha of plantable land had been acquired and 35,000 ha planted. As Anderson (1967) complains, it is not always easy to trace from the Commission's reports how much of the planting was done in Scotland, but it is interesting to note, from the Reports for 1926 and 1930, that land in Scotland was often difficult to obtain at an economic price because of the need to take over 'bound' sheep stocks with the land. This bore out a prediction made by Stirling-Maxwell ten years before – that in the early stages there was a good deal to be said for afforestation in England rather than in Scotland (RSAS *Transactions* 1917). Little progress, moreover, had been made in the subsidiary but important object of creating viable rural employment in the Highlands – one of Lovat's personal preoccupations. Out of a total of 241 Forestry Workers Holdings established by 1926, only 31 were in Scotland (Anderson 1967).

Lovat's energy had been impressive, his vision for forestry wider than most, and his enthusiasm catching. By his example he had induced a number of landowners up and down the country to present land to the nation, notably the estate of Benmore in Argyll, which was a gift from Mr H G Younger to be used as a demonstration forest. It has to be said, however, that under his leadership the Commission was set on a fairly one-track course, which his successors did nothing to correct. His achievement is appropriately summed up by his biographer: 'The miles of barren land now covered with fine woodlands over the length and breadth of the country entitled him to say... *Si monumentum requiris, circumspice*' (Lindley 1935).

Lovat's successors were Lord Clinton and Stirling-Maxwell, both of whose reigns were short, and clouded once again by the spectre of national economic stringency. The Commission's first decade found it in deficit (compared with its initial projection of 1919) to the tune of fifteen per cent in terms of coniferous planting – although the promise of £5.5m for the next ten years was felt to be reasonable in the current economic climate. Private planting, however, remained in the doldrums, partly because of the impact of death duties and partly because of the agricultural depression which had already begun to bite (Annual Report 1929). Moreover in 1931 the Commission had again to face the rigours of national austerity, this time mediated through the May Committee [on National Expenditure]. Its recommendation was that, in order to save money, the Commission should acquire no fresh land and simply plant up the land it had, at a slower rate. After a meeting with the Chancellor of the Exchequer, however, the Commissioners emerged with a somewhat reduced annual provision but with their entitlement maintained to spend at their own discretion (Annual Report 1931). It was not until 1935 that the rate of planting projected in 1929 was resumed.

Under the direction of J D (later Sir John) Sutherland as Assistant Commissioner, the Scottish end of the enterprise gained momentum. Although not a forester by training, he had shown commitment when responsible for forestry within the Scottish Board of Agriculture and as a member of the Acland Committee. Anderson (1967) attributes the Commission's early concentration on Argyll as a forest area to Sutherland's intimate knowledge of West Highland conditions, gained as an agriculturist. No doubt it was also through Sutherland's initiative that in 1935 (by which time he had become a Commissioner) the Commission set up a committee 'to advise how the surplus and unplantable land in the Forests [of the Loch Long area] in the County of Argyll may be put to a use of a public character'. What lay behind this was the bad image the FC had acquired through its afforestation in the Lake District (Sheail 1981). By expending the minimal sum of £5,000 the Commissioners were able to put together with the Scottish Youth Hostels Association, the City of Glasgow and the Carnegie and Jubilee Trusts an attractive package which was grandly entitled a National Forest Park.

Although the committee's report advised the Commission to adopt a low profile, and recoiled from the idea of spending from the Forestry Fund 'on providing facilities for holiday makers', the initiative did in fact mark the start of the FC's very considerable involvement in the tourist business, both commercially and by way of providing amenities in State forests.

The clashes with amenity interests in the Lake District and also in Snowdonia were resolved through an agreement by the FC to refrain from further afforestation in certain key areas. An informal joint committee with the Council for the Preservation of Rural England (and its Welsh counterpart) was established in 1935. No such arrangements were thought necessary in Scotland, where amenity took a decidedly lower place. The FC cannot be required to bear alone the responsibility for this dichotomy: the fact is that public opinion in Scotland was very little exercised about the appearance of forestry, even in the recognised scenic areas. Sutherland met no angry protests when, in addressing the RSAS (now renamed the Royal Scottish Forestry Society) in 1927, he remarked that deer forests had proved a disappointment because in them 'continuous block afforestation as it ought to be practised' was impossible.

By 1936 the Commission's projected planting programme was restored to something like 12,000 ha per annum. This followed representations by the Commission: but far more influential in securing the increase was a desperate move on the part of the Government to counter the unemployment problem which was threatening to become endemic in certain areas, notably NE and NW England and S Wales. These were designated Special Areas, and the FC was invited to suggest means of providing employment within them. The upshot was a further injection into the Forestry Fund, with authority to purchase and afforest 80,000 ha as rapidly as possible, at the same time creating an additional 1000 Forestry Workers Holdings. No such areas were constituted in Scotland, but a significant extent of *de facto* (though unpublicised) Special Area planting was authorised in Argyll (A S Mather, pers. com.).

Table 1: FC Achievements up to 1939

AREA (in 000 ha)

	loc.auth/	Plantable land acquired		Area planted		No. of FWH	
up to	priv. planting	E& W	Scot	E & W	Scot	E & W	Scot
1924	9,300	31,000	24,000	10,000[1]	5,000[1]	-	-
1929	21,800	73,000	52,000	36,000	18,000	620[2]	
1934	41,000	115,000	80,000	70,000	40,000	910	320
1939	50,600	155,000	110,000	85,000	60,000	1020	395

Source: Annual Reports

Notes:

1 The division of planting area figures between England & Wales and Scotland is notional up to 1929.

2 No breakdown of FWHs between England & Wales and Scotland is available for 1929. Up to 1926 the Scottish total was 31 (Anderson 1967).

It was once again a time of forestry expansion, with the Government's mind exercised not only about unemployment but about the possibility of another war. In 1937 a forest census – deferred more than once since 1921 as an economy measure – was put in hand. In 1938 the Scottish Economic Committee invited the FC to consider how forestry could contribute to the economic welfare of the Highlands and Islands. The FC was able to respond quickly because, as explained in the Annual Report for 1938, a special survey was unnecessary in view of the Commissioners' thorough knowledge of the areas suitable for expansion. They were able to identify large areas which, thanks to new techniques of preparation and planting, could now be afforested – and equipped with Forest Workers Holdings – if additional funds could be provided. The Commissioners' cautious insistence on new money reads oddly alongside their actual achievement during this period: by 1938 only 22,000 ha had been acquired in the Special Areas (as against the target of 80,000 ha); and new planting was running at less than 10,000 ha per annum, twenty per cent below the programmed rate. The progress of afforestation and other FC activities in the inter-war period is summarised in Table 1.

The Second World War

The 1939–45 war, to all appearances, marked a significant change in the FC's status and functions. It disappeared altogether as a corporate entity between 1941 and 1945: and when it re-emerged it quickly became subject to a new statutory regime. Yet all the while there was continuity and even development. It was in the midst of the conflict that the blueprint for the succeeding half-century of British forestry was produced – what Ryle describes, with a touch of grandiloquence, as 'without doubt the greatest and most constructive work the Forestry Commissioners have ever undertaken, either before or since'.

The work of the Commission was put on a war footing from the very start. The FC was immediately split into two, with the emphasis on the Timber Production Department which involved, of course, the systematic exploitation of the resource which the FC had been created to conserve and develop. However, the other arm which was entitled the Forest Management Department did a remarkable job not only in continuing to plant throughout the war but in controlling the release of woodland for exploitation according to rational criteria (Ryle 1969). All the same, as in the First World War, Scotland bore the brunt of the fellings. Anderson (1967) quotes evidence from the 1947–48 census suggesting that at least a third of the Scottish forest disappeared in the two wars (the greater part in the Second World War), as against not much more than a tenth of the English forest.

In 1941, because of the timber trade's anxieties that the FC might be managing the market against private landowners, the Timber Production Department was absorbed within the Ministry of Supply. The Forest Management Department remained under the Commissioners throughout the war, headed by Robinson who had held the chairmanship since 1932. Annual reports continued to be produced but were not published: they indicate that new planting continued at a rate of over 11,000 ha per annum until 1941, tailing off thereafter; acquisition of planting land also dwindled (Ryle 1969).

The Commissioners were not merely engaged in a holding operation during the war years. As early as June 1942, Robinson became so engrossed in the need to prepare for post–war reconstruction that he left the Commission's temporary HQ in Bristol and returned to London. Even before that, he had been active in cultivating the then Minister without Portfolio, Sir William Jowitt, so as to gain support for the FC's ambitious plans for the future.

It is simplistic, however, to attribute to the FC the monopoly of forward thinking that took place in the war years. As early as 1937 the Royal Forestry Societies had protested about the continuing neglect of the private sector, which had bred apathy among private owners. The Commission responded by calling a meeting of all private interests, now including the landowners' organisations and the timber merchants, in London the following year, at which the Commission accepted that a new policy comprehending both state and private forestry must be worked out (RSFS Proc. 1939). The only major initiative following this was a countrywide series of meetings organised (in Scotland) by the RSFS with some enthusiasm, 3500 invitations being sent out. The Commission was sceptical of their value (1938 Annual Report) but appeared to have nothing further to offer. The RSFS did not let up, however, and in early 1941 submitted a memorandum with comprehensive proposals for the private sector. These included: the creation of a distinct forest authority charged with the direction of estate forestry; compulsory registration for areas exceeding 8 ha – failure to manage should lead to a take-over by the authority, subject to the owner's right to resume possession on repayment of all charges incurred by the authority; an assured market and price; planting and maintenance grants to be on offer; felling licences to be continued post-war; and rabbit clearance schemes to be introduced. Similar recommendations were made by the English Society. While these proposals indicated a more inward-looking attitude on the part of the RSFS than those made during the First World War, they were far from wholly self-seeking: and they had a significant influence on the private sector policy adopted after the war.

In one respect forestry opinion in Scotland at this time was more open to radical change in land use policy than ever before. It was the height of the great movement towards town and country planning which had begun with Abercrombie in the 1930s and reached a new pitch of enthusiasm following the report of the Scott Committee in 1941 (Sheail 1981). In February 1942 Professor Steven, at that time Chairman of the RSFS, was speaking of the need for a central planning authority to adjudicate between town and country uses, and also between agriculture and forestry in the countryside. When challenged to reconcile this view with the continued existence of a monolithic FC for Great Britain, Steven replied that the FC in its existing form was still necessary to drive forestry forward, and was acceptable on two conditions: that there was a central Scottish authority with the necessary land allocation functions, and that FC's operations in Scotland were effectively devolved to a Scottish Committee (RSFS Proc. 1942).

It was in June 1943 that the Forestry Commissioners published their Report on *Post War Forest Policy* (Cmd 6447). It was a long but punchy document, modelled on the Acland Report of 1918. The Report stated the importance of wood as a raw material and the unfavourable balance of trade so far as Great Britain was concerned. The history of British forestry was up–dated, showing how despite the efforts of the FC since 1919 the supply position had not improved. A major new thrust was needed if an adequate timber reserve was to be created, both for a future war emergency and for peace-time needs. The nation should make up its mind to devote a total of 2m ha to forestry, on a programme spread over 50 years: 1.2m ha should be found by way of afforestation of 'bare' land, which should be achievable against an estimated total of 1.7m ha of afforestable land in Great Britain, half of it in Scotland; the remaining 0.8m ha would be sought by way of systematic management of existing woodland, for which the main machinery would be dedication to forestry aided by 25 per cent grant continued up to the point that the woodland was self-supporting. It would be best to concentrate the bulk of planting – both FC and private – in forest regions characterised by large blocks of forest, mainly spruce: the Moray Firth and Border areas would be particularly suitable.

The Report – again following Acland – went on to spell out in detail the preferred programme for the first decade. Since this would require a massive outlay not only of new money but also of executive effort, some changes in FC administration ought to be made. The need for a single Forest Authority for the whole of Britain remained paramount. Accountability to Parliament through a Minister might now be necessary, however, and the Minister should be the Lord President of the Council. To increase efficiency an increased measure of administrative devolution should be practised, both to executive committees and to executive Commissioners for Scotland and England and Wales respectively.

The supplementary arguments in favour of forestry in the Report went over the familiar ground of provision of rural employment and economic development, but also widened the scope of discussion to include forestry as a valid form of business investment. Also brought into play were the amenity and recreational advantages, and the possibility of increasing the number of Forest Parks.

Early reactions to *Post War Forest Policy* were on the whole positive. Jowitt said that it had stiffened the Government's resolve, though the commitment of funds on the scale outlined would depend on the strength of other post-war claims. The RSFS's observations, submitted in June 1943, took for granted the recommendations about the expansion of forestry, and concentrated – far more than in 1918 – on the place given to Scotland in forestry administration. Since forestry was relatively more important economically in Scotland, and it was there that the majority of additional land was being sought, Scotland should have at least parity of representation on the Commission with England and Wales combined. If not, the Society would consider pressing for a separate Scottish Forest Authority. The existing system for choosing Commissioners was unsatisfactory (only three of the ten signatories of the Report were Scots). Nevertheless, when R E Muirhead, at a meeting of the RSFS in June 1943, moved an amendment to the effect that 'the Society urges the Government to set up a separate Forestry body for Scotland, with its headquarters at St Andrew's House, Edinburgh', he was heavily outvoted (Proc. 1943).

As regards private forestry, the Forestry Societies were unhappy with the details of the 1943 proposals, and after further consultation a further report was published in 1944 entitled *Post War Forest Policy: Private Woodlands* (Cmd 6500). It provided a 'block grant' scheme for approved woodlands as an alternative to dedication; but the Commission stood firm against any idea of a separate division within it to look after private forestry – another reform urged by the Societies.

Forestry Act 1945

The 1945 Bill, which received Royal Assent on 15 June, was one of the last measures of the National Government which had steered Britain through the War. The Act was much less concerned with forestry policy than its 1919 predecessor: this followed directly from one of its main provisions, which was to make the Commission responsible to the two agriculture Ministers jointly (or severally in regard to matters affecting Scotland only or England and Wales only). Thus passed away the remarkable autonomy which the FC had enjoyed since its foundation. The Commissioners obviously did not welcome the change, but made the best of it by reference to the scale on which forestry was to be expanded post–war, and the potential for increased conflict over land use – both of which required Ministers to be in charge of overall policy (1945 Annual Report). In line with this, all land was to be held in the name of one or other Minister, and acquisitions would be made by Ministers, even though still financed out of the Forestry Fund. However, the Commissioners continued to exercise most of the important functions at their own hand.

A corollary of the more direct Departmental status of the Commission was that Members of the House of Commons could no longer be Commissioners. The membership of the Commission was increased from eight to ten, and the requirement that two at least should be knowledgeable about Scottish forestry was dropped (although the condition remained easily satisfied in terms of the four Scots holding office in the new Commission). Of greater significance were the changes in the regional structure of the Commission. Assistant Commissioners and consultative committees for the three countries were abolished, but the Commission was obliged to appoint national committees consisting partly of Commissioners and partly of outsiders, and to devolve upon them such functions as it thought fit. This move was justified on the ground of the increased scale on which forestry was to be practised, calling for vigorous delegation of responsibilities. In addition, regional advisory committees were established on a sub–national scale (and initially on a non-statutory basis), mainly to assist with the promotion of private forestry.

It is instructive to note the fate of these devolutionary provisions. National committees were constituted and actually continue to exist today: but the functions delegated to them initially were insignificant and have now shrunk to vanishing point. Even more important, with the demise of the national Assistant Commissioner posts there was no longer any statutory requirement to keep a national presence in the constituent countries: and although offices were maintained in Scotland, Wales and, for a time, England their significance steadily dwindled. Ryle, who was in charge of the Welsh Directorate for a number of years, illustrates the failure to implement the devolutionary promises of the mid-1940s. In the early 1950s the ratio of administrative and professional staff between headquarters and the national directorates swung from 1:1.8 to 1:1.3 or less, partly through actual cuts in the directorates and partly through a great increase in the number of administrators at the centre (Ryle 1969).

It is not easy to understand how Scottish opinion, which was fully on the alert in 1943 to the need for effective devolution, accepted so passively the FC's drift into a highly centralised monolith. Perhaps Anderson (1967) is right in his diagnosis that the Forestry Society – which was still the custodian of the Scottish forestry conscience at that time – only came to life under the threat of world war, and relapsed into somnolence thereafter. In 1919 Lovat had pacified the fears of his RSAS colleagues with the argument that 'if you have a single authority, Scotsmen can be promoted and this promotion will not necessarily be confined to this Kingdom'. Anderson made the wry comment that it did not seem to have occurred to Lovat that the promotion of Englishmen would not be confined to England. The Commission's report for 1945 suggests that not a single chief officer at that time, including the Director for Scotland, was a Scot. Much the same picture emerges from the details given by Ryle of the professional organisation of the Commission in 1948 – with the additional twist that 'infiltration' had gone further down the line, so that the majority even of Divisional officers in Scotland appear to have come from south of the Border. This does not, of course, point to any sort of conspiracy to 'de-Scotticise' the Commission. It was the direct result of a policy of rigorous interchangeability of professional staff. More profoundly, it was the reflection of a structure increasingly dominated by its headquarters, in which the value of regional variations was at first played down and ultimately came to be feared and proscribed. A variant of this tendency will be seen later, in the story of the Nature Conservancy Council.

The first quinquennium

The decision whether to approve the plan for expansion which formed the main thrust of *Post War Forest Policy* fell to the new Labour government which took office in autumn 1945. The statement made by the Minister of Agriculture in November of that year was positive, if cautious. It in fact granted authority for the full programme requested by the FC, but only for an initial five-year period (which was all that any government could guarantee in any case). During this period planting would be working up to its intended maximum of 60,000 ha per annum but was not expected to exceed a total of 115,000 ha for the quinquennium (distributed between State and private planting roughly in the ratio 4:1). Even so, the five-year financial provision of £20 million was at a rate at least three times as high as the pre-war level.

Actual achievement during the quinquennium fell short of the programmed amount by nearly 30,000 ha or 25 per cent (1951 Annual Report). The major difficulty was an inability to acquire land. The fact was that a national policy for expansion of home food production was being pursued with even greater vigour than the forestry policy, and the Government agricultural officers (especially in Scotland) exercised a *de facto* veto over the release even of land in the possession of the FC (Ryle 1969).

The situation was one which Robinson, with his forceful personality and easy access to Ministers, might have been expected to remedy. But he had retired from the Director–General's post in 1947 (though retaining that of Chairman) and later suffered from ill-health, dying in 1952. In his closing years he was not, according to Ryle, anything like the force he had been.[4]

The turning point

It has been noted how the Commissioners in 1951 were lamenting a shortfall in planting achieved over the first quinquennium of 25 per cent. The next quinquennium was to witness an even greater shortfall, of nearly 40 per cent – 220,000 ha planted, against a target of 365,000 ha for the decade (1956 Annual Report). In terms of land acquisition the situation was even worse, with a shortfall of no less than 73 per cent. This time, however, the FC made no apology for its poor performance, but reasoned that the error lay in setting its sights too high.

It had to be recognised that private owners were reluctant to part with their land, for perfectly valid reasons. The Commission (so it was claimed) was accordingly using persuasion rather than the big stick, and was increasingly learning how to break down landowners' prejudices by offering such inducements as undertakings to maintain fences, keep down foxes, provide fire belts, entertain offers of small as well as large areas, and of lease or feu as against outright purchase. By such means it was hoped to work up to the projected annual rate of 60,000 ha new planting per annum, but over a longer period. A new drive to secure land for special planting in the crofting areas should assist in this.

The Commission's optimism was not shared by the Earl of Dundee, in addressing the annual business meeting of the RSFS in 1955 (*Scottish Forestry* 9). The bugbear remained the attitude of the Department of Agriculture for Scotland (DOAS), whose officials were frustrating the aims of Government policy by refusing to approve the release of land to the FC, under the mistaken belief that more trees meant less sheep. He contrasted with this the recent forestry performance of the private sector, which did not need DOAS clearance in the same way as the Commission. Under the terms of the dedication scheme, and with the capital taxation of woodlands at last being tackled, private owners had come close to fulfilling their admittedly modest target of 200,000 ha new planting in the decade.

It is probable that, given freedom to speak their minds, the Forestry Commissioners would have said a hearty *Amen* to Lord Dundee's comments. Apart from the absolute shortage of land for forestry, their own afforestation was being driven further 'up the hill' on to ever poorer grazings, and also ever further north and west (Mather 1993).

The Commission, however, was being given less and less freedom to speak its mind. The forceful Robinson had been succeeded as Chairman by the diplomatic Earl of Radnor: and while there is no reason to question Ryle's assertion that Radnor was in some measure responsible for the better integration of the private sector, through the setting up in 1954 of the Watson Committee, this seems to have been at least as much a Government initiative. Certainly Radnor was not the man to pitch in heavily when the FC's role was challenged in Whitehall – as was increasingly the case. In 1957 the report of an enquiry into 'Forestry, Agriculture and Marginal Land' – set up by what Anderson calls 'that somewhat detached but interfering personage, the Lord President of the Council', and chaired by Sir Solly Zuckerman – was published. It was on the whole a supportive document, and its main conclusions – that forestry and agriculture should be planned as an integrated whole, that end–uses for forest products should be actively sought, and that there was probably better reason than ever for a national investment in forestry – were entirely welcome to the Commission. But there was a catch. The report made the fairly obvious point that, with the advent of nuclear warfare, it would no longer do to base forestry policy on the notion of three years' self–sufficiency in pit-props. This gave the opening for which the Treasury had long been waiting. An inter-departmental working party of officials was set up in December 1957 'to review the bases and objectives of the forestry programme of Great Britain, taking account of the social, economic and defence considerations involved and in the light of experience gained since the war'.

This working party is notable for being the first instance of forestry policy's being seized from the Commission's grasp and being made to run the gauntlet of examination against the full range of Government criteria. As Ryle puts it, there was consternation within the Forest Service as to why the Government's own statutory forest authority had not been asked to provide Ministers with the appropriate dossier and recommendations on future policy. The working party itself was a shadowy affair, its membership undeclared, its report (dated May 1958) distinguished only by the Cabinet Office number 53485. But its findings were radical. The bases of existing forest policy were one by one removed. Strategic defence considerations were completely set aside. Balance of payments arguments (to which the 1957 report had given some weight) had no long-term validity. Commercial return on capital invested was well short of the Government norm. Employment was the only factor left, and it had relevance only in certain parts of Scotland and Wales: it could not justify the levels of planting in recent years.

The working party's recommendations (in which the FC concurred, with one minor reservation) were equally stringent. Rates of planting, far from being stepped up, should be frozen at the current figure of about 25,000 ha per annum and then brought down steadily to just over half that level – with a heavy weighting towards Scotland. Dedication of private woodland, with the associated grants, should be phased out over at most ten years.

The Government, faced with a report which was unanimous (apart from the views of the Treasury, who favoured even more drastic treatment), endorsed the curtailed planting programme. On private forestry, however, they went in the opposite direction from the working party by increasing maintenance grants for both dedicated and approved woodland. This was in line with the submissions of the forestry and landowner organisations, which had been invited to give evidence to the working party. The RSFS had argued, additionally, for a new deal for forestry associated with agriculture, to be administered by DOAS. It had also come round, at last, to the view that the monolithic FC should be broken up and that a separate forest authority for Scotland was required, responsible to the Secretary of State (*Proc.* Vol 12, April 1958). This recommendation was totally ignored, by the working party, the Government and the FC alike. The days of RSFS's influence in high places were over. But equally, so were the days of the Commission's autonomy.

The close of the 1950s found the FC in reflective mood. The 1959 Annual Report, reviewing 'the first 40 years', commented that, as the strategic aspects of forestry receded, so the social aspects were coming to the fore.

Integration with pastoral farming was now a priority. For the first time, the Commissioners engaged with the environmental objections to their policies, and with the allegation that they had 'ruined huge areas of natural heath, moor and scrub'. Their reply was vigorous. Certainly there were a few areas, like the heart of the Lake District, where large-scale conifer planting might be unacceptable. But elsewhere, 'skilfully planned and intelligently managed' conifer plantations could enhance scenery, once the thicket stage had been passed. It would be as big an aesthetic mistake to plant hardwoods widely as it was to disguise modern houses as Tudor cottages.

The Commission also took the opportunity in the 1959 Annual Report to rehearse its achievements, and to restate its policy, on National Forest Parks. Seven Parks were in existence, with a total area of 170,000 ha, of which less than half were under trees. The Scottish Parks were Argyll, Queen Elizabeth, Glen Trool and Glenmore. The Annual Report observed a careful balance between claiming credit for taking the opportunity 'to meet the growing pressure… for access to open country and especially to the hills' and avoiding any suggestion of extravagance in the use of public money: provision of footpaths and camping sites was on a modest scale and undertaken only 'as funds permit'. At one time, as chronicled by Sheail (1981), the FC had been bidding – with some encouragement from the Treasury – to become the national park authority. That opportunity had passed, and the Commission was now content to let forest park expansion cease and to leave the parks themselves to be run on a care and maintenance basis. No new initiatives were to be taken until the 1990s.

The decade of expansion

At the start of the 1960s few would have predicted that the close of the decade would witness a rate of expansion of forest cover higher than that at any other time in British history. The causes were various and complex, and owed little to government or FC strategy.

At a major symposium on Natural Resources held at the Royal Society of Edinburgh in October 1960 under the auspices of the Scottish Council (Development and Industry), the prevailing view was that forestry had lost its way. E M Nicholson, the guru of the Nature Conservancy, claimed that 'land use is absolutely hit-or-miss – the basis of the forestry programme won't bear scientific examination'. W A P Black, a distinguished research chemist, commented that, despite the exhortations of the Zuckerman report of 1958, there was still no coherent strategy for disposing of the product of the forest which was increasingly coming on stream. In reply James Macdonald, Deputy Director–General of FC, accepted the need for a large pulp mill to absorb the product: this however merely reinforced the need for single–species planting, since manufacturers did not like to vary their chemical formulae, and they needed a cast–iron guarantee of supply. In fact, said Macdonald, a big expansion of Scottish forestry was needed. Why must we accept the current orthodoxy (stated earlier by the Director of the Grassland Institute) which restricted 'nimble foresters' to the steep slopes and boulder-fields, while 'stiff-jointed shepherds' (and sheep) had the run of the smooth and gentle slopes?

What Macdonald pleaded for was about to happen, though not perhaps in the way he would have preferred. It proved, if anything, more difficult for the FC to get hold of Scottish hill land, thanks to the clearance procedure which still had to be operated with DOAS. As a result FC planting did not even rise to the annual ceilings imposed following the 1958 working party report. But private planting, which was in practice exempt from DOAS clearance, shot ahead. This resulted from three factors. The first was economic. In the 1960s the market for mature (wedder) mutton collapsed, as did the market for wool. Sheep production therefore shifted to the lamb side of the market, and so to intensification on better ground, with the abandonment or disposal of outlying hirsels (W E S Mutch, pers. com.). The second factor was technical in nature, with the development of mechanical site preparation and aerial application of fertiliser, mainly phosphate, which allowed afforestation to proceed on the poorest sites. From now on the site could, to a significant extent, be adapted to the species, rather than the species to the site – leading to a marked increase in the use of the popular and fast–growing Sitka spruce (Malcolm 1991). The third new factor was the emergence of what Ryle calls 'syndicates of land investors'. These, in effect forest developers, were able to acquire large stretches of land in southern Scotland which were not accessible to the FC, and to attract private investment with the incentives both of planting grant and of tax concessions (Mather 1993). Thus there arose a new type of plantation – distinct from both estate and Commission afforestation – with a particularly hard-edged commercial slant, and owned by 'clients' not necessarily having any forestry (or landowning) background or allegiance.

It was in 1962 that the Commission's Annual Report, for the first time, totalled the area of FC and private planting. This indicated a recognition that the private sector had come of age and was now a partner in and not a mere appendage to the afforestation programme. 1962 was also notable as the year in which Scottish planting first exceeded 50 per cent of the Great Britain total – a trend which has continued and become more marked with the passing years.

Planting targets had been allocated to the three countries as early as 1958, when the inter–departmental working party, in recommending a cutback in FC afforestation, accepted that it should not bite so hard on Scotland or Wales because of the employment situation there. Now that the time had arrived for a review of the five–year programme instituted in 1958, another working party of officials in effect formalised the policy by laying down separate criteria for the three countries. The programme of new planting for 1964–73 (to be cut back still further to a total of 180,000 ha) should be concentrated on upland Scotland and Wales, where the maximum social and economic benefit could be expected. Elsewhere, land should be acquired only where distinct economic advantages could be expected, or where planting would enhance landscape beauty. In the Forestry Review of 1963 the Commission was instructed to devote more attention generally to considerations of beauty, public access and recreation. In compliance with this, the following year the FC engaged Sylvia Crowe, a distinguished landscape architect, to advise on the principles and practice of forest design. Her work was influential south of the Border, but was not thought to have much application in the remote 'tree factories' of the North. The wedge between economic and environmental considerations was being driven deeper and given a geographical dimension.

Another sign of the times was an unusual statute entitled the Fort William Pulp and Paper Mills Act 1963. This did not betoken the existence of a mill or mills at Fort William. It was an enabling Act, and was coupled with a formal assurance on the part of government that supplies would be available, whether from the FC or private sources, to keep the project running without intermission. This demonstrated the FC's practical interest in the disposal of the product – an issue which was coming to be of increasing concern. But it did not completely satisfy the main architect of the project, Dr T H Frankel, whose request for the ownership of three or four state forests to be transferred to the mill company was refused by the FC (McNicoll et al. 1991). Selling off to the private sector would have been politically anathema at that time: but in any case it was foreign to the ethos of the FC, which had by this time acquired a strong proprietary interest in 'its' forests.

In 1964 it was the turn of the Commission (after a lapse of fifteen years) to come under the scrutiny of the House of Commons Select Committee on Estimates. This was not a particularly intimidating summons, concerned as it normally was at that time with nothing more than arcane matters of accounting procedure. The Committee, however, was in a mood to take a broad view of its terms of reference. It went widely, but not deeply, into every aspect of the

Commission's functions and organisation. DOAS was asked if it saw any virtue in a separate Forestry Commission for Scotland, and replied that it saw none at all. The Ministry of Agriculture, asked for an opinion on the composition of the Commission, declined to comment. Nevertheless, prompted by a submission from W M F Vane MP, the Select Committee pronounced the FC to be weak on the commercial side of its work, and recommended that Ministers look into the need for some changes both in the membership of the Commission and in its management structure.

No doubt the FC would have been willing to assist Ministers in responding to the Select Committee's findings, but once again the matter was taken completely out of its hands. A Working Party on Forest Organisation, chaired by Sir William Murrie (at that time Permanent Secretary at the Scottish Office), was given more or less *carte blanche* in considering how the FC should be reorganised. It interviewed chief officers of the Commission and the chairman of the Home Grown Timber Advisory Committee, but otherwise consulted no one in the outside world before finalising its findings: and its confidential report was available only to Ministers.

The Working Party's report (1965) went far beyond that of the Estimates Committee in its criticisms of the Commission, which it castigated as 'an unsatisfactory compromise between an effective Board of Directors and a Committee representative of forestry interests'. It was not a matter of adding one or two Commissioners who were more commercially aware: the notion of a part–time Commission needed to be scrapped and replaced by 'a body of an executive nature on the lines of a Board of a nationalised industry, which would be able to give continuous attention to the business of the Commission'. This was a simplistic view of an organ of government whose functions increasingly embraced the sponsorship both of private planting and of the downstream use of forest products. However, the nationalised industry model was closely followed in the Working Party's recommendations. It stopped short of proposing a Commission consisting wholly of full–time paid officials, but insisted that they should form the core of the executive. The top structure should consist of a part-time Chairman, a full-time Director-General and four full-time functional Commissioners, responsible respectively for forest management, harvesting and marketing, administration and finance, and research – with a leavening of part–time members representing forest interests.

It was hardly surprising that the Working Party saw no place for National directorates, which 'weaken Headquarters control by removing some of its authority'. National boundaries, so it was said, now had little meaning. The directorates were simply a fifth wheel exercising functions which either were trivial or else interfered with management responsibilities which should be exercised centrally. Designated officers might still be needed in Scotland and Wales, to liaise with the authorities there: but there was no such need in England. For the National Committees the Working Party could scarcely conceal its scorn. It might, for presentational reasons, 'be impolitic to abolish the National Committees at the same time as abolishing the posts of national Director', but they should be made entirely advisory, meet less frequently, and (it was implied) be buried as quickly as this could be decently managed.

The Working Party's report was implemented more or less as soon as it was received. The Commissioners were invited to place their appointments at the disposal of Ministers, and a virtual clean sweep ensued at Board level. Whether

gramme. The policy review is therefore of paramount importance to the future of the Commission.

It was no doubt under the stimulus of the policy review that the FC began to sharpen up its own policy intentions. The same Annual Report announced two initiatives, both germane to the announced terms of reference of the review. The first had to do with up-dating the corporate plan (which had formed one of the pillars of the 'efficiency' shake-up of 1965, but had since fallen into a decline). The other was concerned with the ancillary objectives of forestry. A Conservation and Recreation Branch was established, and a statement of policy on recreation was made, accompanied by a press conference. The intention was to develop recreational facilities, and the recreational potential of the forests, to the maximum degree consonant with the primary objective of timber production.

The reader of the Annual Report was also reminded of the Commission's sensitivity to 'the role which the forests play in the character of the countryside'. Substantial areas were planted with larch and other species of conifer, 'in order to bring a variety of shades of green' to the forest. The lower commercial return, in comparison with spruce, was accepted because of the importance of amenity considerations. What was not mentioned was the area of 'other' conifers thus planted, and their geographical distribution. For some time the Commission had ceased to publish such details, probably because the proportion of Sitka planting, especially in Scotland, was embarrassingly high (and the proportion of the decorative evergreens virtually zero). The increasing adoption of double standards was also shown in the publicity given to a 'new mandate' for the management of the New Forest in Hampshire, in which an absolute priority was to be assigned to the conservation of its traditional character as against timber production. All this at a time when planting, in both public and private sectors, was going strongly ahead, almost exclusively on 'bare' ground in the Scottish uplands, and with scant regard for species variety or forest design.

While the policy review was going on a parallel inquiry, of wider scope and of great interest to Scotland, was initiated under Parliamentary auspices. A Commons Select Committee on Scottish Affairs, appointed in May 1971, decided to look into 'the usage of land resources in the rural and urban areas of Scotland', and it divided into two sub-committees (rural and urban) for that purpose. The non-partisan nature of the inquiry was emphasised by the choice of an Opposition MP to chair the rural sub-committee, and by the appointment of an academic geographer (Professor J T Coppock of Edinburgh University) as its specialist adviser. The sub-committee concentrated on two aspects – the policy underlying land use allocation, and the administrative machinery through which policy was effected (HC 1972 511–i).

Evidence, both written and oral, was received in great quantity from all the private interests and public authorities, giving a comprehensive view of informed opinion on all aspects of Scottish land use. The overwhelming picture was of a near-total 'absence of concerted land use policy on the part of the Government' (a quotation from G B Ryle put to FC witnesses in the course of oral evidence), and a corresponding degree of confusion in the objectives and methods of the numerous agencies concerned with land use. Evidence to this effect in relation to forestry was submitted by the RSFS, but it shied away violently from any idea of a commission to co-ordinate or direct land uses (HC 1971–72 51–v).

The FC evidence to the sub-committee was circumscribed by the fact that the forestry policy review was going on simultaneously. On every issue relating to objectives, or the co-ordination of policies, its witnesses were able to evade the force of the question or to imply that no problems existed (a position strongly backed up by the later evidence of the Scottish Ministers themselves). In fact the main interest of the FC evidence lies in the references to amenity. Pressed as to whether the FC would refuse a grant for private planting of Sitka spruce because of Countryside Commission objections, the Secretary (J J V Summers) said:

> Yes, indeed we would... It is a very real situation in the south of England, but as yet there are not quite the sort of amenity pressures or, indeed, the anti-coniferous prejudices in Scotland which arise south of the border'.

The Director-General (J A Dickson) tried to modify the impression thus created in his answer to a later question about FC planting:

> We are not going to get in future any more of these solid blocks of Sitka spruce?
>
> **A**: You will find this is the case with the new plantings. I am sorry they are there in the old plantings, and we cannot do very much about it.'
>
> (HC 1971–72 51–iv)

Oddly, as it seems now, the issue of the FC's Scottish administration scarcely came up during the sub-committee's inquiry. It was not mentioned in the evidence of the RSFS. The National Farmers Union of Scotland alone commented, in the following terms (HC 1971–72 51–v):

> When there was a Director of Forestry for Scotland frequent meetings and exchanges of opinions between the Union and the Commission took place and... there was...in Scotland a forestry 'presence' which recognised the advantage of close liaison with the agricultural industry. When the Forestry Commission down-graded its Scottish establishment, the possibility of meaningful consultation vanished and very few, if any, communications have been received from the Commission's Headquarters – and certainly none which sought our opinion or advice on the levels of planting to be undertaken.

The Select Committee reported in October 1972 (HC 1971–72 511–i). So far as rural matters were concerned its conclusions were far from radical. The four 'heavyweight' official institutions concerned with land use – the Department of Agriculture, the FC, the Nature Conservancy and the Countryside Commission – should continue to 'flourish', in a state of 'constructive tension': forestry, however, should be less circumscribed *vis-à-vis* agriculture. A proposal by Dr W E S Mutch of Edinburgh University (HC 1971–72 51–xviii) for a new executive Scottish department of state embracing these and other minor agencies was rejected. However, a Land Use Council should be set up by the Secretary of State 'to act as a central forum for discussion of rural affairs', including the creation of protection forests and the transfer of land from agriculture to forestry. The Council would be backed by a Land Use Unit of professional planners, with special responsibilities with regard to potentially conflicting uses and multi-purpose use.

It was not to be expected that a Conservative government would have much time for even these modest extensions of bureaucracy. In the Secretary of State's response to the Select Committee (1973 Cmnd 5428) the proposed Land Use Council and Land Use Unit were dismissed as incompatible with the proper exercise of the responsibilities of elected central and local government. Instead, a standing conference of the new regional councils should meet under Ministerial chairmanship to consider *inter alia* national guidelines on land use matters; and a standing committee of officials from central government agencies should provide technical back–up on rural land use. In fact, the standing conference never got off the ground, and the Standing Committee on Rural Land Use (SCRLU) limped along for about ten years before being wound up by the next Conservative administration. The problem of conflicting land uses was overcome by a virtual denial that any such problem existed.

Meanwhile, forestry policy for Great Britain was being reviewed as if the Select Committee's inquiry had never existed. A consultation paper (albeit with a good deal of firm changes of policy built in) was published in June 1972, entitled *Forestry Policy*, along with the findings of an interdepartmental cost/benefit study. Once again the FC was involved in the official working group, becoming a reluctant signatory of its findings. The Countryside Commission for England and Wales was consulted but not the Countryside Commission for Scotland. Representations by the RSFS and the Society of Foresters were more or less ignored.

The findings of the Government's review were simple, even simplistic. The FC's operations over the previous half-century were stated to be uneconomic – for understandable reasons. Thus it would be reasonable to write down substantially the notional debt on the FC enterprise. But, in order to import a greater degree of financial discipline, the FC would be set a target rate of three per cent return on all its trading activities (other than those carried out for social reasons). The difference between three per cent and the current rate of interest would be expressed in the trading account as a notional subsidy. Some of the shortfall (between three per cent and the then current interest rate of ten per cent) could be attributed to the social, recreational and amenity benefits of forestry, but not all. It followed that forestry involved a significant resource cost to the economy.

In terms of future forest policy the findings of the review were equally simple, even if their rationale was more difficult to detect. The Commission was relieved to hear that its programme of new planting was to continue at a marginally reduced rate (22,000 instead of 24,000 ha per annum), but angled towards employment creation in Scotland, Wales and N England. Grants for private forestry should be given only in respect of employment creation (in specified areas) or for amenity: the dedication and other grant schemes would be closed forthwith. Tax concessions available for private planting should continue.

The flaws in the logic of *Forestry Policy* were quickly exposed. In a trenchant paper (submitted to the House of Commons Select Committee, which was still sitting), Mutch showed that the cost/benefit approach adopted by the inter-Departmental review was relevant in assessing the return from a standing crop managed for sustained yield, but not at all in relation to an asset which was in process of creation, and which had been initiated for strategic reasons, not for profit. The Commission had been in grave error in accepting, since 1958, commercial criteria for rate of return on an asset which was not commercial. The real reasons for continuing to extend the nation's forests (both public and private) were quite different (HC 1971–72 511–v). The RSFS questioned the job creation assumptions of the consultation paper: direct employment close to the forest was diminishing, but on a wider canvas new jobs were being generated in the area, both in forestry and downstream (*SF* 26). Colin Price (an economist teaching at Oxford and, later, at Bangor) attacked on virtually every front. The application of a ten per cent test discount rate to forestry to discover its value to society was absurd because it took a snap view of an ultra long-range activity. The method of evaluating recreational and amenity value was riddled with fallacies, chief among which was the assumption that forestry conferred benefits but not costs. In relation to private forestry, tax concessions should have been the first to go, because they benefited the large investor and yielded the smallest social and amenity returns (*Forestry* 44 and 49).

Criticisms of this kind, however cogent, did not have any effect on Government thinking: but pressure mounted in the right quarter did. The Minister of State at the Ministry of Agriculture announced in October 1973 that the dedication of private planting would not only continue on a countrywide basis but be operated under relaxed conditions. The dedication covenant would expire with felling, and would no longer be a burden on the land. The Commission would offer an outright payment based on the area of planting, subject to the continuance of sound management, integration with agriculture and environmental safeguards, 'together with such opportunities for recreation as may be appropriate'. Departures from a plan of operations could involve recovery of the grant.

It was immediately obvious, however, that with the abolition of continued management payments enforcement of these conditions would be a dead letter. Provided an applicant could get his proposals through the initial sieve, he was in practice free from supervision – and it did not even matter if the trees did not grow. It could hardly be said that this was an unforeseen consequence of the new policy: *Forestry Policy* had grumbled about the cost of running the old dedication scheme, and had stressed that under any revised scheme grants should be payable 'with maximum simplicity of administration'.

The only concession the Government offered to the growing unrest over private forestry was to make the initial sieve a little finer. The Commission was obliged, in administering grant aid, to consult with the Agriculture Departments and local planning authorities on land use and amenity aspects of woodland owners' proposals. This was a significant change, especially as it marked an entrée, however modest, into forestry for the new Scottish regional and district authorities. In another way, however, its effect was negative. Once the FC had specialist bodies to consult on land use and amenity, it tended to wash its hands of direct responsibility for these aspects. Worse, it gradually turned into a kind of sponsor for the private sector, in the sense not of promoting standards within that sector but of standing behind grant applicants and assisting them in minimising the impact of agricultural and amenity objections (1974–75, 1978–79, 1981–82 Annual Reports). The same tendency was apparent in the reconstitution of FC's Regional Advisory Committees (supposedly to give greater weight to amenity factors in the consideration of grant applications). This was carried through without any visible effect on the balance of the Regional Advisory Committees, which remained packed with representatives of private forestry (1973–74, 1974–75, 1975–76 Annual Reports).

In one sense, the acceptance by the FC of a sponsorship role was a move forward, since it marked the long overdue recognition of the private sector as an essential partner in the development of the nation's forestry. But it happened at an unfortunate time, when the forestry companies, with their emphasis on investment and profit rather than on silvicultural standards, were rapidly displacing the traditional estate type of afforestation.

The private growers – especially the forestry companies – responded to the renewed confidence placed in them, as well as to a favourable taxation regime. Throughout the Heath administration the annual area of new planting by the private sector continued to increase – from under 20,000 ha in 1970 to 24,000 ha in 1972 and the following years (roughly ²/₃ of it in Scotland). A watershed was reached in 1973, when for the first time this century private planting exceeded that of the FC (by then pegged back to 22,000 ha per annum).

The 1972 review continued to cast a baleful shadow over the FC and its operations. Notwithstanding the specious nature of the cost/benefit exercise, the Commission was trapped by the requirement to show a three per cent return on the enterprise, and this showed. The 1972–73 Annual Report recorded a drop in employment of industrial staff from 6650 to 6150, or 7.5 per cent in a single year. In the 1973–74 Annual Report the Commissioners beat their breasts over their employment objectives: where special circumstances called for an emphasis on providing jobs, there could be marginal exceptions to the adoption of mechanised methods, but only if no additional cost were entailed. The main aim of the Forestry Enterprise remained that of producing wood as economically as possible: amenity was a subordinate objective, because it reduced the final return.

It was the private sector that was to bear the brunt of the next shock to forestry. In the spring of 1974 the Heath government was ousted. In July the incoming Labour administration adopted the dedication scheme outlined by its predecessor, though with a reduced planting grant for conifers (and, of course, no supplementary management grant). A month afterwards, however, came a crushing blow in the shape of the replacement of death duties by Capital Transfer Tax (CTT), and the threat of a wealth tax later. The CTT concessions subsequently offered to forestry were largely illusory (*SF* 30): and private sector confidence collapsed. In the two years from 1973 to 1975 new planting dropped from 19,000 ha to 9,000 ha per annum, with a proportionate decrease in Scotland. The Commission expressed concern over this development, but took no initiative towards reversing it. The private sector appeared to lose confidence in the FC as sponsor, complaining that it looked only to its own future and not that of the forestry industry as a whole (*Forestry* 50; *SF* 30).

The opening by the Secretary of State for Scotland of the new FC headquarters in Edinburgh also occurred in 1975. The move to Edinburgh was no new decision: it had been announced as long ago as 1971, with the object of unifying the then divided administrative offices in order to improve efficiency, and also 'to bring the headquarters more closely in touch with those parts of the Commission's estate where the weight of commercial interests will increasingly lie' (1971–72 Annual Report). Commenting on this decision, the National Farmers Union of Scotland had expressed the hope that it would lead to better liaison within Scotland (HC 1971–72 51–v). In a sense this hope was fulfilled, because it became at once physically easier for Scottish interests to gain access to FC headquarters. Since 1970 the FC Chairman had been Lord Taylor of Gryfe – the first Scotsman, as was noted in the Annual Report for that year, to hold the post since 1932 (and it has been filled by a Scot ever since). The membership of the Commission still held to its quota of four Scottish representatives – a larger share than any other of the constituent countries.

Nevertheless, the move to Edinburgh failed to establish a Scottish leadership, or to strengthen Scottish links in the way that NFUS had desired. With the FC based in Edinburgh, it was deemed to be a nonsense to retain any longer the title, or the residual functions, of a Chief Officer for Scotland. Scotland (as well as Wales and England) finally ceased to be meaningful administrative entities for forestry purposes. Moreover, the senior staff lists for the 1970s suggest that the average proportion of Scots amounted to one full-time Commissioner (out of four) and one officer of Director status (out of eight). Finally, the change of headquarters paradoxically put the FC at a greater distance from the Secretary of State for Scotland, who spent most of his time in Whitehall. The lead Minister on forestry continued to be the Minister of Agriculture, Fisheries and Food.

Meanwhile the furore over the application of Capital Transfer Tax to forestry refused to go away. Addressing the annual meeting of the Scottish Woodland Owners Association (SWOA) in May 1976, the Under-Secretary of State at the Scottish Office, Hugh Brown (speaking from a FC brief), claimed that the Government had 'struck about the right balance' between fiscal equity and the needs of particular interests. Mr Brown blamed the decline in private forestry on the national economic situation and the slump in the world market for timber. The private owners totally disagreed, and demanded CTT reform (*SF* 30). The Government quickly caved in and yet another interdepartmental group was set up, under Treasury auspices, to review 'the taxation and grant arrangements for private forestry taking account of economic, fiscal and environmental considerations and to report by 31 December 1976'.

Evidence was not slow in coming forward to the interdepartmental group, and advantage was taken of the group's surprisingly wide terms of reference. A curious feature of the Government's stance had been that forestry expansion might be holding back agricultural production. The RSFS rejected this with some scorn. They pointed out that it was the private sector which had been urging integration of forestry with agriculture – a matter on which they had greater knowledge than either the FC or the Government's agricultural services. Grants should be given specifically for farm–forestry and angled towards smaller blocks of planting. The Scottish National Party agreed, but saw the chief lack in forestry policy as being the absence of an ambitious target – in their submission, one of 80,000 ha per annum until the turn of the century (*SF* 30). At a conference in Edinburgh organised by the indefatigable Dr Mutch, M S Philip of Aberdeen University pointed the finger at the FC in its capacity as Forest Authority, noting its lack of commitment to the private sector, as well as the secrecy in which its advice to Ministers over taxation and other matters was shrouded (*Forestry* 50). Mutch himself (*SF* 29), had urged a total reconstruction of capital taxation of forestry so as to reflect its 'sustention value', in other words tax would be minimised if the crop was harvested at the proper rotation age.

The interdepartmental group proved to be fairly sympathetic, accepting the need to restore confidence in private forestry, and shaping its recommendations to that end. It proposed ending the requirement to enter the dedication scheme in order to qualify for the existing capital taxation relief; allowing in addition business relief at 30 per cent; greatly enhancing the levels of planting grants; reintroducing management grants and a small woods scheme; and regularising the process of grant and taxation reviews in the future. The recommendations were accepted almost *in toto*, and in the 1977 Budget the Government went one better by raising the CTT business relief to 50 per cent. It was only after the 1978 growing season, however, that the Commission was able to report signs of returning confidence in the private sector.

It was not the private sector alone that hit rock bottom in the late 1970s. The Commission was finding it impossible to acquire land except in Scotland, and difficult even there. Planting by the FC fell to 17,000 ha in 1977-78, nearly 25 per cent below the target rate; and the total planting figure for that year of

Figure 2: New Planting[1] in Scotland[2] 1971–1991 (000 ha per annum)

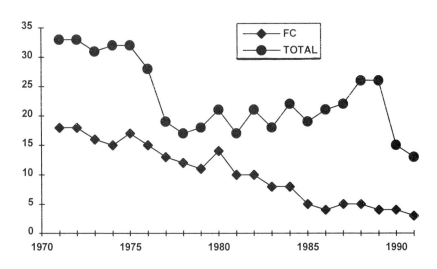

Source: FC Annual Reports

Notes:
1 Excluding replanting
2 New planting in Scotland averaged about 85% of the total
       GB figure throughout the period.

The Thatcher years

It is appropriate to sum up very briefly the UK land use and forestry scene as it appeared on the arrival of the Conservative government under Mrs Thatcher. Agriculture was flourishing and land prices at or near an all-time high, particularly in Scotland (Mackay 1990). As a result, FC acquisitions were dwindling and its rate of new planting had fallen to around 14,000 ha per annum; private sector activity, by contrast, had begun to recover, so that the total programme of new planting was in the region of 22,000 ha per annum. Afforestation was virtually confined to the uplands and still raised few hackles there: the single issue which exercised the major interest groups was farm/forest integration, on which a working party was set up in 1978 with representation from the Commission, the Department of Agriculture and Fisheries for Scotland (DAFS), the Scottish Woodland Owners Association, the National Farmers Union of Scotland, and the Scottish Landowners Federation. In other ways the FC was reaching out: it was involved with the Standing Committee on Rural Land Use (SCRLU) – the only child of the 1971–72 Commons Select Committee – on land capability mapping for forestry; with CCS on the implications of National Scenic Areas; and with DAFS on the scope of consultation for private sector forestry grant applications. New statements were issued on the implications for forestry of nature and landscape conservation (1978–79 Annual Report).

The incoming Government demanded of the FC a rationale of its spending and planting plans; and the FC responded with a Ministerial paper dated November 1980 – prepared within the Commission, without consultation with the Treasury or other Departments. It leant heavily on the arguments of the Wood Production Outlook of 1977 (and also those of the study by the Centre for Agricultural Strategy which was about to be published) – viz: that forestry expansion was still justified in view of supply/demand projections, which foresaw a possible world shortage developing by 2025; that continued national investment in forestry could not be justified if the required rate of return exceeded five per cent; but that it seemed entirely reasonable to use a very modest proportion of oil revenues to create a renewable raw material resource on land that had a low potential as a source of food.

In several important respects, however, the Ministerial paper backtracked on the Wood Production Outlook (and even more so on the findings of the Centre for Agricultural Strategy, published in February 1980). This was because Ministers had already given indications of their thinking, summed up concisely in the final three heads of the FC response: 1. The Public and Private Sector Roles in Afforestation; 2. Sales of FC Plantations – Policy Implications; and 3. Reduction of the Grant in Aid to FC. Thus the paper hastened to assure Ministers that precise targets for annual rates of planting and for the ultimate forest area were neither necessary nor appropriate; and that on a projection of current trends the FC share of new planting would go down anyway, and the private sector's share would go up.

Beyond that, however, the paper was defensive. If FC afforestation yielded only a modest return to the Exchequer, the return on private planting was zero or negative. Only a continued FC programme could offer the guarantee of future supply required by the processing industry, and safeguard fragile areas of Scotland from disastrous loss of employment. Sales of FC plantations would require legislation and would be controversial and difficult: not much land could be put on the market at any one time, and sales would realise much less than the cost of establishment.

The Commission's arguments did not prevail. They were up against a government committed to the ideals of privatisation and the test of the market – and much influenced, of course, by the propaganda of right wing think-tanks such as the Adam Smith Institute. The Ministerial statement (made by the Secretary of State for Scotland in December 1980) marks a further watershed in the story of the FC. Its terms were not all that dramatic: expansion of the nation's forests should continue, to supply the domestic processing industry and to reduce dependence on imports in the long term; scope existed for continued planting at broadly the rate of the past 25 years (ie around 30,000 ha per annum); the Commission was not to be dismembered, and it was to continue to have a planting programme, particularly in remote areas. But the private sector was to become the major partner; the FC's grant–in–aid was to be progressively reduced; and specific targets for sales of FC plantations would be set.

If the FC did not welcome the wind of change, at any rate it did not make the mistake of confronting it head on. It took comfort from the fact that the Commission itself was not to be dismantled, and began seriously to seek its *raison d'être* in the sponsorship of the private sector. Unfortunately, however, it did not take seriously the concerns of estate forestry, which were focused upon integration with hill farming. Studies had been launched under the auspices of Edinburgh University into ways in which agriculture could not only coexist with but benefit from afforestation on the farm, but these were not followed up in terms of grant policy. Instead, a new Forestry Grant Scheme (1981) boosted the rates for large scale planting, while the tax incentives (preserved under the 1980 Ministerial statement) proved an increasing attraction to investment forestry but remained of little use to struggling hill farmers. Indeed this was the period in which Scottish hill farming came under the greatest pressure (Mather 1993b), with the forestry companies seeking (with FC blessing) to take over progressively entire Highland straths and glens, and DAFS supplying the only measure of resistance to the process (neither NCC nor CCS played any significant part in vetting grant applications at that time).

The engine of sustained coniferous planting at this time was, of course, the projected demand from the downstream processing industry. It was ironic that in 1980 the domestic pulp sector collapsed, and the major pulp mills at Fort William and Ellesmere Port (Cheshire) were forced to close (also, later, the particle board mill at Irvine in Ayrshire). The collapse was brought about by a combination of circumstances – economic stringency at home and severe competition from larger and more modern plant overseas (McNicoll et al. 1991). Pulpwood and roundwood had to be exported in order to keep the work force (mainly FC, but to an increasing degree private forestry as well) in employment. The FC, however, kept its nerve and took the lead in seeking new outlets and in founding, along with the HIDB, the Scottish Forest Products Development Group (1982). Its confidence was justified: by 1985 the market for domestic pulp was buoyant, and in addition there was scope for a much more diversified range of products which made more complete use of the raw timber.

In every direction, it seemed, the FC was being obliged to rethink its traditional role as a planter and to concentrate instead on its Forestry Authority functions. Plantations were put up for sale: the private sector, however, was reluctant not only to buy but to allow the Commission to sell at too fast a rate, lest the land market should be affected. The Treasury nevertheless kept up the pressure and forced on the FC an increased target of £80 million of sales over a five year period. A Select Committee – this time of the House of Lords – homed in on the Commission's failure to promote or even to appreciate the need for fundamental research in forestry, leaving the responsibility to others. It recommended that the FC should appoint a Chief Scientist, who should concern himself, inter alia, with the integration of land uses, at both the national and local levels (HL 1979–80 381–I). The Government refused to authorise such an appointment (on economy grounds) but approved the setting up of a Forestry Research Co-ordinating Committee chaired by the Commission. At the international level, the UK (advised by the FC) had long resisted the adoption of any forestry policy by the European Community, as being outside the scope of the Treaty of Rome. In 1983, however, the UK was forced to accept the integration of forestry with agriculture as an element in certain structural measures, mainly for the benefit of the poorer Mediterranean countries. This proved to be the foot in the door which enlarged into the very comprehensive array of EC forestry incentives on offer by the end of the decade.

The major new factor to which the FC had increasingly to adjust during the 1980s was the growth of environmental awareness, especially in Scotland. It has been noted how at various stages the Commission was forced to take account of strong feelings about the effects of conifers on the landscape, first in the Lake District, then more widely in England and Wales. The Commission's perception, as expressed in the 1979-80 Annual Report, was that 'the national drive to acquire land and plant trees following two world wars temporarily blunted awareness' of amenity considerations but that, following the appointment of Sylvia Crowe as landscape consultant in 1965, such attitudes belonged merely to history. All this time, nevertheless, Scotland was treated as 'different', so that even when general statements were made about the FC's sensitivity to scenic factors it was understood that they did not apply with the same force there. This was especially true of private sector planting.

In May 1982 an efficiency study under the auspices of Lord Rayner recommended changes in the exercise of the FC's regulatory functions, in order to save money and manpower. The Commission responded by proposing fewer consultations with the agricultural Departments over planting grant applications, and also with local authorities, which should be encouraged to concentrate on the more environmentally sensitive areas and issues (1983–84 Annual Report). But this was swimming against the tide. The Countryside Commission (CCEW) had already called for planning permission to be sought for planting of over 50 ha in the uplands – a proposition strongly opposed by the FC. Rather less forcefully, CCS had argued for consultation over planting in the National Scenic Areas of Scotland.

Nature conservation came well behind landscape in terms of public consciousness about the implications of forestry, and even in the thinking of NCC. Until the late 1970s it had been common ground between the FC and NCC that the latter's interest in forestry was broadly confined to natural woodland and to the effects of planting in SSSIs and nature reserves. The NCC's report for 1977–78 congratulated the FC and foresters generally on 'increasingly recognising the needs of conservation and amenity and...adapting forest management to take account of them'. In its 1979–80 Annual Report the FC acknowledged the compliment by commenting that, 'by tradition, foresters are sensitive to nature conservation... though this is being sharpened by co-operation with NCC and the voluntary organisations'. It took the passing of the Wildlife and Countryside Act 1981 to show the unconscious irony implicit in this claim.

The stormy proceedings on the Wildlife and Countryside Bill (recounted in greater detail in Part III of this volume) did not engage the attention of the FC to any great extent. In the late stages, however, amendments were accepted which had the effect of requiring farmers to inform NCC of any operations affecting an SSSI, and conversely of requiring NCC, if it objected to such operations, to pay compensation for any profit forgone, including the value of Government grants that might have been payable. The amendments were not well drafted and failed to cover the full range of agricultural, let alone forestry, grants. It was agreed nevertheless, under a code of practice drawn up under the Act, that all forestry as well as farming operations affecting SSSIs should be notified and compensated. The Act also required NCC – for the first time – to notify owners and occupiers of both the existence and the extent of SSSIs and also of the operations within them that would be damaging to the scientific interest. Afforestation, of course, is the operation which above all transforms the character of a natural site, so it featured in the great majority of NCC's lists of 'potentially damaging operations'. The scene was set not only for massive confrontation between NCC and bona fide woodland owners, but also for exploitation of the compensation provisions by others, who had no serious interest in forestry and, but for the provisions, would not have been applying for grant.

Among the exchanges to which these provisions of the Act gave rise none was more tense than that concerning Creag Meagaidh (1984–86). Fountain Forestry, one of the more aggressive development companies, successfully applied for grant to afforest a mountain slope on the north side of Loch Laggan (Badenoch and Strathspey) and rejected NCC's offer of compensation for not doing so. The issue went to the Secretary of State for Scotland, with the FC presenting the company's case. The decision was a compromise, with the company's planting proposals halved: but so concerned was NCC over the outcome that it purchased the entire site from Fountain Forestry and declared it a nature reserve.

In April 1986 NCC published a major report entitled *Nature Conservation and Afforestation in Great Britain*. It was a well–researched and fairly hard-hitting commentary on FC policy and practice, especially with regard to the administration of the grant schemes. It singled out for special attention the tendency in recent years to plant in unfavourable situations, where the only harvest to be reaped would be grant and tax benefits. It also recommended that the FC should make adoption of appropriate design and management practices a condition of grant aid; and that government should remove the automatic award of tax relief and should institute a regime of planting licences, to be administered by the FC. In spite of these radical recommendations, the report was fairly conciliatory in tone, giving the Commission credit for a certain amount of progress in its attitude towards nature conservation and its measures to promote it.

Behind the report, however, lay a long and fairly tempestuous history, and a long series of drafts, stretching right back to 1976. The pre-publication draft, issued for consultation in 1985, had a very different tone, described by CCS as partisan. The SLF commented that NCC had failed to recognise forestry as a natural resource, essential to the retention of the rural population. The RSFS simply dismissed the report as containing 'so many factual errors that its conclusions have little validity' (*SF* 40). The Commission said little in public, merely regretting 'the wide circulation of the paper before full consultation within Government had been completed'. Behind the scenes, however, it had savaged an earlier draft more or less from start to finish, and had insisted on wholesale rewriting. Although the main differences were resolved, the relationship between the FC and NCC had become strained, with serious consequences which were to surface before long.

The Commission's main reason for feeling aggrieved with the environmentalists was that it considered that it had done enough in the recent past to put its nature conservation house in order. All applicants under the Forestry Grants Scheme had to commit themselves to manage their woodland in a way that would secure environmental benefits (1983–84 Annual Report). An extensive consultative exercise in 1984 had preceded the launch the following year of a generous grant scheme for the planting of pure broadleaves (a scheme which had some success south of the Border but was much criticised in Scotland, where it was contended that broadleaves could be grown commercially only in mixtures). Other developments in 1985 had included the appointment of Dr J M Boyd, recently retired NCC Director for Scotland, as FC nature conservation consultant; the acceptance, with fairly good grace, of a statutory duty on FC to achieve a reasonable balance between forestry and conservation; and the publication by Timber Growers UK of a Forestry and Woodland Code giving guidance to private owners on environment-friendly forestry practice. In 1986 a revised policy paper *The Forestry Commission and Conservation* was published, along with statements of intent about the management of FC SSSIs, conservation plans for FC forests as a whole, and the setting up of local consultative panels on environmental issues. A further review of the much criticised Regional Advisory Committees was announced, with a view to achieving a better balance within their membership among environmental, farming and forestry interests (1985–86 Annual Report). But the FC had stood out strongly against the imposition of planning control on forestry. It was also opposed, in terms of public pronouncements, to the notion of a planting licensing system administered by the Commission, which had been proposed by CCS in *Forestry in Scotland: a Policy Paper* (1986) and by the Convention of Scottish Local Authorities (COSLA) in *Forestry in Scotland: Planning the Way Ahead* (1987) and endorsed by the House of Lords EC Committee (1985–86 HL 259–I). Privately, however, the Commission had advocated such a system as early as 1985, but it did not receive Ministerial backing (P J Clarke, pers. com.).

Meanwhile profound changes were afoot on the agricultural front. The issue of EC farm surpluses, which had been long suppressed, could not be contained any longer – if only because it had begun to place an intolerable strain on the EC budget. Measures which would actually curb production were not yet on the horizon: but already the EC Commission was putting out ideas for the alternative use of farm land, most significantly in a discussion paper entitled *Community Action in the Forestry Sector* (COM(86)26, January 1986). For the first time for many years, there was a real incentive towards common cause between the FC and the agricultural Departments. In September 1985 a Government consultation paper entitled *Woodlands as a Farm Crop* made some modest proposals for the integration of farming and forestry, for which the forestry societies had been crusading (without much response from either the FC or the Departments) for many years. It was to be another two years before a Farm Woodland Scheme, with grants also on a very modest scale, was introduced.

The Commission's eyes were still very much more on the hills than on the general run of farm land. After considerable pressure, DAFS was induced to relax somewhat the criteria for releasing land on hill farms for forestry. As its Permanent Secretary admitted in addressing the 1986 Annual Meeting of the RSFS, the Department's protective attitude had become something of an ingrained habit, but it had now to be accepted that 'forestry was a clear front runner as an alternative use of land' (*SF* 40). The new rules were meant to encourage integration of hill farming and forestry: in practice they did little more than open up the way for increased acquisitions by the forestry investment companies, with consequent abandonment of hill farms (Mather 1993b).

In spite of all the environmental concern, the FC was holding its own and persuading forestry Ministers that expansion was still the watchword. In early 1986 the Commission survived a political assault which sought to privatise its entire estate (1985–86 Annual Report). The annual target rate for new planting, which

from the narrow, rather simplistic forestry policy which has dominated the last 70 years to a new, multi–purpose framework' which would endure into the twenty-first century.

'Multi–purpose forestry' was certainly the buzz-word of the time. It featured not merely in the Agriculture Committee's recommendations but also in the Government's response and in the tone and content of the Annual Reports for 1989-90 onwards. But there was a dour insistence in the pronouncements of both Government and the FC on the importance of continued forestry expansion and of fulfilling the target for new planting of 33,000 ha per annum (on which performance always fell lamentably short).

This was now justified on a wide variety of criteria instead of one or two, but it was not explained how the target had been arrived at or how it could be met without a continuance of the mass afforestation of the Scottish uplands. A somewhat worrying example of this underlying bias emerged in connection with a grant application for new planting extending to over 1000 ha at Glen Dye in Grampian Region. Notwithstanding strong objections from nature conservation and landscape interests and from the District Council, the application was given final approval with minor modifications in November 1990. So dissatisfied was the Council with the procedures that had been followed by the Regional Advisory Committee and the Commission that it sought a judicial review of the decision. It lost the case, on the technical ground that, although an environmental assessment was required by EC directive for a scheme of this magnitude, the grant application had been made before the UK regulations implementing the directive had come into effect (1990–91 Annual Report and *SF* 46 and 47).

To round off the account of the Thatcher years it may be of interest to focus on the enquiry of the House of Commons Agriculture Committee in 1989. The Commission was closely questioned on various aspects of its policies, and forestry Ministers were pressed on the FC structure – both on the possibility of devolution to the separate countries and on the division of the FC into a separate Enterprise and Authority.[5] In its report the Committee called for this functional separation: and it deplored the FC's intention to abolish the national advisory committees for the three countries as 'a move in the wrong direction, reducing the Commission's responsiveness to national variations, at a time when these factors require greater recognition' (HC 1989–90 16–i). But the Government gave the Committee's recommendations short shrift. They simply asserted that 'the present structure of the Commission provides an effective means of implementing the Government's forestry policies' (Second Special Report of House of Commons Agriculture Committee 1989–90, May 1990).

The great divide

In September 1990 a new Director-General took over at FC Headquarters – Robin Cutler, formerly Secretary of Forestry in the New Zealand Ministry of Forestry. For the first time in its history, the Commission's chief executive was an outsider – more ready, perhaps, to listen to the ideas which had begun to circulate within the Commission following the intake of a new generation of more environmentally–conscious staff (W E S Mutch, pers. com.)

It was not by coincidence that a very significant change ensued within months of Cutler's arrival on the scene. It is true that the FC Chairman was also a new broom – for the first time, an individual without forestry connections – and that

Ian Lang had succeeded Malcolm Rifkind as Secretary of State for Scotland and, therefore, 'lead' forestry Minister. But it was neither of these that turned the policy of May 1990 on its head. In March 1991 the Secretary of State announced that the Government had endorsed a proposal by the Forestry Commissioners that the FC's management structure should be reorganised so as to distinguish clearly between its regulatory and its forest management functions. In other words, a self-standing Forestry Authority and Forest Enterprise were being created.

The announcement acknowledged no debt to the House of Commons Agriculture Committee: on the contrary, it confirmed the Government's rejection of the Committee's recommendation, stressing that the reorganisation was an internal matter. To most people, this sounded like protesting too much. The truth was that the FC, under new leadership, had begun to recognise that the alarm bells were sounding. Unless it moved with the tide of events and of public opinion, it would find itself stranded, just as NCC had recently found.

This did not mean that the reform went all the way that outside commentators would have wished. It was in fact an ingenious compromise. As it was to be later worked out in detail, the Authority functions were to be exercised within the Commission as a Department of Forestry, which would also contain a Policy and Resources Group serving 'the Commission as a whole' (1991–92 Annual Report). The Authority was to have its own Chief Executive, and to be supported by national offices in Cambridge, Aberystwyth and Glasgow (the terms English, Welsh and Scottish were coyly avoided) for administrative purposes. The Enterprise, in contrast, was to have five regional offices, two in Scotland, two in England and one in Wales. Its operations were to be formally subject to oversight by the Authority. Overall control, however, would remain in the hands of the Commission as before. In a sense the FC was correct in claiming that the changes were of organisational rather than constitutional significance.

If the House of Commons Agriculture Committee had been gratuitously snubbed over its principal recommendation – the formal separation of the Authority from the Enterprise – there was evidence that many of its detailed suggestions were being heeded. In the course of 1990 and 1991 grants to private owners became multi-purpose, encouraging rather than penalising variation in species and design; management grants returned; woodland on farms was lavishly assisted; crofting forestry was made a practical possibility; a start was made on tackling the problem of public access to grant–aided woodlands and sold-off FC plantations; and the membership and procedures of Regional Advisory Committees were drastically overhauled. On three points, however, no ground was given – mainly, it would appear, because of pressure from the forestry lobby. Planting licensing was rejected; grants continued at the same rate for restocking as for new planting; and no steps were taken to improve the flow of information as to the different types of private sector interests engaging in new planting.

Moreover, the Committee had asked for a general review of forestry policy, to ensure its coherence and acceptability. The Government's reply was that existing policy was coherent and reflected changing perceptions: however, they compromised to the extent of bringing together the various strands of policy in a single statement (1990-91 Annual Report). This was predictably bland, except for the dogged restatement of the target figure of 33,000 ha of new planting per annum.

In their report for 1990–91, the Home Grown Timber Advisory Committee

tee, whose Secretary had to beg the Society to submit one. In response the Society advised that the Government should carefully consider methods by which production by private owners might be encouraged, including reduction of railway charges, readjustment of rates and taxes, subsidised borrowing, generous grants for research, and amendments to the rights of life tenants. A Forestry Council should be established, its members to be unpaid and to be appointed by the interested bodies. Schemes of large-scale afforestation should be considered, but only in the event of serious post-war unemployment (*Quarterly Journal*, Vol XII, pp256–257). It is not surprising that the Acland Committee found this submission unhelpful. When it produced recommendations along entirely different lines, the English Society changed its tune and welcomed the Report, stressing however that, as 97.5 per cent of woodlands were privately owned, it was essential to secure the landowners' cooperation (*Quarterly Journal*, Vol XIII, p78).

3. In his note of reservation Lovat castigated the total obstruction which Scottish forestry had experienced at the hands of the Board of Agriculture and the Development Commission, using this as the main ground of his contention that nothing would serve except a 'definite break with the past', and an Authority which could not only develop a forest policy for the British Isles but also carry it into effect. Lindley (1935) mentions a sustained rearguard action by the Scottish Office, after the Report had been submitted, to have its main recommendation subverted; and claims that it took all of Lovat's backstairs diplomacy to secure the necessary Cabinet support. He comments that Lovat – an ardent Scot and opponent of centralisation – was nevertheless the first to insist upon centralisation when he saw it as necessary. In this he was reflecting the prevailing view within the RSAS, of which he was an active member throughout his life.

4. This is perhaps the point at which to assess the contribution made by Robinson to the work of the FC, particularly in its bearing on Scotland. His positive qualities are not in dispute. Everyone who has left a record testifies to his outstanding intellect, energy, selflessness, patience and diplomacy. He became, even more than Lovat, the genius of British forestry, and virtually directed its course for 25 years. Ryle, speaking as a close colleague, pays tribute to his vision and professional insight, and his ability to inspire and lead from the front. On the other hand, Ryle admits that Robinson's single–mindedness led him to underplay 'the impact of the forests on human beings'. His impatience with private forestry has already been referred to: although Long (1953) and Anderson (1967) record a later change of mind, it is probable that Robinson must be held to some extent responsible for the bad relations between the FC and the private sector which prevailed for the first 40 years of the Commission's life. Moreover, though he was not alone in this, Robinson set his seal to the policy of block afforestation and monoculture which characterise so much of the Commission's early plantings, particularly in Scotland. On this issue also he appears to have had something of a change of heart. At a meeting of the British Ecological Society in July 1943 Robinson referred to 'one leading consideration which has gradually forced its way into my mind, namely the necessity of basing British forestry more squarely on Nature'. He went on to admit the unnaturalness and the dangers of pure plantations, which he defended on the ground of the need to recreate the timber reserve in the shortest possible time; but conceded that 'we ought at least to begin to provide our successors with the data on which to decide the advisability of turning over to mixed forests on the second rotation' (*Forestry* XVII, 1944). Some of this later thinking, acknowledging the importance of ecology and soil science, came through in Post War Forest Policy. But it was far from satisfying Lord Glentanar (writing in *Scottish Forestry Journal* 1945). Are we to be content, he asked – in the face of all the ecological advice now available – only to provide our successors with data? Pure stands of trees might be easier to manage: mixed planting was known to be preferable from every other point of view, and was the only kind that we should wish to hand on to our successors.

Finally, although Robinson was, on Ryle's evidence, a forester first and last and no empire-builder, his intensity of purpose must have laid the foundation for the FC's centralist tendencies and its impatience of regional autonomy. Anderson attributes to Robinson personally the reservation of forestry research and education exclusively to the Commissioners, without any measure of delegation to the constituent countries. The centralisation of research work at Alice Holt in Surrey was undoubtedly due to him, and was harmful to Scottish interests (Anderson 1967). PWFP states without any supporting argument that 'The Commission reserves to itself questions of Policy, Finance, Personnel, Research, Education, and Publications. All Acquisitions and Disposals of land come before it for approval.' One can almost hear Robinson's voice in this passage, which virtually spelled the death–knell for the effectiveness of any delegation to National Committees.

In defending the provisions of the 1945 Bill in the House of Commons (in particular the need for a unitary FC, the decision not to provide for a separate Commission for Scotland, and the adequacy of National Committees), Tom Johnston assured the House that the Chairman of the Commission would have direct access to the Minister of Agriculture and the Secretary of State for Scotland. The RSFS's Parliamentary reporter saw that as a threat rather than a promise: 'There is, at the present time, a danger that the personal views of the Chairman may be given too much prominence' (*Scottish Forestry Journal* 1946). Robinson was not only not a Scot but had not, as most of his senior colleagues had done, either studied at a Scottish university or spent part of his professional career in Scotland. Although intimate with the Scottish lairds who played such a vital role in the setting up of the Commission, and deeply knowledgeable about Scottish forestry, he appears to have had little feeling for the aspirations and political sensitivities of the Scots. To Robinson, Scotland was a resource of planting land and not much more.

5. During the interrogation of Ministers by the House of Commons Agriculture Committee on 22 November 1989, Mr Calum MacDonald raised in the first instance the matter of the hiving off of the Scottish end of NCC, asking whether the logic behind this was that circumstances were so different in Scotland that a separate Scottish agency was desirable. Lord Sanderson of Bowden (Minister of State at the Scottish Office) replied that this was part of the reason: the trouble with NCC was that it did not allow delegation of decision–making to England, Scotland and Wales. Mr MacDonald immediately followed up with the question why the same logic did not apply to the FC. Lord Sanderson replied that, unlike NCC, the FC was a Government department (a fact which he himself sometimes forgot) and was separately answerable to Ministers in the three countries for decisions affecting each country. The junior environment Minister (Mr David Trippier) went on to explain that, besides the reason given by Lord Sanderson, there had been disquiet in Scotland and Wales about the failure of NCC in bringing about 'the form of nature conservation that people would like to see on the ground'. If Ministers were under the same kind of pressure to split up the FC geographically, Mr MacDonald might well have a point. But, so far as he knew, there was no such pressure (QQ 898–901).

Mr Eric Martlew then posed the question (910) to Lord Sanderson whether the FC should be 'broken up' into two sections, the enterprise side and the authority side. This time the Minister responded with greater vigour and fluency. The case for dividing up the Commission was not a strong one. The argument that the FC was judge and jury in regard to its own operations was invalid because it applied to its planting programme the same scrupulous and dispassionate consideration that it gave to grant applications from the private sector. There was nothing unusual in a government Department having a promotional as well as a regulatory role. The fact that staff could be and were interchanged between the Enterprise and the Authority side was a great source of strength to the Commission: it gave individual officers the hands-on experience which the public valued in dealing with FC, and it allowed a much more economical and effective use of staff. The short answer to the question was therefore 'No'. Mr Martlew thanked the Minister for putting up 'such a defence for the Forestry Commission': whereupon the Committee Chairman (Mr Jerry Wiggin, a former junior agriculture Minister) commented that it might have been well rehearsed.

When it came to a vote on this issue at the end of the Committee's proceedings – the only issue on which the Committee was divided – Mr Martlew was on his own in defending the status quo, while the rest of the Committee recommended the complete separation of the two functions and the vesting of the Authority function 'within the appropriate government departments' for England, Scotland and Wales (HC 1989–90 16–i, paras 135ff).

3

ORGANISATION AND EFFECTIVENESS

The previous chapter traced the origin and development of the Forestry Commission, concentrating on what appear to have been the most significant trends and the critical points in its history, especially so far as Scotland is concerned. A good deal has been said, in passing, about FC organisation and its relevance to the achievement of the Commission's objectives. It is important to look into these aspects more systematically, and to note views that have been expressed, from time to time, about the FC's effectiveness as an agency.

Constitution

The Commission is unique among UK Government agencies in having the status of a Department of State. Whether it has always had this status is a matter of debate: however, Anderson (1967) seems to be correct in dating it from 1945. What is not open to dispute is that its constitution was specifically framed from the start to give it the maximum stability and independence. Unlike the general run of agencies, which are designed by sponsor Departments with at least half an eye to how they can be effectively restrained, the FC was designed by a committee determined that it should be free from the conventional restraints. As the Acland Report (1918) put it:

> ...the afforestation policy of the State, once embarked upon, should be as little as possible liable to be disturbed by political changes or moulded by political pressure... When Parliament has once adopted a policy of afforestation the decisions that have to be taken as that policy develops should not be taken by politicians'.

These extraordinary statements were plausible only against the background of the urgent need then felt for an effective forest policy, and the total failure of the existing arms of Government to achieve it. However – in spite of the protests of the Treasury member of the Committee – they were persuasive, and the Commission took the form that Acland devised. This has proved remarkably durable, though whether it has best served the interests of the nation, or of the FC itself, is more open to question.

The Commission as constituted under the Forestry Act 1919 consisted of eight persons, of whom one had to be a technically qualified forest officer, two had to have 'special knowledge and experience of forestry in Scotland', and up to three could be paid as full-timers. For many years the only paid Commissioner was Robinson, the Technical Commissioner, though others gave their services free on something approaching a full-time basis (Lindley 1935, Ryle 1969). The choice of Commissioners seems to have been left very much to the Chairman. Anderson (1967) comments, in his usual acidic fashion:

> ...the principle that appointments should not be political has meant, in fact, that political appointments have usually been made, and few of the Commissioners

could claim to be very conversant with forestry, even in its political implications. The result has been that the technical staff and especially the Technical Commissioner have had an important say in running the State forest service.

This last sentence, unusually for Anderson, is an understatement: since the Robinson epoch the Commission has been a virtual technocracy.

It is sometimes supposed that the FC was set up to carry out afforestation and nothing else. This is not the case. Acland had identified four principal duties: carrying out schemes of afforestation; improving the management of existing woods; collecting statistics about forestry and timber usage; and keeping an eye on the total supply position in UK, including imports. Although the Forestry Act 1919 did not spell out these duties, it provided FC with the powers to fulfil them: the Commission was a forestry authority from the very start.

Constitutional questions came to the fore again with the proposals in *Post War Forest Policy* (1943) for a further massive increase in afforestation. The Commissioners recognised that their existing anomalous status, without responsibility to a Minister, might require attention. They suggested, without enthusiasm, that the Commission might report to Parliament through the Lord President of the Council (a government Minister without Portfolio) – adding plaintively: 'There is the obvious danger that a change of Minister might entail a change of Policy'. They also recommended that the practice of appointing to the Commission representatives of the political parties should be continued, so as to minimise party controversy.

The Government responded positively to the Commissioners' proposals for forestry expansion but not to their constitutional ideas. In the Forestry Act 1945 MPs became ineligible for appointment to the Commission; and the FC was made answerable to not one Minister but two, in the shape of the Minister of Agriculture & Fisheries and the Secretary of State for Scotland. Moreover the Ministers could give directions to the Commission, acting either separately (in respect of matters affecting one country) or jointly. If these new powers sent shivers of apprehension through the Commissioners, they soon learned that there was no need to worry. Their accountability was to the Ministers personally and not through the agriculture Departments (*Hansard* 4 May 1945), so in effect they had two spokesmen in Cabinet, and no critical Civil Service filter to penetrate. Anderson comments somewhat enigmatically: 'If this arrangement is working then some part of it is shirking its responsibilities'.

It had become clear by the Second World War that the FC was not properly set up to promote private forestry. Although making sympathetic noises, Post War Forest Policy failed to address the problem. The private sector had asked for the appointment of a special Commissioner to look after their interests, with his own staff and allocation of funds. This was rejected, as cutting across the general organisation of the Commission. So incensed were the private owners at the FC's high-handed treatment that they pressed for and obtained a further report, entitled *Post War Forest Policy: Private Woodlands* (1944 Cmd 6500). It made acceptable proposals for forestry grants: but on the question of constitutional change within the FC itself the owners met a blank wall. The notion of separate divisions, one to manage the nationalised enterprise and the other to foster the private sector, was one which, in Ryle's words, 'the Commissioners could not support... The two sectors clearly ought to merge at all possible points and levels'.

During the 1950s no important constitutional issues arose affecting the Commission. However, 1957 marked the first of an apparently endless series of inquiries, sparked off by the Treasury, into FC policies and programmes. And more drastic intervention was to follow. Reference has already been made to the Murrie Working Party of officials (1965) which sought to align the Commission with the model of the nationalised industries of the period. In so doing it brushed aside the FC's responsibility for the private sector – not simply by confirming the Commission in its preference for a monolithic structure, but by the changes which its findings enforced on the membership of the Commission. The report noted that, of the ten Commissioners (all part-time), five – in addition to the Chairman – were woodland owners. It recommended that instead the core of the Commission should consist of four full-time members – the Director-General (who should also be Deputy Chairman) and three other civil service members, responsible for Forest Management, Harvesting and Marketing, and Administration and Finance. The Chairman should continue to be a part-timer; and the remaining members (also part–time) should include a 'business man with the right sort of background and experience'. The Committee put a good deal of emphasis on the Commissioner for Administration and Finance: he would be 'the normal point of contact with the Treasury in all matters. We should expect him to move on, probably to a higher post within the Civil Service, after some years in the Commission'.

These recommendations were implemented almost at once. No legislation was needed, although the changes were, from a constitutional point of view, as great as any that had overtaken the Commission during its lifetime. The representation of the private forestry sector dropped from seven out of ten in 1964 to three out of ten in 1965 (Ryle 1969). In spite of the Murrie emphasis on alignment with the civil service and with business practice, the Commission was now dominated by full-time forestry professionals.

Although the FC was subject to constant upheavals in the succeeding 25 years, none of these was of constitutional significance. One administrative incident is worth pausing over, dating from the start of the Thatcher era. It has been noted earlier how the status of the FC as a Department in its own right was asserted from time to time, as well as its independence of the agriculture Departments. However, it had become the practice, following the move to Edinburgh in 1975, for the Commission to submit Ministerial briefs, answers to Parliamentary Questions and so on, through DAFS – no doubt because of the FC's lack of experience in this area. In time, the Commission chafed under this imposition, and a minute was duly circulated from the Secretary of State's office in 1980 stating the constitutional position and ordaining that FC briefs were henceforth to pass direct to Ministers, without intermediate editing by DAFS. At the same time there was reasserted the principle which had been laid down in the Murrie report of 1965, that Ministers were entitled to seek advice from their own senior officers as well as from the FC on the broader aspects of forestry.

New statutory provisions were required in 1981 to allow the Commission to engage in large–scale disposals, but thanks to back–bench pressure the caveat was inserted that 'Ministers... shall have regard to the national interest in maintaining and expanding the forestry resources of Great Britain'. In 1985 a Private Member's measure obliged the FC to achieve a reasonable balance between forestry and conservation – a duty which the Commissioners professed themselves glad to accept (1984-85 Annual Report).

Legislation was again required (1991 Forestry Act) for the relatively trivial

two years after the Commission had moved to Edinburgh, Scots were still in a small minority among the senior management and they have remained so ever since.

Figure 4: Management Structure of the Forestry Commission at 31 March 1993

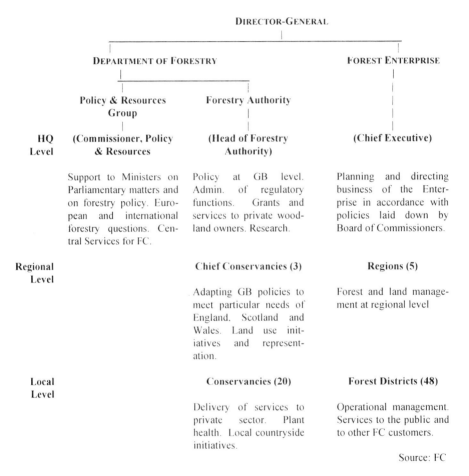

		DIRECTOR-GENERAL	
	DEPARTMENT OF FORESTRY		**FOREST ENTERPRISE**
	Policy & Resources Group	**Forestry Authority**	
HQ Level	**(Commissioner, Policy & Resources**	**(Head of Forestry Authority)**	**(Chief Executive)**
	Support to Ministers on Parliamentary matters and on forestry policy. European and international forestry questions. Central Services for FC.	Policy at GB level. Admin. of regulatory functions. Grants and services to private woodland owners. Research.	Planning and directing business of the Enterprise in accordance with policies laid down by Board of Commissioners.
Regional Level		**Chief Conservancies (3)**	**Regions (5)**
		Adapting GB policies to meet particular needs of England, Scotland and Wales. Land use initiatives and representation.	Forest and land management at regional level
Local Level		**Conservancies (20)**	**Forest Districts (48)**
		Delivery of services to private sector. Plant health. Local countryside initiatives.	Operational management. Services to the public and to other FC customers.

Source: FC

Why Scots have failed to figure prominently in the higher echelons of the FC is not easy to unravel. While it has been deemed politically prudent to ensure that the membership of the Commission is heavily weighted towards Scotland, at the career level Scotsmen must, of course, compete on equal terms, and it may be argued that they have simply not excelled. But still, considering the high proportion of FC activity going on in Scotland, the outstanding quality of the Forestry schools at Edinburgh and Aberdeen universities, and the location for the past eighteen years of the FC Headquarters in Edinburgh, it may be wondered why the representation of Scots remains so relatively low. It may be contrasted with the Great Britain private sector forestry companies – Fountain Forestry, Tilhill, the Economic Forestry Group – where the managing directors have tended to be Scots (W E S Mutch, pers. com.).

Glen Dye – bulldozed forestry track

Perhaps an explanation may be sought in the very characteristic which the Scottish advocates of the Commission insisted on in the early days – its uncompromisingly unitary structure. The obverse of this has been its unwillingness to tolerate a devolved administration, or a Scottish interface. Anderson (1967) commented that many Scots foresters refused promotion if it meant working, as he put it, 'abroad' (II, p498): and it may be that Scots forestry administrators have felt the FC Headquarters to be a piece of alien territory – whether situated in Savile Row or in Corstorphine Road. The creation of a Scottish national office for the new Forestry Authority, with a substantial measure of devolution, may mark the turn of the tide in this respect.

The advisory committees

The 1991-92 Annual Report records – like its predecessors since 1988 – that National Committees exist for England, Scotland and Wales, but that they held no meetings during the year. This simply reflects the position under the Forestry Act 1945: that the FC was to establish National Committees, consisting partly of Commissioners and partly of outsiders, and to delegate to them such functions as it saw fit. The delegation to the Committees shrank over the years, so that the Murrie working party of 1965 saw them as a useless appendage which should be abolished when it became politic to do so. So far, it has not been deemed politic.

The Regional Advisory Committees (RACs) are another story. *Post War Forest Policy* recommended the formation of small advisory committees in each Conservancy, on which woodland owners and others would be represented. They were made statutory in the Forestry Act 1951. Anderson (1967) defines their role as: i: stimulating forestry; ii: solving forestry problems; and iii: promoting good relations between forestry and agriculture – and regrets that they were not given executive powers. In 1965 Murrie saw them as having a useful function.

In 1974, when the newly elected Labour administration announced the terms of the new dedication scheme for private woodlands, a wider role was intimated for RACs. They were to assist in reconciliation where differences of view remained on the acceptability of particular grant applications, especially in regard to environmental and land use issues. In addition the Commission would consult RACs over local authorities' structure and local plans. Accordingly, RACs would be reconstituted to include representatives of agriculture, planning and environmental interests, though without enlargement of their membership (which remained at nine each). What the announcement did not mention was that these interests were to get one seat each, leaving the majority of the membership (including in almost every case the chairman) representative of the forestry and landowning interest. As a means of giving dispassionate attention to land use issues, therefore, the reconstituted RACs were a face-saver and little more. It was true, as the FC repeatedly pointed out, that RACs were for reconciliation and not for adjudication, and that the proportion of cases that went to them was very small anyway: but the absence of any other forum for considering the merits of sensitive grant applications put an undue weight on what appeared to be an inappropriate piece of machinery.

Increasingly instances were highlighted in which RACs behaved in a far from even-handed way, some of their members actually voting on cases in which they were personally concerned. Tompkins (1986) mentions a Perthshire case where, after the RAC decided to reject the grant application, two of its members who had an interest announced that they were going ahead with planting anyway. This was embarrassing to the Commissioners, and they persuaded the applicants to seek retrospective approval – which was duly given, along with the grant.

In January 1985, responding to a report on the uplands by the Countryside Commission for England and Wales, the Government endorsed the FC's consultative procedures, but added that the Commission was 'looking at ways of achieving greater public accountability' for RACs. The upshot was a consultation paper, issued in March 1986, proposing an increase (from nine to twelve) in the membership of RACs to give additional places to environmental and farming interests; greater care in the choice of individual RAC members and chairmen; and procedures allowing the public to submit views on cases under dispute. The results of consultation were published in December 1987. They confirmed the FC in all their proposals (except that some respondents would have wished to go much further). But virtually nothing happened. The reason was – as eventually explained to the House of Commons Agriculture Committee in 1990 – that the increase in RAC membership required legislation, and the Government were still waiting for a suitable legislative opportunity. This came, at long last, through a Private Member's Bill which became law in September 1991.

'Headquarters' committees

The most significant statutory committee is the Home Grown Timber Advisory Committee (HGTAC). It was set up by the Board of Trade in 1949 and became, under the Forestry Act 1951, a kind of sounding board for the FC with private forestry, with special reference to the downstream sector. The Committee was however far from an effective source of outside advice: and it was not until 1963, following the recommendation of the Watson Report of 1956 (on private forestry), that it was given an independent chairman and a fully independent membership (Ryle 1969). It is a large (25) and active Committee, which has given the FC fairly uncritical support down the years, except where private interests were thought to be adversely affected. In other words, it acts as a kind of official pressure group. Since 1978, however, the Committee has had two members appointed to it to represent environmental interests, and in 1992 it appointed an environment sub-committee 'drawn from a balanced cross-section of persons representing forestry and environmental interests' (1991-92 Annual Report). These changes in the constitution of HGTAC bear some resemblance to the measures taken to improve the image of RACs at the Conservancy level. They hardly justify the hope, expressed in the 1991-92 Annual Report, that the FC will thereby be materially assisted in 'fulfilling our statutory duty to balance the needs of productive forestry with those of the environment'.

The overall impression left by the FC committee organisation is one of fairly complete ineffectiveness in letting in the light of general public opinion to the Commission's operations. The committee structure appears to have been designed from the start to admit special interests only, and that only to the extent that suited the FC. Concessions were made piecemeal and with reluctance, and rarely ended up by satisfying the demands which had given rise to them.

Efficiency

There is very little literature bearing strictly on the question: *Is the FC efficient?* Efficiency is essentially the extent to which stated ends are achieved with the minimum of expense and of internal friction. The trouble with forestry in Britain is that there is very little agreement over stating ends, so that those who start out to consider efficiency, whether in the FC or in the private sector, are very quickly diverted into discussing ultimate values and objectives.

In a way, the FC itself has made this question all the harder to answer. The standard means of analysing efficiency in modern practice is to require the agency under scrutiny to lay out its own objectives in a systematic way and to break down its expenditure under each objective or sub–objective. This allows certain techniques to be applied in a rigorous fashion – eg unit costs, year-on-year comparisons, and cost/benefit analysis. In the very early days the Commission, anxious to demonstrate its careful stewardship of public funds, was exemplary in its layout of costs. Each main service was reported on, and its expenditure disaggregated, under a separate subhead, with common services allocated among subheads, so as to give 'a clear view of the true cost of the effective services on which expenditure has been incurred' (1st Annual Report, 1919-1920). Such simplicity was of course easy to observe, and entirely adequate, when the only main services were buying land and planting trees, and expenditure was measured in a few hundreds of thousands of pounds per annum. Of course, as the enterprise grew in size and complexity, service headings became much less of an aid to financial appraisal. In 1974, when the FC stated its objectives in a revised corporate plan, the opportunity presented itself to reshape its accounts around the objectives. The Commission did not grasp the opportunity, but stuck to the familiar service headings, which continued to be used up to and including the 1991-92 Annual Report. The only performance indicators were global ones for the Forest Enterprise – for plantations over GB as a whole and for recreation and amenity as a whole. In this respect the Commission lagged behind Government departments and almost all public agencies.

It is not clear why the FC has been allowed to be so backward in providing measures of efficiency – whether in terms of objectives, or of geographical breakdown, or of performance tests. One possible reason – which has already been adduced in this investigation – is that it is neither fish nor flesh, neither classical Department nor typical agency. If it were a Department, it would long since have been brought within the mesh of the Government's management initiatives, which involve ever closer targeting and performance measurement. If it were an agency, it would have had the same management regime imposed upon it by its parent Department. As it is, the only kind of management discipline that can be imposed upon it is an external one, usually through Parliamentary scrutiny of accounts. And that can only be spasmodic and unsystematic, as is brought out elsewhere in this chapter.

Select Committees on Estimates reviewed the FC's finances in 1929, 1937 and 1948–49, but only came up with such platitudes as 'The Commission is doing a fine work of national importance, which will in the future secure for the nation satisfactory dividends on their investment' (1948–49). This implied that technically the Commission was efficient, planting trees which would on the whole come to maturity, and was succeeding in keeping its costs down. It did not carry any sort of quantitative judgment as to what the returns to the nation might actually be (because the Committee was thinking only or mainly in terms of insurance against a future war). It was the Select Committee of 1964 which for the first time recommended that a realistic assessment of the value of State forests should be made at regular intervals, and that annual reports should include a summary of financial results.

In 1971-72, the Heath government's cost/benefit study and *Forestry Policy* consultation paper were published. These consolidated what Stewart (1987) calls 'the Forestry Commission's obsessive concern with net discounted revenue as the criterion for all decisions'. It was certainly not helpful to the pursuit of effi-ciency in day–to–day management, because revenue from past investment, how-ever calculated, was not within the control of managers making decisions about future investment.

The next significant enquiry into FC efficiency can be found in the *Review of Forestry Commission Objectives and Achievements* (National Audit Office 1986), which is considered in greater detail below. What should be noted here is para 2.5, which deserves to be quoted at length:

> The absence of more clearly defined objectives or quantifiable performance tar-gets makes it difficult to assess the Commission's performance other than in broad terms, and does not provide the Commission with a clearly defensible mechanism for recognising any imbalance of effort and determining the correc-tive action in a calculated way. NAO's assessment, based on an overall view of the Commission's work, was that the Commission had achieved a reasonable balance in directing its efforts and resources across its different activities.

This verdict, which the FC accepted with complacency, was in fact quite a se-vere one so far as efficiency was concerned. It confirmed that the FC had still not made the effort that had been lacking all along to clarify its own objectives, or those that had been handed down to it, in a way that would enable the Comm-ission itself or anyone else to test actual performance. In that light, NAO's judgment that the FC had achieved a reasonable balance in its use of resources was virtually meaningless – a conclusion to which the Public Accounts Commit-tee was driven in its subsequent Report (HC 185, April 1987).

Nothing in the Annual Reports for the succeeding years would indicate that the FC intended to take remedial action in this area. In fact it has taken the new management reorganisation to show any signs of progress. In the initial state-ment regarding the new Forest Enterprise there is a commitment to specifying objectives (including environmental goals), applying financial and performance disciplines, and ensuring that line management will operate under full account-ability for the services it provides, both to the industry and to the general public (1991–92 Annual Report).

Unfortunately there is no similar commitment from the new Forestry Author-ity – although the need for objective-setting and performance testing is even more clamant there (1986–87 HC 185).

Effectiveness

In most commercial organisations the line between efficiency and effectiveness is difficult to draw: being efficient means making a profit, and making a profit is a large element in being effective. As we have seen, it is hard to tell whether the FC, although in large part a commercial organisation, is in fact making a profit – a problem which afflicts forest services throughout the world (Clawson 1977). But that is not the only factor that makes a verdict on the Commission's effectiveness difficult: there is the problem of the criteria by which effectiveness is to be judged. Not only are forestry policy criteria widely in dispute: even in so far as they are agreed to be relevant and important individually, they cannot all be satisfied together. Clawson lists five such criteria: biological feasibility, economic efficiency, economic equity, cultural acceptability, and administrative practicality; and argues cogently that it is impossible either to maximise the values of each simultaneously, or even to compare one directly with another, because they are qualitatively different.

This section is not attempting to assess the FC's effectiveness, but only to summarise the opinions that have been expressed on that topic. Fortunately – despite the difficulties noted above – few observers have hesitated to express an opinion, favourable or otherwise. These will be summarised under categories of observer – first Parliamentary committees, then Ministers, next the FC itself, environmental writers, and finally Scottish commentators. The opinions of the forestry lobby – or the client group – form part of the subject matter of the next chapter.

Parliamentary committees

As mentioned above, Parliamentary scrutiny of the FC up to the 1960s was minimal, and was conditioned by the unquestioning acceptance of the need to build up a strategic forest reserve. In a sense, the same can be said of scrutiny on the floor of the House of Lords up to the 1990s. As pointed out by Tompkins (1989), although forestry has been regularly debated in the House, the object is not to criticise but to press for increased afforestation: 'The House of Lords is the heart of the forestry lobby'. It is principally in the Commons, or rather in its committees, that useful appraisal of the FC and of forestry policy has taken place.

The Commons Estimates Committee of 1964 gave the Commission good marks overall and did not challenge its objectives directly. The main question marks were over the Commission's financial procedures and targets, and its organisation. The Committee's recommendations on these points were influential, but only because they were applied with extraordinary rigour by the Murrie Working Party. The Committee Chairman, on hearing of the full range of the enforced changes, exclaimed to the House that the baby was being thrown out with the bath water (Ryle 1969).

The Commons Committee on Public Accounts (PAC) looked at the FC in 1979, concentrating again on financial targets, which it pronounced not sufficiently demanding. This was a superficial scrutiny, as was that of 1983-84: but the Committee's next summons, in 1986-87, was a different matter altogether. It was preceded, as has been noted above, by the National Audit Office's review of the Commission's objectives and achievements. This registered an impressive increase in the forested area of Britain and a corresponding increase in production, but detected an alarming vagueness as to the financial and economic returns from afforestation, particularly in the north of Scotland, and as to the alleged value of the secondary objectives (mainly in the environmental field). The PAC went further. While observing the proprieties through declining to comment on 'the merits of the policy objectives set for the Commission', the Committee took note of evidence that forestry had negative as well as positive impacts on recreation and the environment and that there had been a failure to identify these, let alone to quantify them. The return on the subsidies to private owners was a particularly grey area (HC 1986–87 185).

In 1987-88 the Commons Environment Committee issued a report (HC 270) in which the FC was taken to task for failing to take seriously the effect of air pollution on trees – and, through them, on soil and water. The House of Lords Select Committee on Science and Technology, on a wider front, found the FC to be wanting in urgency in identifying the need, and pressing the case, for increased forestry research (HL 1988–89 13–I). But in effect the Government drew most of this criticism in upon itself, by declining to provide any more research funds 'in the present economic circumstances'.

The final item to be noted in the list of Parliamentary scrutinies of the FC, though by no means the least in thoroughness and importance, is the Commons Agriculture Committee's report of 1989-90 on Land Use and Forestry (HC 16–1). Its recommendation on the Commission's structure has already been discussed. The Committee, while sparing in its direct strictures on the Commission, used freely the device of quoting with implied approval critical evidence that had been put to it in the course of its enquiry. Reading thus between the lines, one can infer that the Committee considered the FC as having failed to achieve a reasonable balance between forestry and other countryside interests, and between commercial and amenity planting; as having dragged its feet on the question of indicative forestry strategies, and on the reform of RACs; as having neglected to develop locally-based employment; and as being too much in the pocket of the private sector to be given responsibility for the task of environmental assessment, or to fulfil the role of Forestry Authority.

All this, coming from a Committee which was certainly not anti-forestry, represents a fairly serious indictment: but it was not one which the Commission took particularly seriously, if the official response (the Parliamentary statement of July 1990) is any guide.

Looking back over the range of Parliamentary enquiries, one is conscious of, first, an acceptance of the case for increased afforestation, and of the need for a Commission; and second, an increasing degree of irritation with the FC – for its failure to specify its objectives, and for its slackness in observing them.

The Government

An interesting finding to emerge from this investigation is how reluctant Ministers are to pronounce on the performance of agencies, compared with their readiness to interfere in their organisation and even their day-to-day running. The Commission is an extreme example. In one way that is perfectly understandable, because the FC is a government Department, and Ministers do not normally pronounce on their Departments. But then, neither do they normally interfere in their organisation or day-to-day running: whereas the Commission has been subject to almost constant interference. Forestry Ministers do of course often make statements about forestry policy, in which the role and performance of the Commission are referred to. But in the great majority of these the wording will follow closely that of the draft put forward by the FC, which is after all the Minister's Department for forestry purposes. In many cases the Minister will agree with the FC line. In others, he might have wished for a second opinion from a less committed source, but he accepts the FC advice because it is constitutionally difficult to get access to a second opinion. So the scope for a statement which genuinely represents the Minister's mind, as distinct from that of the Commission, is limited.

It is to some extent speculation, but there is evidence that some forestry Ministers find this situation frustrating. How can they find relief? One way is to refer their problem to a political think-tank. Another is to talk to Ministerial colleagues, who – especially if they belong to the Treasury – will not be slow to suggest ways in which forestry policy can be looked at collectively. This perhaps explains the unusual number of forestry policy initiatives which have originated from outside FC. Ryle (1969) chronicles the first of these, in 1958. Others followed in 1963, 1965, 1970-72, 1976-77, 1979 80, 1985-86, 1988 and 1993 – all as detailed at various points in the previous chapter. Each of them implies some (unspoken) Ministerial judgment on the Commission's performance. It is far from clear that their net result has been to improve that performance: some of the changes have been mutually contradictory, and they certainly have not all had regard either to the need for continuity in forestry policy or to the principle of 'reasonable balance'. What they do undoubtedly indicate is a lack of Ministerial confidence in the FC's ability to see straight and to act, in concert with other Departments, so as to fulfil the broad aims of Government policy – whatever these may be at any particular time.

The Commission itself

The judgment of the FC on its own performance is even harder to discern than that of Ministers. Commissioners are not given to beating their collective breast as, for example, NCC occasionally did. That, however, is a reflection of the Commission's status as a government Department. Departments are nothing more than an embodiment of their Ministers and their policies, as was emphasised in the 1971-72 Annual Report. Any public acknowledgment of shortcoming could be construed as a slur on the government of the day.

Thus it is of little use scouring Annual Reports for evidence of self-appraisal by the Commission. They are consistently low-key, even in their celebration of achievement. The nearest one gets to an admission of failure (usually in the distant past) is in remarks such as 'It has been a deliberate policy of ours *since the early 1970s* [author's emphasis] to take account of the needs of other land users and of the views of those who care for the countryside' (1985-86) and 'The days of insensitive monoculture are over' (1991-92). In their absorption of criticism the Annual Reports achieve a remarkable mastery of understatement. When some unpalatable judgment is uttered or awaited, or some change of practice is forced upon the Commission, the usual formula is 'We were interested in...' or 'We welcomed...' (eg Annual Reports 1985-86 paras 21, 52; 1986-87 para 34; 1988-89 paras 29, 54; 1989-90 para 28; 1990-91 para 93; 1991-92 para 43). Not infrequently, of course, new initiatives are announced with the object of 'enabling the Commission to discharge its obligations more effectively': but rarely is it made clear what shortfall in effectiveness preceded the initiative in question.

Even in cross-examination by Parliamentary Committees and other enquiries, FC representatives have provided little indication of the self-questioning which one imagines goes on at Headquarters. To get at this kind of information would require access to the minutes of Commission meetings, although it is likely that the minutes are kept Cabinet-style and do not give very much away.

North of Loch Rannoch – blanket planting

Environmental writers

Because of its many facets, forestry attracts attention from a wide variety of commentators – scientific, technical, economic and environmental/political. However, interest in the FC as an institution – the theme of the present investigation – is usually limited to the last–named category. That does not mean that the literature on the subject is limited in extent or scope.

Among environmental writers, the FC has few allies. It was not always thus: up to the 1950s the Commission was widely welcomed as doing a good and useful job, even if its horizons were thought to be a bit restricted. As late as 1972 Fraser Darling, giving evidence to the Select Committee on Scottish Affairs, was inclined to view even FC's blanket Sitka spruce as a benefit, because 'after it is thinned out and some of it gone, other stuff could be used which are pleasanter trees altogether... The more forest there is the better' (HC 1971–72 51–xvi). More recently, it has been hard to find an ecologist or an environmentalist who will speak up for the Commission or its policies. Paradoxically that does not mean that they would be happy to see the FC disappear. During one of the recent alarms about privatisation the Director-General was moved to say 'We never knew we had so many friends' (Stewart 1987).

Criticisms of the Commission cluster around a number of themes. The first is policy, or rather the lack of it. Commentators point to the successive reasons that have been advanced since 1919 for forestry expansion, often of very temporary plausibility but always replaced by some other reason when the need for it arose. To them, forestry in Britain looks like an activity in permanent pursuit of a rationale (Stewart 1987). If it is objected that policy is a government rather than an FC responsibility, these critics will ask where governments are supposed to get their policies from, if not the functional Department concerned. Besides, the Commission has come out openly again and again (eg in 1943, 1977 and 1991) in favour of expansion, as if there were no other possible choice.

A second focus of discontent is with the results of afforestation, as practised by the FC itself and promoted through the various dedication and grant schemes. Here the pack has been led by the official conservation bodies (NCC and the Countryside Commissions) and notably by the Royal Society for the Protection of Birds. These critics would deny that they are anti-forestry: indeed they would mostly accept that the woodland coverage of Britain is still too low and ought to be increased. Nor would they wholly discount the value of what the FC has achieved over the last 70 years. But they point to a wide discrepancy between what has been achieved and what could have been achieved. They assert that in the area of the alleged supplementary benefits of afforestation – eg recreation, integration with agriculture, nature conservation and amenity – the balance sheet is often negative; that in the pursuit of quantity, the opportunity to build in or improve quality has been not so much let slip as cast aside; and that the FC has been guilty of double-talk over a long period in asserting its own environmental concern (RSPB 1985; NCC 1986 and 1987; Bowers 1987; Tompkins 1989; Mattingly 1991). Grove (1983) has developed the line of thought that the Commission's attitudes in this respect flow from the adoption of the block afforestation model of forestry prevalent in Germany at the turn of the century, and popularised in this country by Sir William Schlich – who was a member of the Acland Committee. Certainly the complaints of environmentalists in this country are by no means unfamiliar on the mainland of Europe and further afield, which may suggest that there is something structural at work here.

A further line of criticism attacks the FC directly as an institution. This comes in several forms. The first takes issue with the extreme centralisation and mobility of staff practised by the Commission, which have tended to promote uniformity and stifle the development of local tradition (Stewart 1987, echoing a complaint by Anderson 1967). A second focuses on the 'forestry mind', a frame of thinking conditioned by the recruitment of FC staff from a small number of teaching centres which interact more with the Commission's thought-world than with other academic disciplines (Stewart 1987, Tompkins 1989). That this again is not a purely British phenomenon is indicated by the work of Kennedy (1985), who reported that foresters in US 'tend to be a proud, cohesive professional group', untrained to be sensitive to 'social values' – and, moreover, attracted by personality 'to the perceived tranquility of working in and with forests' and to the avoidance of 'heavy human interaction and confrontation in the normal workday'. This, if correct, is a fairly intractable problem, but it is contended by Stewart that it is exacerbated by the tightly centralised structure of the Commission.

A final thrust of criticism aimed at the Commission as an institution will be mentioned briefly here and dealt with in detail in the following chapter. It is developed with great ferocity by Tompkins (1989), who was himself an employee both of the FC and of a private forestry company. Its flavour can be deduced from his quotation from a speech by Lord Taylor of Gryfe:

> The great thing about forestry is that it is a partnership. The dreary debates between public and private sectors which bedevil other areas of our national economic life do not apply to the rational world of men and women who grow trees. It was therefore an easy transition when I ceased to be chairman of the Forestry Commission and became chairman of the Economic Forestry Group.

It is an axiom with those who adopt this line of attack that a Commission which is on such cosy terms with the private forestry and downstream sectors cannot be fit to be a forestry authority, since its judgment in that capacity will be affected both by its interests *qua* Forestry Enterprise and by its commitment to the commercial aims of the private sector, especially in regard to forest expansion. This once more is not a problem unique to Great Britain.

The Scottish perception

The Scottish influence in the formation of the Forestry Commission has already been discussed at some length – in particular, the insistence of the Scots on the Commission's being the kind of monolithic object that it became and still is, to a large extent. It is clear that the movement behind its formation was headed by a small number of enthusiasts who might be seen as the embryo of the forestry lobby of today. But the movement was a much wider one, representing a desire on the part of ordinary citizens and MPs of all parties to see a more productive use of what were regarded as the barren wastes of hill land and deer forest. It is therefore instructive to trace how Scottish attitudes to the FC have developed over the past 70 years, and how its performance is viewed now from a Scottish perspective.

As in Great Britain as a whole, Scottish reaction to the FC's early policies and practice was muted, and amounted to little more than the occasional complaint regarding the neglect of the private sector. When in 1945 the devolution of pow-

some schemes implemented in the 1980s, have attracted many times more opposition and opprobrium. Particular outrage was expressed over the afforesting with mixed species, at a grant cost of £2m, of 2000 ha of Strath Cuileannach in Sutherland, which had been the scene of notorious cruelty during the Highland clearances during the nineteenth century: but it emerged that the scheme did not have the depopulating effects which its opponents had attributed to it, and that it had the prior approval of SNH. On the credit side, the Commission has been widely praised for its part in the Central Scotland Woodlands Project (1991), designed to transform much of the bleak landscape between Glasgow and Edinburgh into a complex of productive and amenity forest. But the negative publicity continues greatly to exceed the positive: and the FC's image seems likely to suffer so long as its grant-awarding and regulative roles are combined.

In summary, therefore, the FC started out with a good image, which it began to lose in the 1970s – just at the time when the environmental movement was gathering pace in this country. Its reputation hit rock bottom in the late 1980s, but has experienced something of a revival since then, paradoxically through the perceived threats to the continued existence of the Commission.

In Scottish terms, confidence in the FC, which has tended to be higher than in the rest of Britain, is now probably lower, because of the increase in environmental awareness and the higher level of afforestation in Scotland.

4

THE FORESTRY CLIENT GROUP

The term 'client group' has a particular slant in the case of forestry in that, of the three agency functions under review in this investigation, forestry alone has a major commercial aspect. It is no accident, therefore, that in the case of the FC the client group currently takes the form of an interest group. This is not in itself a reason for covering the forestry lobby with abuse, as some do – although it must condition one's attitude to its pronouncements.

History

The forestry client group is, in its current form, probably unique in British experience in having been called into being by government, rather than having developed of its own accord. There have been, of course, forestry societies (ie associations of people who are keen on forestry) in the UK for well over a century, and they played a crucial role in the creation of the FC. But having done so, they did not instantly mutate into an interest group. The Royal Societies for Scotland and for England, Wales and Northern Ireland relapsed into a largely 'enthusiast' role for many years after 1919 – though in so far as they began *faute de mieux* to represent the interest of private woodland developers *vis-à-vis* the Commission the term enthusiast was scarcely appropriate. The sluggishness of the FC in stimulating planting by the private sector seemed to be communicated to the Societies, so that up to 1935 or so it was accepted on all sides, in practical terms, that the decent thing for the private landowner to do was to make his land available and for the Commission to buy and plant it. In 1937 the Societies so far roused themselves, and the FC, as to hold a series of meetings designed to stir up private planting but, according to Ryle (1969), with little effect.

By 1943 the private woodlands had been ravaged again to support the war effort. *Post War Forest Policy* made various proposals for reinvigorating private forestry to make good the losses, but it took a supplementary report and a separate Act of 1947 to generate a new 'dedication' regime which stood a chance of achieving the desired object. In 1945 the RSFS revised its constitution to take account of its obligations to private forestry, and in 1946 a most significant step was taken – the appointment of a Scottish Joint Forestry Committee comprising representatives of the Society, the landowners and the timber merchants (Anderson 1967). It was the first of what was to be a long series of joint bodies, some evanescent and others with greater stability.

The main concern of the private owners at the time – and indeed right on into the 1980s – was their lack of confidence in the FC to give due attention to their welfare. In 1947 the Commissioners rejected out of hand the plea of the Societies and the landowners for a separate Authority to foster the private sector.

Somewhat inconsistently, in 1949 Robinson insisted on the sector itself creating a single body for the Commission to negotiate with (Anderson 1967). So a body called the UK Forestry Committee was set up (representing owners only) and it hobbled along until 1959.

Other consultative entities set up during the 1940s, on an unofficial basis, were the RACs (at Conservancy level) and the Home Grown Timber Advisory Committee (on the initiative of the Board of Trade). These were made statutory in the Forestry Act 1951. However, the private sector remained uncertain and fragmented: and the Government was concerned enough, in 1954, to ask Sir Hugh Watson to head a committee to investigate its problems. Its terms of reference were limited and did not include the power to look at the FC's own organisation. But it did confirm its approval of 'the ideal of partnership between State and private enterprise on which British forestry is founded'. It recommended the formation, with initial assistance from the FC, of a strong woodland owners' association for the UK, with the functions of negotiating with the Commission, the timber trade, and other interests; of building up and disseminating information for the use of its members; and (optionally) of providing professional and commercial services for its own members. Scotland quickly went its own way with the creation of the Scottish Woodland Owners Association, carrying out all the above functions. England and Wales moved more slowly to form the Timber Growers Organisation (TGO) which did not offer the optional services. The two organisations were rather loosely joined under the umbrella of the Forestry Committee of Great Britain, which replaced the moribund UK Forestry Committee. HGTAC was also reconstituted, following another Watson recommendation, under independent chairmanship and with a more definite brief to cover the interests of the entire timber industry, including its downstream elements.

This brief historical survey illustrates how unfair is the characterisation of the structure, current among the anti-forestry lobby, as a 'disreputable cartel' for which the FC is at once 'a PR organisation, their tame planning authority, the trough through which subsidies are funnelled, and the obliging escalator of land values in remote places' (Wright 1992). The fact is that the structure was imposed on a none too enthusiastic FC and a torpid industry, at a time when encouragement of forestry was still the national watchword – and very few would have been found to say a word against it.

The two national bodies – SWOA and TGO – gradually gained strength over the following 25 years, though with many vicissitudes as a result of changes in Government policy towards the private sector and hiccups in the world and domestic timber markets. It was not until 1983, after the Thatcher government had come out for the first time in favour of private as against State planting, that the two bodies completed the logic of the Watson recommendation by uniting in the form of Timber Growers UK. This has a strong regional structure and a headquarters organisation based in Edinburgh. There is also a Forestry Industry Committee of Great Britain – a voluntary combination of the growers and processors, as against the statutory HGTAC. Finally the Royal Forestry Societies and the professional Institute of Chartered Foresters continue with very much the same orientation as they have had all along.

The client group as a lobby

The forestry client group obviously has its own varied functions, which occupy most of its time and attention. Many of these are technical, others are to do with internal interfaces in what is a multi–faceted industry; but it serves no purpose to minimise the extent to which the group is an interest group. There is very little of the 'merely' academic or enthusiast participation of the kind that is found, for example, in the US forest scene. Whether this will change, and the membership of the various constituents of the client group will broaden, with the introduction of grants for multi-purpose and amenity forestry, remains to be seen. It has scarcely happened yet.

The client group is, of course, an active and effective lobby. It had its first real success with the interdepartmental review of taxation in 1976: *Forestry and British Timber* reported that the Chancellor of the Exchequer 'had learned the error of his ways, thanks partly to powerful lobbying'. It is not so clear what part the client group played directly in the Conservative government's espousal of private forestry in 1980: probably other forces came into action. The massive campaign launched by the Forestry Industry Committee of Great Britain to counter the NAO report of 1986 – which had cast serious doubt on the public benefits to be gained from subsidies for private planting – was undoubtedly effective, in damage limitation if nothing more. Following the removal of tax incentives in the 1988 Budget – announced by the Chancellor without prior consultation – the lobby has been thrown into some confusion. But it has regrouped around the standard of the need for new regulative mechanisms (FICGB 1989), for improved management grants (TGUK 1991) and for a new forest strategy (FICGB 1992).

The client group as a vested interest

The sentiments uttered by Wright (see above) are commonplace among not merely environmental journalists but also environmental writers. Tompkins (1989) is the most thoroughgoing, although not the most extreme, in his attack on the client group. His charges – taken up sporadically by other commentators – fall under four headings: the group as a cartel, as a propaganda machine, as a corrupt promoter of the forestry cause, and as a mindless 'belief system'. In respect of all four the client group is bracketed closely with the FC as a fellow-conspirator.

The cartel accusation is based on the notion that the timber growers operate within a 'forest-industrial complex' along with the FC, investors and processors to rig the market, both in wood products and in land. This seems unsustainable. The timber market is a world market, in which the UK industry is entirely passive so far as price is concerned (Arnold 1991). The links that have been formed within the industry are quite open and of long standing, the object being to create a measure of mutual support in order to counteract, to a slight extent, the externalities of trade (McNicoll et al. 1991). As for the land market, it is certainly the case that afforestation, and the size of the grants available, have distorted the price of land in remote areas. But the wide range of interests represented in the forestry lobby, including both losers and gainers from distorted prices, makes the conspiracy theory implausible.

The view of the interest group as a propaganda machine does not rest solely on its efficiency in that regard, but more particularly on its lack of scruple. This is a charge which is difficult either to sustain or to disprove. Tompkins (1989) quotes as an example the parrot cry of the forestry industry that 'mistakes have been made in the past, but we have learned better now'. This is certainly disingenuous, but not particularly subtle. Indeed, since another of Tompkins' charges is that foresters are stupid it is difficult to take the combination of charges seriously. The writer's view is that, taken over the piece, the propaganda of the British forestry industry has been relatively restrained and reasoned in character. If it has been lavish in expenditure terms, at any rate the costs have mostly been incurred in hiring serious academic analysis rather than advertising agents.

The accusation that corrupt methods are used in promoting the interests of forestry is not often made directly, although Wright (quoted above) does not shrink from it. It is put in its mildest form by Callander (1987) who draws attention to the enormous concentration of land ownership in Scotland in the hands of a few – all of them with an interest in the encouragement of private forestry. Tompkins (1989) takes this a stage further in highlighting the 'kindly interest' taken by the House of Lords in forestry, especially by the 'backwoodsmen'. More serious is the charge that politicians are regularly 'nobbled', mainly by being appointed to the boards of forestry companies, and that there is far too steady a flow of FC Commissioners in the same direction.

The fourth type of criticism is not so much a charge of vested interest as a warning regarding foresters that 'such men are dangerous'. Tompkins (1989) alleges that they display symptoms of 'group-think' akin to members of certain religious sects or ideological groupings, the common features of which are inward-lookingness and unreality. This is echoed, but much more plausibly, by Stewart (1987) who speaks of foresters developing a 'defensive solidarity' among themselves. An early example of this characteristic is perhaps to be found in the pages of *Forestry* (1971: Vol 45), where the editor had to defend himself against two eminent foresters for including an article critical of private planting and the activities of the forestry companies. His reply was to the effect that foresters were merely an extreme example of a tendency in all professionals, whether road engineers or aircraft designers or whatever, to think that an ever greater supply of their product must unquestionably be a good thing. If the editor's diagnosis is correct, the fault is in principle a venial one: although Tompkins is no doubt justified in drawing attention to its potential dangers if the whole complex of decision-making about forestry expansion and planting grants is in the hands of, or is unduly influenced by, people of too homogeneous backgrounds and outlook.

A final word is needed on the allegation that the FC and the private sector are too much in each other's pockets. It is evident to anyone who looks at the history that for most of the time the two have been far too much at arm's length. The Watson Committee of 1956 had to remind FC forcibly that it was responsible for the welfare of private forestry. In the 1970s the FC, although it had ceased to regulate grant–aided planting effectively, was far from being a reliable ally to the private sector. In its submission to the incoming Thatcher government in 1979 the Commission depreciated the contribution that could be made by private planting – not unfairly, but in a mode more akin to that of the Treasury or NAO than of a sponsor Department.

If throughout most of the 1980s the Commission and the private sector seemed to march closely in step, it may have been more that their interests happened to coincide. However, since the tax changes in 1988 the client group has fallen into its habitual mood of suspicion of the FC. Commenting in April 1991 on the working party set up by the industry to formulate a new forest strategy, the Chairman of TGUK expressed the hope that the Commission 'would join in the deliberations because they were, after all, the Department responsible for the formulation of advice to Government on forestry policy in Great Britain'. In June 1992 he went further, stating that Government policy was 'becoming rapidly discredited' and that the private sector was taking over the policy–making role. And while the Director General of the FC was assuring the industry that the Commission had not sold out to environmental pressure groups, TGUK was emphasising that it entirely accepted the current environmental constraints, claiming that the organisation set the pace in 1985 with its Forestry and Woodland Code, which had since been imitated by the FC. Finally, a survey of forest owners, carried out on behalf of TGUK in the summer of 1992, indicated that only 26 per cent considered that the FC provided adequate leadership to the industry.

The overall picture, therefore, is that the view taken of the FC by its client group has been not much different from that taken by its clients of another Great Britain body, the Nature Conservancy Council, which will be considered in the next chapter. While looked at from the outside the interests of the agency and the client group might appear to be identical, in reality the two have generally lived in a state of considerable tension, and not always constructive tension.

Conclusion

The forestry client group, as at present constituted, is a combination of grower and user interests, and scarcely as yet embraces the increasing number of 'outsiders' who are interested in forests and concerned about their future development – usually with a 'green' orientation. Such people either organise themselves separately or participate in environmental organisations. The client group as such is therefore perceived – and justifiably so – as commercially oriented and concerned to bring pressure on FC mainly in terms of increased grants and higher afforestation targets.

While the situation is a fluid one, there are few signs yet of the FC taking the initiative in reconstituting and redirecting its client group so as to reflect the wider objectives which forestry ought to serve in the future.

Creag Meagaidh NNR, Badenoch

III

NATURE CONSERVATION

5

The Nature Conservancy/Nature Conservancy Council

Anyone trying to trace the administration of nature conservation in Great Britain from its beginnings at once comes up against a problem – and one which is at its most acute north of the Border. Since 1949, there have been no fewer than five bodies operating in Scotland – independent Nature Conservancy 1949-65; Nature Conservancy as part of the Natural Environment Research Council (NERC) 1965-73; Nature Conservancy Council 1973-91; NCC for Scotland (NCCS) 1991-92; and part of SNH 1992 onwards. Moreover, although the responsible body has remained throughout a 'non–Departmental public body' in Government parlance, or an agency for the purposes of this volume, the legal status has subtly changed in each of the five manifestations. This makes it necessary to review the status and development of nature conservation under each of the regimes – briefly for the early stages, and in somewhat greater detail as we move towards the present day.

Even before that, it is essential to trace the movements leading up to the formation of the Nature Conservancy in 1949, because so much of what happened then has significance for subsequent developments, down to the present day. This is not the place to write history – and in any case it has been well written up by Sheail (1976, 1981, 1984, 1992), Adams (1986), Evans (1992) and others. It will be enough to set down the most important features in summary form – particularly since otherwise there might be undue overlap with Chapter 9, the corresponding countryside chapter in this volume.

1. Nature study has a long history in Britain – both amateur (manifesting itself publicly in protection societies) and, in the twentieth century, increasingly professional (Sheail 1976).

2. Alongside this, there is a long tradition of enthusiasm for the countryside, for mountains, for the refreshment of the spirit through nature. However, the custodians of the two traditions have been, on the whole, different groups of people (Smout 1991). In this respect Britain differs from most other countries where the nature movement has been more broadly based (Boyd 1983).

3. Thus although in the 1930s and 1940s the two (nature study and countryside) came together in the National Park movement, it was a temporary alliance and the interests soon diverged. The great founding statute of 1949 – the National Parks and Access to the

Countryside Act – said comparatively little about nature conservation: it established the National Parks Commission but not the Nature Conservancy.

4. The Conservancy took its rise directly from the work of the Wild Life Conservation Special Committee for England and Wales, appointed in 1945 to consider, primarily, the wildlife issues thrown up by a previous National Parks report (1945 Cmd 6628). In the end, the Wild Life Committee did not relate its findings at all closely to national parks, but went instead for a National Biological Service which would acquire the best sites from a natural interest point of view – wherever they might be found – and manage them in the interests of science and, ultimately, for the benefit of man (1947 Cmd 7122).

5. In respect of both landscape and nature, the situation in Scotland was different from that in England and Wales. Even in the early years of this century, interest in nature in Scotland was less narrowly biological and made room for a broader ecology including man (Smout 1991). As regards national parks, the emphasis was much less on *safeguarding* (which was not seen as a priority because of the extent of 'wild unspoilt country which is incapable of recreational development') than on *promoting* active recreation, fostering of rural industries, and indeed making a financial return (Report of Scottish National Parks and Wild Life Conservation Committee, 1947 Cmd 7235 – the Ramsay Committee). Moreover a significant proportion of the proposed national parks was deemed to be of nature conservation interest, and although a measure of seasonal restriction might be desirable there, the public would be the gainers from 'the surplus population of animals' which would spread over the unrestricted area of the park.

6. In the end, Scotland and England & Wales went their different ways. There were (and are) no national parks in Scotland (though in the five major areas identified by the National Parks Committee special planning restrictions were imposed). The big landlords, and the fledgling Hydro–Electric Board, heaved a deep sigh of relief (Sheail 1976). However, by a narrow margin the Wild Life Conservation Committee (a kind of sub-committee of the National Parks Committee, headed by Professor James Ritchie) agreed, under the influence of Fraser Darling, to support a common 'Biological Service' for Great Britain. The Committee made it abundantly clear, nevertheless, that the Scottish arm of the Service should be differently run from that for England and Wales, because of the different physical conditions, administrative arrangements and political sensibilities that prevailed on the two sides of the Border. The Scottish division (or 'Scottish Biological Service' – the Report never seemed to make up its mind on the nomenclature) should be fully devolved, separately financed, and overseen by an independent executive organisation which should, moreover, be adequately represented on the Nature Conservation Board for Great Britain. How far this recommendation was honoured,

reserves and acquiring new ones – hoping that the necessary staff and facilities could be afforded later. Stamp's advocacy of new purchases – under the watchword 'Now or never!' – carried the day (Stamp 1969). Similarly Morton Boyd, Scottish Director of NCC from 1971 to 1985, writes of the exhilaration of the early days, when the yardstick of success was the number of NNRs appearing in each succeeding Annual Report, which had risen to 100 by 1961 (Boyd 1991). By 1965 the total had reached 113, with an aggregate area of around 100,000 hectares (NERC Report 1965-66).

If the expansion of the nature reserve estate swallowed up much of the Conservancy' s energy – and funding – in this first phase, there was also the more mundane but still significant function arising from the Royal Charter – the work of developing research and scientific services. This was akin to that of a Research Council, and it was overseen by a Scientific Policy Committee. The 1955-56 Annual Report describes with enthusiasm a meeting in June 1956, hosted by the Nature Conservancy in Edinburgh, of the International Union for the Conservation of Nature and Natural Resources. This occasion showed how ecological knowledge could be brought to bear on matters as widely varied as engineering, town and country planning, forestry and agriculture. In return, it was piously hoped, ecologists could gain insights into problems of administration and land use. How far this interchange between Nature Conservancy staff and the outside world could have been realised, had official responsibility for ecological research remained exclusively within the Conservancy, will be discussed below.

1965–1973

In October 1963 a government Committee of Enquiry into the Organisation of Civil Science submitted its report (Cmnd 2171). It was concerned mainly with rationalising the structure of the national scientific Research Councils, which was thought to have developed rather haphazardly. No doubt the formation of a new Natural Environment Research Council (NERC), tidying up the various institutes of oceanography, seismology, hydrology, geology and forestry, would have seemed one of the least controversial parts of the report. But the question arose: What was to be done with the awkward body responsible for nature conservation, with its Royal Charter and nominal supervision by a committee of the Privy Council? The solution was a typical British compromise: the Conservancy as a working unit continued, but its controlling Council became in 1965 a Nature Conservation Committee of NERC.

The effects of the change were, on the surface, minimal. Nature reserves went on being declared – at a slower pace, but this might have reflected the approaching completion of the task. However, the NCC's *Nature Conservation in Great Britain* (NCGB 1984) says, a little cryptically:

> The enthusiasm of Cmd 7122 [the 1947 report of the Wild Life Special Committee for England and Wales] for survey of the biological and physical resources of Britain did not...carry over into the established science policy of the Nature Conservancy... Concern to ensure a more adequate NNR series...led in 1966 to the launching of a Nature Conservation Review to identify the areas of national biological importance to nature conservation in Britain.

At about the same time the scientific side of the Nature Conservancy was reconstituted into eight habitat teams, covering the main plant and animal communities – mountain/moorland, wetland etc – (NERC Annual Report 1966–67). The timing of these moves might suggest a certain irritation on the part of the new NERC overlord at the random, intuitive approach of the old Nature Conservancy, and a desire to direct its efforts into more orderly scientific channels. This however would be over-simplistic, since the initiatives in question had been launched before NERC took over. It seems more likely that the discomfort felt by NERC related to the duty of the Conservancy to *promote* nature conservation, which seemed to prejudice the Council's jealously-guarded objectivity (Poore 1987).

Whether or not there was irritation on the one side, there was certainly frustration on the other. Looking back from the perspective of 1990, Sir William Wilkinson, Chairman of NCC, recalled the 'Research Council' status as a strait-jacket, from which the Conservancy could escape temporarily only by participation in, for instance, wider national and international conferences. The full and informative Annual Report of the Conservancy had been reduced to a brief chapter in a dry-as-dust NERC Annual Report – though the Conservancy sought to make up this gap by publishing periodic accounts of research and reserve management. The *Nature Conservation Review* mentioned above was completed during this period, although its publication was suppressed until 1977 – apparently because of fears for the reaction to a massive declaration of new sites of nature reserve status (Adams 1986). Direct access to Ministers was lost, and although funding of nature conservation continued to grow it had to be obtained by increasingly bureaucratic procedures.

Nature Conservancy Council

1973–1991

Nature Conservation in Great Britain succinctly attributes the escape from the NERC web to 'growing stresses from the Nature Conservancy's uneasy relocation as a promotional agency within a Research Council', as well as to the Government's acceptance of the Rothschild advocacy of consistent customer–contractor arrangements for applied research and development.[1] The Nature Conservancy Council Act of 1973 constituted a *Council* responsible for nature conservation, under the aegis of the Department of the Environment. What was lost was the direct responsibility for ecological research, which remained with NERC in the form of a new Institute of Terrestrial Ecology (ITE) along with the various research establishments which had been set up over the years under the Nature Conservancy's Charter. The function of the Nature Conservancy Council became that of commissioning or supporting relevant research, although it retained supplementary powers to carry out its own research. In line with this, funding for research was severely cut, apart from a transitional grant allied to the continuance of work commissioned from ITE.

The emergence of NCC as a promotional agency was not accidental. The Government had stressed in the course of the 1973 legislation that the Council was being given this degree of autonomy so that it could take a strong and independent line on major issues when necessary. But its role as an official environmental 'conscience' did not develop in a day: some Council members were not too comfortable with the change. The early Annual Reports are more concerned with assessing the management responsibilities inherited from the old

Conservancy, and with surveying the new areas for investigation and future action. Three areas were thus identified: agriculture, forestry and water.

Nature Conservation and Agriculture arrived in 1977, as the first of NCC's large glossy publications. It drew attention for the first time to the fairly drastic effects on the nature conservation interest of intensive agriculture, which had been promoted since the Second World War through production subsidies and capital grants, and consolidated following Britain's entry into the European Community in 1973. Among the effects highlighted were the loss of wetland, the removal of trees, hedges and field headlands, and the increasing load of pollution by fertilisers and pesticides in the wider environment. The publication bore the marks of the personality of Norman Moore, NCC's Chief Advisory Officer, whose experience and interests lay predominantly in the lowlands: very little was said about the uplands, in which the focus for future conflicts was to lie. The tone of *Nature Conservation and Agriculture* is described by Adams (1986) as 'calm and polite', and the recommendations were moderate: better advice to farmers, a plea for incentives to farmers to notify changes of management affecting SSSIs, and a plea to Government departments to recognise their environmental duty by making grant aid available for conservation from developmental budgets. As Moore put it in 1987: 'We must pay for our heritage'. These modest demands fell on relatively deaf ears.

The *Nature Conservation Review* has already been mentioned. It finally emerged in 1977 as a two-volume blockbuster costing what was at that time an astronomic £60, putting it beyond the reach of all but specialist readers (Steele 1978). The work is a monument to the immense industry of NCC's Chief Scientist, Derek Ratcliffe. It not only listed every biological site in Great Britain considered worthy of protected status but classified these sites according to habitat and inherent merit, and provided a detailed rationale for selection.

The political significance of the *Nature Conservation Review* had been perceived as far back as 1970, when the work was completed (interestingly, publication was to have been jointly by NCC and NERC, but NERC later withdrew). Instead of a total of 128 NNRs (37 in Scotland) extending over 110,000 hectares – 75,000 in Scotland (NERC Report for 1969-70)[2] – it envisaged an expansion to 702 protected sites covering nearly a million hectares (Table 3).

Table 3: Nature Conservation Review: number and extent of 'key' sites

	Grade 1		Grade 2		Total	
	No	000 ha	No	000 ha	No	000 ha
England	238	297	165	74	403	371
Wales	41	57	30	19	71	76
Scotland	116	273	112	193	228	466
Total	395	627	307	286	702	913

Source: *Nature Conservation Review* (1977) (p383)

This apparently insatiable appetite for designation has been variously diagnosed by different writers. Moore (1987), writing from his lowland perspective, argued that, since croplands were becoming less and less suitable for wildlife, reliance had to be placed on a network of specially designated reserves. Adams (1986) saw NC/NCC's strategy in enlarging its nature reserve estate as deliberate, responding to the inadequacy of powers to protect areas outside reserves (ie SSSIs). But the *Nature Conservation Review* embraced both NNRs and some SSSIs (the 'top-quality' sites, which it was assumed at that time would in due course be designated NNR), and there is evidence from the records that even in its earliest years NCC was not too happy about the protection available in some NNRs. Ratcliffe himself, in his defence of the *Review*'s proposals, laid emphasis on the enlarged understanding that NCC had acquired both of the nature of the threats to different types of habitat and of the inherent interest of the habitats themselves. In a contribution to a 1977 Royal Society symposium, he admitted that 'science' had become too pretentious and that it would be more honest to stop describing sites in terms of their scientific importance and to substitute 'nature conservation value' – an explicitly subjective criterion.

Subjective it may have been, but in Ratcliffe's eyes the judgment of value had to be made by scientists. The *Nature Conservation Review* awarded gradings of 1–4 (Grades 1 and 2 qualifying as 'key sites'). It abounded in references to sites of national or international importance, which tended to attract to themselves an authority liable to bemuse lay people, and even the rank and file scientists within NCC itself. This went hand in hand with an increased status for the Chief Scientist Directorate at NCC headquarters. Originally created in 1974 to manage the commissioned research programme, the Directorate soon became 'primarily a scientific advisory service to the whole organisation' (NCGB 1984). This reflected the weakening links with NERC and, specifically, with the Institute of Terrestrial Ecology. In a carefully worded paper dated December 1974 Martin Holdgate, formerly a Nature Conservancy employee but at that time Director of ITE, warned NCC that NERC's ecological stance would be 'neutral in terms of value judgment' and that ITE's advisory role was bound to differ from NCC's for that reason. Although NERC repeatedly undertook to continue collaboration with NCC, it naturally expected redeployment of NCC funds, especially to support such tasks as survey and monitoring which 'were not the most welcome work in ITE' (NCC Minutes July 1977). By 1979 Ratcliffe was admitting to his Council that 'attempts to persuade others to undertake research had not been over–successful' and that ITE was expecting to be contracted for almost all the work they did. In return NCC felt itself released from the moral obligation to continue funding NERC for commissioned work at the current level (NCC Minutes, September 1979). After that the proportion of research commissioned from NERC went steadily down, though ITE remained one of NCC's more important contractors.

The 1981 Act

Many commentators – though not NCC itself – regard the Wildlife and Countryside Act 1981 as marking a major epoch in the Council's existence. The perceptions of the Act are not what might have been expected: the general view is that it ended up as a farmers' charter and made the work of NCC harder and more contentious, whereas NCC never wavered in its support for the Act.

It is part of the mythology that, whereas other interests were fully brought into the consultations which preceded and accompanied the proceedings on the Bill, NCC was kept at arm's length (Blunden and Curry 1985, Adams 1986). This will not stand examination.

As early as 1974 NCC was angling for stronger protection for important sites: the proposal was that 'a decision to permit damaging development on a Grade 1 SSSI shall only be taken at Ministerial level'. In January 1979, in a Council discussion on forestry, the Chief Scientist put forward the view that 'sites of greatest importance should be inviolate'. It was hardly a mark of Ministerial indifference to NCC's views, then, that the Conservative government elected in May of the same year should have responded with a consultation document in which it was proposed, as regards habitat, that certain special sites designated by Ministers should have penal sanctions attaching to any operation liable to damage their special features. It is true that this provision (which was eventually enacted in the form of Section 29 of the 1981 Act) did not find favour with NCC, because it wanted to do the designation itself. But the Government, through the Department of the Environment (DoE), showed themselves ready not only to consult but to heed the NCC point of view as the Wildlife and Countryside Bill slowly gestated.

It was in fact the voluntary bodies that rocked the boat on the habitat provisions of the Bill. In December 1979 they told the NCC Chairman that they were not content with the statutory protection of special sites only: in their opinion all SSSIs should be protected, by prior notification of potentially damaging operations. This threw NCC into confusion. At the Council meeting in January 1980 alarm was expressed at the 'massive loss of goodwill among landowners and occupiers' which prior notification would lead to, and at the intolerable burden on NCC staff which would result. Accordingly the Council decided to adhere to the DoE scheme, with the caveat that it would eventually wish to notify to Ministers as requiring special protection all the sites in NCR Categories 1 and 2 (other than those in NNRs or otherwise safeguarded already). By then, however, work on the Bill had lost momentum and it was postponed to the following session.

The voluntary bodies did not let the grass grow under their feet. They came together under the banner of the Council for Environmental Cooperation, the Chairman of whose Wildlife Committee, the Labour politician Lord Melchett, addressed the NCC Council in November 1980. As a result, NCC changed its ground and wrote at once to the Secretary of State for the Environment to signify its endorsement of 'the principle of a statutory requirement for prior notice of all deleterious change on all SSSIs' and that, failing a Government amendment to that effect, it would seek recourse to an all-Party amendment (NCC Minutes November 1980).

Events then moved fast. The agricultural and landowning lobby, alarmed by the prospect of their members having to submit to prior notification and possible veto of farming activities on all SSSIs, turned the tables by moving amendments which required NCC itself to renotify all SSSIs and, moreover, provided for NCC to pay compensation where farming activities were restricted thereby. It is still held against NCC by the wildlife lobby that its tame acceptance of the principle of these amendments swayed the House of Lords into narrowly approving them (Lowe et al. 1986).

The 1981 Act changed the role of NCC more, perhaps, than NCC itself was prepared to admit. Throughout it had clung to the 'voluntary principle' to which the landowning interests also adhered. The Council had always shunned open confrontation and the publicity that went with it, preferring quiet diplomacy and persuasion. It was not until 1985 that it got round to appointing its first public relations officer. Now, compelled as it saw it by the terms of the Act, it took two decisions which were to influence its policy and relations with the public for the rest of the NCC epoch. The first was to drop the categorisation of sites into Grades 1, 2, 3 and 4 and treat all SSSIs on the same level. The second was to interpret Section 28(4) of the Act (requiring it to notify to the owner or occupier of an SSSI any operation appearing to the Council to be likely to damage flora, fauna etc) as covering *every* operation, however unlikely, that would have a damaging effect if carried out. It was NCC's contention all along that no other interpretation was legally possible: and so it felt obliged to present each occupier with a list of up to 32 'potentially damaging operations' from which only a small number would have been crossed out as (in the particular circumstances) either technically unfeasible or harmless. To the outside observer, it would appear less confrontational for NCC to have approached the problem from the other end and started with a short list of really live options for land use change – or, better still, entered into dialogue with the occupier about his future plans before serving formal notice on him. In practice, NCC staff increasingly did this in later years.

The code of practice governing the assessment of compensation was, from the beginning, heavily weighted against NCC and in favour of the claimant. That NCC accepted it without demur was due to two factors. The first was it genuinely regretted the sharp feelings which had been polarised by the Bill (1980-81 Annual Report): nature conservation was best achieved by consent. In the second place, the Council seems to have felt that it was time to present the Government with the real costs of conservation, and to use the estimates of compensation payments made possible by the existence of the code as a lever to obtain additional funds from DoE. The resource implications of the Bill (and, later, the Act) formed a constant refrain in the Council's own thinking and in its submissions to Government. In this objective the Council was entirely successful. Its grant-in-aid rose, in cash terms, from £8m in 1979-80 to £41.5m ten years later. However, there was a price to pay. The sheer effort of the task of renotification took a heavy toll on NCC staff: and in the end the costs to DoE may well have been a factor in bringing about the break–up of the agency.

Nature Conservation Strategy

No published document exists with the title 'Nature Conservation Strategy'. Yet this was the heading under which NCC struggled for several years to clarify its role and the thrust which nature conservation should take in the years up to 2000 (1983-84 Annual Report). This effort was stimulated by the World Conservation Strategy of 1980 with its memorable watchword of 'sustainable development'. The Council, having been deeply involved in the launch of the Strategy, felt bound to respond, and once again commissioned its most creative thinker, Derek Ratcliffe, to undertake the task. Early drafts of the response, in 1982, show Ratcliffe struggling with the concepts that were forming in his mind as early as 1977. Dissatisfied with 'science' as the engine of nature conservation, he nevertheless pinned his faith to the principles of Tansley's Wild Life Conservation Special Committee and its 1947 Report (Cmd 7122). (This is odd, because to the general reader Cmd 7122 sounds like a manifesto for the biological scientist.) At any rate, by 1982 Ratcliffe was edging towards an alliance with the Countryside Commissions, and urging on his own Council a policy of conserving wildlife and habitat 'as a cultural resource for aesthetic and recreational reasons'. The NCC Council did not encourage him in this line of thinking, and he dropped it. Accordingly, his next draft drew trenchant criticism on the opposite flank from Richard Mabey, a writer about countryside problems and a member of the Council. Mabey found the draft tending towards the 'centralised, institutional and traditional', compromised by expressions such as 'nature conservation has a fine record of achievements', characterised by elitism, and stand-offish towards other movements and sectors of society from which NCC might be able to learn.

The response eventually appeared in 1984 as NCC's second major glossy publication, with the title *Nature Conservation in Great Britain*. It took an interesting posture midway between Mabey's and the one he criticised, drawing a boundary between cultural and economic purpose and, within the cultural, a boundary between scenic beauty and 'the tangible phenomena of flora, fauna and physical features' with which nature conservation must deal. It advocated 'the planned integration of conservation with development', but acknowledged that the nature conservation bodies could not themselves be integrators but must remain 'a sectional or partisan interest'. The Council would seek to improve its understanding of the economics of land and resource use, but chiefly for adversarial, not cooperative, purposes. It was the task of the UK Government to build environmental objectives into revised land use policies. In line with this, against nineteen recommendations concerned with sites of special importance, the document contains only six recommendations designed to secure conservation in the wider environment. In 1984 NCC was essentially protective in its attitude, looking outwards mainly in order to remind others of their obligations.

No less interesting, for the purposes of this investigation, than the future objectives set out in *Nature Conservation in Great Britain* are the chapters entitled 'Successes' and 'Failures'. The 'Success' chapter contains only six pages, one of which curiously is a table headed 'Post–1950 decline in breeding bird populations in Britain'. Items identified as successful are the designation of nature reserves, both national and local; the battle against indiscriminate use of pesticides (incidentally, one of NCC's most effective campaigns, but one for which it has never been given sufficient credit); the growth of the conservation movement and the heightened level of public awareness of conservation issues; and the strengthening of the law protecting both species and habitats.

The 'Failures' chapter is 22 pages long. It bemoans, in the first place, the absence of 'the broad and integrated kind of conservation which was the great vision of Cmd 7122' [the Wild Life Report of 1947]. Thus NCC's narrow view of its own remit is described as an inevitable compression brought about by 'the nation's failure' to develop an overall land use strategy. Following this, the catastrophic losses of different types of habitat are detailed, though more in an illustrative than a comprehensive fashion. The villains of the piece are identified as intensive agriculture and, to a lesser extent, afforestation: the prospective effects of these were grossly under-estimated in the 1949 legislation. The 1981 Act, although effective in relation to designated areas, came much too late and did little for the wider environment. There was no common cause among the countryside organisations. Within NCC itself, the task of biological survey was skimped from the start. The splitting of the old Nature Conservancy in 1973 impoverished the new NCC in terms of an 'enormous reservoir of scientific knowledge' and the residual funding of research was virtually halved. Among the greatest disappointments was the failure of successive governments to support NCC with more than a mere pittance from the national budget. In all this catalogue of woes there is very little self–criticism: blame is heaped upon the nation and the Government, and nothing is said to indicate what NCC would have done with extra resources had it been given them.

Afforestation

It was as far back as 1975 that NCC formed the intention to publish a paper on Forestry, as part of a trilogy with Agriculture and Water (the Water paper never materialised, although numerous aspects of freshwater problems were tackled in the 1980s). The first paper, on Agriculture, has already been discussed. Forestry gave more trouble. The earliest draft was the work of George Peterken, a forestry specialist, and came under criticism in the NCC Council as being too diffuse to form the basis of a policy document. The subject was remitted to a working group chaired by Dr Jean Balfour, a member of Council, which took until 1979 to report. When it did, its findings met with further criticism from Ratcliffe, on the grounds that it was too soft on modern-style afforestation and that there was no attempt to widen the debate to include economic factors and so bring in other interests, such as hill farming and water supply, which might wish to support nature conservation.

The upshot was that Ratcliffe and Jean Balfour were sent away to think yet again: their joint effort was considered at the Council's meeting in February 1980. It was admitted to be a compromise between the single-minded expression of the nature conservation case and the recognition that other land uses had a right to be considered. After intense discussion it was agreed to publish the paper with only minor editing, but as a think-piece and not a policy document. It was used as the basis of NCC evidence to the House of Lords Committee on Scientific Aspects of Forestry (1979–80 HL 381), but attracted little notice.

The Wildlife and Countryside Bill and its aftermath took up most of the NCC's energies for the next few years, and consideration of forestry went on the back burner. When it was actively resumed, it was Derek Ratcliffe once again who was commissioned to do the writing. It was 1985 before the draft of *Afforestation and Nature Conservation in Great Britain* appeared, and this time it met with fairly general approval from the Council. Much had been learned since 1980 about the impacts of new forests on wildlife; equally, afforestation had advanced markedly in the intervening years, particularly in the private sector. It was decided, however, to circulate the draft widely for comments before publication. The reaction to the draft took NCC by surprise. While the environmental lobby welcomed it with open arms, the response within Government was violently hostile. DoE called its tone 'shrill and assertive' and regarded its circulation outside Government as an act of betrayal. The Scottish Office felt that it could only engender public confrontation, as did CCS. What the FC thought has already been described.

In general, however, it was the tone rather than the content of the paper that came under fire, and NCC was able to publish the final document (with 'Nature Conservation' placed first in the title!) in May 1986, only a matter of months after the circulation of the draft. It was a more solid piece of work than *Nature*

Conservation and Agriculture. The science had been more thoroughly researched. Account had also been taken of the silvicultural point of view, and of the economics of forestry and its social effects. Attention was no longer confined to forestry within SSSIs, and the paper was able to examine how forestry and other interests could live together. Indeed it invited the forestry industry to consider expanding its activities in the lowlands – a surprising point of view at the time, but one which has been vindicated by subsequent events. No longer were the anti-conservation forces able to depict the authors of the report as a mere group of eco-enthusiasts. The launch of the document – simultaneously in London and Edinburgh – went off well and was celebrated by the signing of a concordat with FC over the protection of SSSIs on Commission land. If the final response of the Government to the report – in the form of a letter signed by the Secretary of State for Scotland as forestry Minister – was eighteen months late and so blandly complacent as to elicit a sharp response from the NCC Chairman, at least the Government were unable to pick holes in the document itself.

The final years

The overwhelming focus of attention for NCC in the years 1986-1989 was the afforestation of the so-called flow country of Caithness and Sutherland. This is not the author's opinion alone but that of NCC, for the subject dominates the Annual Reports for these years and indeed is described in the 1986-87 Report as the most important nature conservation issue of the last 30 years. It was certainly so for NCC, because it was the trigger for the Council's disbandment.

The story of the flow country is of course a Scottish one, and so belongs to the next chapter, on NCC in Scotland. The final events in the life of the Council, however, fall in this section and will be briefly summarised below.

In other respects the years 1986-89 might have been seen as a fairly quiet and even prosperous period. The back of the heart–breaking task of renotifying SSSIs had been broken. Gloomy predictions about the overall cost of SSSI management agreements were falsified. Adams (1986) had stated: 'One can be fairly sure that the cost of agreements will rise to £20 million [per annum] at the very least within 2–3 years'. The actual total for 1988-89 was £6.4 million. What lay behind this, of course, was the sharp decline in agriculture and the virtual collapse of private afforestation, brought about by the withdrawal of tax concessions in the March 1988 Budget. These were on the whole bonuses for nature conservation. Meanwhile NCC's grant-in-aid had risen from £21 million in 1985-86 to £39 million in 1988-89.

Yet there is ample evidence of an unease on the part of NCC – an uncertainty over its role, strategy and relationship with the outside world. At the end of 1986 William Waldegrave, then Minister for the Environment, took occasion to administer a few sharp rebukes to the members of Council. They should regard the purchase of nature reserves as a last resort, looking to less expensive options and encouraging voluntary bodies to take on more responsibilities. They should collaborate more with Research Councils and avoid wasteful duplication. They should remember that NCC was not a campaigning organisation, but part of the state machine: it should seek to emulate the Royal Commission on Environmental Pollution in its restrained presentation of a sound scientific case. There was a big task to be done in informing the public and responding to requests for advice, but without overlapping on the fields of other bodies. He was against a merger with 'the Countryside Commission'.

Within the Council there were signs of strain. On the same day that Waldegrave addressed the Council, misgivings were expressed by members about the content and control of the forward research programme and the adequacy of 'peer review'. At a Council meeting some months later the Deputy Chairman was critical of NCC's handling of publicity and regional sensitivities. During consideration of a paper on National Nature Reserve strategy it emerged that the Chief Scientist Directorate's plans provided for an additional 250 or more NNRs – to the great dismay of the NCC Council, which was envisaging an increase of perhaps 25. Another indication of tension was the reference by Derek Ratcliffe in his retirement message (June 1989) to the 'vast internalisation of energy within NCC'. By this he meant the weight of bureaucracy imposed by Government controls, added to 'an inevitably top–heavy internal management structure', using up energy which should have been directed to attacking the real problems of nature conservation on the ground.

All this time, apparently unbeknown to NCC, pressures were building up for major changes in the conduct of nature conservation in Britain. As early as autumn 1987 the Secretary of State for the Environment, Nicholas Ridley, had asked for consideration to be given to hiving off NCC operations in Scotland. It was the expected cost of management agreements in Caithness and Sutherland that prompted Ridley's enquiry: he saw no reason why Scotland should not bear the costs of its own nature conservation. The request was conveyed to the Scottish Office, which undertook to look into both the principle and the mechanics of such a change, as quickly as staff resources permitted. By January 1988 consideration had got far enough for the Scottish Office to show DoE some figures of possible staff needs for a separate Scottish organisation. At about the same time – and also in pursuance of Ridley's initiative – the Scottish Development Department (SDD) put a paper to Scottish Ministers outlining ideas for detaching the Scottish end of NCC and combining it with the Countryside Commission for Scotland.

The further progress of these ideas within Government was kept very much under wraps. There is evidence, however, that certain soundings were taken outside Government and that ideas were hardening throughout 1988 (J Balfour pers. com.) – though nothing was said to NCC itself for fear of an organised backlash.

In July 1988 a new Director–General was appointed to NCC, following the usual processes of advertisement and interview – in this case somewhat protracted in order to secure a wider field of candidates. The successful applicant was Timothy Hornsby, up to that time under–secretary at DoE in charge of rural affairs. On arrival at NCC, he took stock of the existing organisation, noting *inter alia* the strong and increasing centralist tendencies, on both the scientific and the administrative sides, which are commented on elsewhere in this narrative. Encouraged by the Chairman, William Wilkinson, Hornsby initiated a drive towards extensive delegation to the 'country' committees and headquarters, which acquired the title 'federalism'. It is reasonable to suppose that the new Director–General – apart from his own assessment of the organisational failings of NCC – had some inkling from his previous post of what was brewing in Government circles, and was using all available means to outflank it. In December 1988 the federalism proposals were reported to DoE Ministers, who responded favourably. Hornsby's internal studies of federalism patterns went ahead in the early months of 1989, but with some obstruction

6

Nature Conservation in Scotland

Reference has already been made to the recommendation of the Scottish Wild Life Conservation Committee (the Ritchie Committee) that there should be a single Biological or Wild Life Service for Great Britain. The caveats attending that recommendation bear repetition and expansion. In its Scottish manifestation the Service required to be administered in close consultation with the Scottish Home Department, the Department of Health for Scotland, the Scottish Education Department, the Department of Agriculture for Scotland and the 'Scottish Branch' of the Forestry Commission. It had to be noted, also, that the legal systems north and south of the Border were fundamentally different. Terrain, geology, even flora and fauna in Scotland were distinct, as was the significance of economic factors. 'Above all', said the Committee, 'we are convinced that wildlife conservation in Scotland can be fully effective only if it has the backing and whole-hearted support of the Scottish people generally, and such support is most likely to be gained by there being centred in Edinburgh a Scottish Division of the Biological or Wild Life Service of Great Britain'.

The Committee recommended that, in consultation with the Secretary of State for Scotland, an executive organisation called the Scottish Wild Life Committee, composed of scientists with appropriate qualifications, should be appointed to organise the Scottish Division – that is, supervise its research and survey programmes, and advise other authorities on wild life questions within the land under their control. These responsibilities were to be exercised not just in nature reserves but throughout the whole of Scotland – an emphasis lacking in the England and Wales Report (Cmnd 7122).

Characteristically, perhaps, the Scottish Committee laid stress on financial matters: the new executive committee should be given a block grant to administer at its own discretion, and also be able to carry out investigations on contract from Scottish government Departments or other authorities or individuals. Members of the Committee should receive adequate remuneration in view of the economic potential of their work.

Whatever the virtue of these very specific recommendations, it is clear that they were passed over when the Nature Conservancy came to be set up. 'Rejected' would be too strong a term: they just did not fit into the unified framework which, following Cmd 7122, was imposed on Great Britain as a whole.

As has been noted, evidence of Scottish unease over the failure to devolve responsibilities is simply lacking.

The Nature Conservancy

1949–65

In practice, Scotland was from the start allowed a large measure of practical autonomy. The 'Scottish Committee' was a unique feature of the NC, and although its powers and duties were not specified it was clearly allowed to go its own way in many respects. This was possible because, in the early days, finance was really no constraint. In its first three years the Conservancy underspent its allocation by £160,000 or nearly 40 per cent, which annoyed the Treasury much more than an overspend would have done (Annual Report to 30 September 1952). Scotland made the running in the creation of National Nature Reserves. Beinn Eighe, an enormous tract of land, was acquired in 1951, and Cairngorm – even larger – was established in 1954. It seems that landowners were willing, even keen, to enter into nature reserve agreements in order to avoid what they saw as the greater threat of national parks (J M Boyd, pers. com.).

Personalities were also of some importance. Smout (1991) has chronicled the immense care that was taken with the appointment of the first Director for Scotland (a post with no counterpart in the south) – Dr John Berry, a distinguished biologist, but also a member of the Scottish Landowners Federation. The founding membership of the Scottish Committee also reads like a rollcall of the scientific and landowning establishment of the day – the Earl of Wemyss and March, Sir Henry Beresford-Peirse, Sir Basil Neven-Spence, along with Fraser Darling and Professors Matthews, Peacock, Ritchie, Walton and Yonge. Men of that calibre (women did not appear on the scene for another sixteen years) were easily able to get alongside and gain the confidence of the major landowners, which seemed at that stage a high priority. When in 1953 a Scottish landowner – Arthur Duncan of Tynron, near Dumfries – became Chairman of the Conservancy itself, Scottish sensitivities were lulled to the point of complacency, a situation that prevailed until the early 1970s.

It is not easy to recapture the carefree spirit of these early years, except by the silence of the contemporary records towards what would nowadays be recognised as threats to the natural environment. A flavour may however be gleaned from papers read at a symposium of the Royal Society of Edinburgh in October 1960 on 'Natural Resources in Scotland'. Even then the contributors from the nature conservation side were almost exclusively concerned with the question (as one of them put it) of 'how to take the maximum crop without depleting the stock'. Dr Eggeling, at that time the NC's Conservation Officer for Scotland, called conservation 'another name for wise use', and Fraser Darling himself summed up by pronouncing:

> Utilisation of natural resources, and particularly of wildlife, I feel to be one of the main foundations of its ultimate conservation.

It is difficult to imagine the conservation case being expressed in that sort of way in a comparable conference held at that time south of the Border.

1965–73

Although the absorption of the NC within the Natural Environment Research Council (NERC) made little difference to the everyday running of the Conservancy, it affected Scotland in a far–reaching though indirect way.

The *de facto* separateness of Scotland – its possession of a formal Committee, a national Director and a substantial headquarters – became eroded, not by the abolition of any of these institutions, but by the 'levelling up' of the rest of the country. Since the NC was itself a fairly minor component of NERC, it was not to be expected that subtle distinctions within the NC would continue to be recognised.

During this period took place the important activity of the Select Committee on Scottish Affairs which resulted in the Report on Land Resource Use (HC 1972 511 – i). Rejecting evidence (HC 51 – xviii) to the effect that all agencies dealing with rural land use in Scotland should be amalgamated into a department of rural affairs, the Select Committee nevertheless recommended the setting up of a Land Use Council to act as a central forum for discussion of rural land use questions. One of its first tasks would be to examine ways in which the NC (and the recently formed Countryside Commission for Scotland) could more effectively police the activities of public bodies affecting the natural beauty and amenity of the countryside. This reflected a rather far-sighted body of evidence, both written and oral (HC 51 – iii), from the Conservancy which concentrated not on the importance of designated sites but on the conservation of nature throughout the countryside. Less forward-looking was NC's view that there was virtually no overlap between its field and that of the Countryside Commissions. The Select Committee's recommendations were in any case given fairly short shrift in the Government's response (Cmnd 5428, September 1973). This provided for a standing conference of the new elected regional authorities – a promise which was never redeemed – and for a possibly strengthened advisory role for the new Nature Conservancy Council once it had been set up.

Nature Conservancy Council

1973–1991

The Nature Conservancy Council Act 1973 completed the demise of the Ritchie concept of the administration of nature conservation in Scotland. It did this in three ways. First, it put the Scottish Committee on the same level as those for Wales and England, and declared all three to be advisory in character (the nature of the Scottish Committee having been previously undefined, as we have seen). Second, it brought the sponsorship of NCC, and its financing, under the Department of the Environment – essentially a *territorial* department, with England as its predominant field of interest. Third, it made appointments to the Advisory Committee for Scotland subject to the approval of the Secretary of State. In constitutional theory, this term can cover any of 'Her Majesty's Principal Secretaries of State'; but in practice the Secretary of State for the Environment became the confirming authority, at least throughout most of the 1970s. The stage was set for the centralisation of NCC which reached an extreme in the 1980s; and for the increasing emphasis on the natural environment of Scotland as part of a Great Britain resource, rather than as a Scottish resource.

Of more immediate concern was the loss to the new NCC of the research function and the research establishments (including stations at Edinburgh and on Deeside) which remained with NERC. In their report the Select Committee on Scottish Affairs had commented that, although they were unable to take fully into account the implications of the Government's decision, it would be difficult in a Scottish context to separate research and advice on conservation, for example in the case of grouse. They quoted Max Nicholson, a former Director–General of the Conservancy, as an exponent of the view that combining the two functions had led to the strongest single ecological team in the world, and that their separation would be stupid or at least misguided. No such qualms appear to have been felt within the Conservancy itself. In evidence to the Select Committee the then Director, Dr Duncan Poore, flanked by two of his Scottish colleagues, expressed the hope that the changes would be beneficial. At the inaugural meeting of the NCC's Scottish Advisory Committee (SAC) in June 1974, the Council Chairman, Sir David Serpell, spoke of the great advantage of the Council's now being a statutory body; and the Scottish Committee Chairman, Mr Hamish Maxwell, saw no problem in commissioning research from the Institute of Terrestrial Ecology and elsewhere, apart from the need to choose priorities carefully among limited funds.

The work of NCC in Scotland continued along similar lines to what had gone before. There was close liaison with the Scottish Office over the planning of North Sea oil and gas installations and in the drawing up of National Planning Guidelines, which brought NCC more formally into the town and country planning framework by requiring clearance by the Council of development proposals on or affecting SSSIs deemed to be of national importance. The Scottish Director (Dr Morton Boyd) was deeply involved in the Standing Committee on Rural Land Use, one of the few positive outcomes of the work of the 1971-72 Select Committee, and in the assembly of data on rural land use on an all–Scotland basis. Administratively, NCC staff in Scotland were grouped in four regions, though with rather limited delegation of authority.

In November 1975 the Government published a White Paper on devolution of government to Scotland and Wales (Cmnd 6348). The Council of NCC hastened to welcome the White Paper proposal that nature conservation should not be devolved. This displeased the SAC, not because it disagreed with the Council's stance, but because it had not been consulted (SAC Minutes January 1976). Thereafter much debate focused on the question whether, and how far, the new Scottish Assembly and Executive should be required to take nature conservation into account in the discharge of their functions, which included land use planning and countryside. By the following year a majority of the Committee had come round to the view that this was not practicable unless certain nature conservation functions were devolved (SAC Minutes January 1977). Sir David Serpell quickly arranged to be present at the Committee's March meeting. The Committee was assured that its views had been noted and that it would be further consulted if the current legislative proposals were proceeded with. The meeting then moved on to consider the question of internal delegation within NCC, a step which had been encouraged by the Council, not without reference to the devolution proposals. The main point made by the Scottish Committee was that there should be a greater scientific capacity based at Scottish HQ 'to serve Scotland', and under the control of the Director (Scotland), not the Chief Scientist (SAC Minutes March 1977).

The Scotland Bill as published (November 1977) did not devolve any of NCC's functions, though it did give NCC a statutory advisory role towards the new administration. Members of SAC expressed concern about possible confusion and conflict if the Bill were enacted. They agreed however that the most important point was that NCC in Scotland should be adequately staffed and have sufficient delegated authority to respond to the needs of the Assembly and Executive (SAC Minutes January 1978).

What happened in the counsels of NCC when the Scotland Act foundered, following the consultative referendum held in March 1979, is not to be found in any of the Council's records. From personal recollection, however, the Scottish Director tells how, when the news came through, a colleague reacted instantly with the comment 'There goes our extra staffing and our delegated authority!' (J M Boyd, pers. com.). A tiny scientific unit had indeed been outposted to Scottish Headquarters, but under the control of the Chief Scientist, not the Director (Scotland). No other change, beneficial or otherwise, resulted. The next challenge which the Scottish Headquarters had to face was not the absorption of additional staff but the threat of losing staff following a reduction in the NCC's grant-in-aid (1979–80 Annual Report).

That this threat did not materialise was a consequence of the Wildlife and Countryside Act 1981 and NCC's successful efforts to convince the Government that implementation of the Act required massive extra resources. Scotland received its share, along with the toilsome drudgery and increased paper work that went with renotification of SSSIs. Even so, we find a 'Rayner scrutiny' of NCC – which awarded the organisation, in total, a modest increase in staff – sniping at one or two advisory and administrative posts in Scottish Headquarters under a serious misapprehension as to 'the volume and level of work generated by the existence of separate Scottish Departments and agencies, acting under specifically Scottish legislation and procedures, and which cannot be dealt with effectively from GB HQ' (SAC Minutes June 1983).

It was not merely the volume of work (which was massively augmented by case–work thrown up by oil developments) that was getting on top of the Scottish NCC. Its image, and relations with local communities, were suffering because of procedures introduced by the 1981 Act. In a discussion at its meeting in May 1984, the Advisory Committee highlighted factors which were causing misunderstanding and even demonstrations of hostility. These included the following: the list of Potentially Damaging Operations (PDOs) in terms of Section 28(4) of the Act was long, detailed and forbidding, and was construed as a list of prohibitions; an owner who wished to carry out a PDO might get compensation, but not de-designation; there was no provision for independent assessment of sites, and no appeal against designation. Better training for NCC staff in the art of communication was suggested as one remedy, but ways of improving the presentation of PDOs were also required.

This sense of Scottish unease was articulated eloquently in a valedictory paper given in in January 1985 by Morton Boyd, the retiring Director (Scotland) who had served with distinction in that capacity since 1970. Although it is entitled 'Nature Conservation in the Highlands and Islands of Scotland', some of its strictures may be taken as applying more widely throughout Scotland.

Dr Boyd began by reviewing the course of Highland history, which had left deep scars of resentment and of folk memory relating to incomers seeking either to exploit the native population or to change their way of life. On the whole, that way of life had been in balance with the natural environment.

The notification process for SSSIs assumed an exactly specified natural interest, readily identifiable PDOs, easily defined boundaries, and known owners, occupiers and land rights. In other words, the SSSI was visualised as being a small lowland site of uniform habitat-type. In the Highlands, by contrast, SSSIs tended to be vast, superficially indistinguishable from the surrounding area, and requiring management in sympathy with neighbouring estates rather than in contrast to them. If Scotland had been legislated for separately, said Boyd, it would have been a somewhat different Wildlife Act. Agriculture was the predominant occupation in the Highlands, and yet over large areas which were of outstanding wildlife interest it was necessary, in terms of the 1981 Act, to declare the most basic agricultural practices as damaging. Even where consent was given to continue such practices – as was usually the case – the notion of 'consent' smacked of arrogance and made for a bad start in negotiations with owners and occupiers. Where the NCC negotiators had lacked the necessary cultural rapport with Highland, especially Gaelic-speaking, communities the stage was set for disastrous misunderstanding, likely to be eagerly seized upon and inflated by the media. The same problem occurred when NCC was obliged to comment unfavourably on commercial developments which affected SSSIs or the wider environment but were perceived locally as the economic salvation of the area. Boyd concluded with a call to NCC to develop a different emphasis and approach, to reflect the value judgments of the whole community, and to exercise the degree of flexibility necessary to ensure that the legislation was in fact workable 'in the land and among the people'. In this he was echoing the appeal of the Scottish Wild Life Conservation Committee of 1947 for effective devolution of nature conservation to Scotland.

Boyd's paper was unfinished. A final chapter was projected, entitled 'The Future', and outlining a series of long-term targets for harmonised land use in the Highlands and Islands, as well as touching on the functions of other official bodies, such as the Countryside Commission for Scotland. But the paper was not destined to see the light of day. It was given a warm welcome in the SAC for its 'inspirational message' (Minutes, February 1985), and was thought to have the support of the Council Chairman. But the paper had attracted criticism from some members who thought that it could be politically controversial and potentially damaging to the NCC's operations in the Highlands and Islands, even if clearly understood to be an expression of Boyd's personal views. Accordingly it was decided to reconsider publication in 1987, giving Boyd a chance to revise it in the meantime (NCC Minutes, June 1985). It is hardly surprising that nothing was heard of it again.

Indeed, far from Boyd's warnings being heeded a new development hastened the move towards centralisation and uniform treatment throughout Great Britain. At the very meeting at which his paper was suppressed Council heard a warning that recent court cases had called into question the efficacy of the 1981 Act provisions for notifying SSSIs. Although legislative means were found of curing the particular defect in question, Council became increasingly wary over the defensibility of its procedures; and in time it had occasion to seek the advice of Treasury Counsel on a further issue. Since 1973 the Advisory Committees had been given a wide range of delegated responsibilities, including that of deciding on the notification of SSSIs. The legality of this was now challenged: and Counsel, after considerable hesitation, gave it as his view that, in terms of Section 28 of the 1981 Act, all notifications and renotifications had to be confirmed by the Council itself (NCC Minutes November 1987). The effect so far as Scotland was concerned was disastrous. Not only did reference to the Council eat into the already limited time for consulting owners and occupiers, but the actual consultations increasingly came into the hands of the Peterborough-based

Chief Scientist Directorate, which was already showing centralist tendencies and notoriously lacked the sensitive local touch that Boyd had pleaded for (A R Trotter, pers. com.). Even before this, the Council had begun to assert a more proprietorial interest in Scottish matters, reflecting what the Chairman later described as 'less supportive' attitudes there towards nature conservation (1989-90 Annual Report).

The first effects of this changed posture were seen in relation to Islay, an island with a great variety and extent of nature conservation – as well as agricultural – importance. In July 1984 the Secretary of State for Scotland gave Scottish Malt Distillers Ltd planning permission for peat extraction from Duich Moss, proposed as a Grade I SSSI on account of its importance for roosting barnacle geese (although, by a curious quirk of local NCC adaptability, not formally notified as SSSI until the day after the planning consent had been granted). The Secretary of State invited NCC to take part in discussions on conditions that might be attached to the planning permission so as to minimise damage to the Moss. These discussions made little progress, and meanwhile a great deal of interest was focused on the area by the RSPB and other conservation bodies. Under pressure from these, NCC reported the affair to the European Commission, who responded by seeking an injunction in the European Court of Justice requiring the Secretary of State to revoke the planning permission. In the end the matter was resolved by the Malt Distillers being assisted to develop an alternative site (SAC Minutes May 1986). However, NCC had set a precedent by providing advice not for Ministers but against them, praying in aid its responsibilities for international as well as domestic conservation.

An even more contentious issue was that of the Rinns of Islay, a large, significantly agricultural, area where the conservation interest was somewhat diffuse but was thought to be at risk from afforestation. There was no difference in principle between the Committee for Scotland (as it had by this time been renamed) and the Council on the notification of the entire area as an SSSI, but the feeling of the Committee was that more time should be allowed in order to resolve the exceedingly complex and fraught preliminary consultations with individual owners and occupiers. This was not forthcoming (NCC Minutes, September 1987; A R Trotter, pers. com.).

The effect of this and other restrictions on Islay was to create a climate of hostility there towards NCC which persisted for years.

The Flow Country Debate

'The flow country' is a grandiose and non-indigenous title conferred on the peat-covered area of Caithness and Sutherland, amounting in total to about 400,000 ha or 45 per cent of the land surface of these counties. 'Peatlands' is a more useful description, but even then it obscures the immense variety of habitats, ranging from thin broken blanket peat, as found on numerous hill slopes equally in other parts of the Highlands, to the fully developed raised bogs (mainly on the Caithness/Sutherland border) which properly merit the title of 'flows'.

Caithness and Sutherland do not stand out in the 1977 *Nature Conservation Review*, being represented by only seven sites, with a total area of 16,000 ha. When advanced forestry methods began to allow planting on deep peat, both the FC and one of the large forestry groups saw the north of Scotland, with its large uninhabited spaces and cheap land, as promising territory for expansion, and they met little opposition from NCC in exploiting it.

Even as late as 1984, *Nature Conservation in Great Britain* failed to identify the flow country as under particular threat. It was only with the publication of *Nature Conservation and Afforestation in Britain* (1986) that NCC began to highlight the extent of actual and potential habitat and wildlife loss (although the RSPB had already been focusing attention on Caithness and Sutherland for some time). This is put down, in nature conservation circles, to a failure in NCC's survey programme which was not systematic enough, and which only began to pick up the significance of the northern peatlands from about 1979 (O W Heal and M Usher, pers. comm.).

Accordingly, when the Committee for Scotland received a report on afforestation in Caithness and Sutherland in May 1986, it was simply to the effect that the Director (Scotland), Dr John Francis, had joined in a discussion at the Scottish Office Departmental Group on the Countryside at which it was agreed to formulate a 'simple framework of locational principles' for land use in the area, and in that context to look at an overlay of plantable land produced by the Forestry Commission. The Group would return to the subject later in the year.

By October 1986, however, the matter had taken on a different complexion, and NCC participation in the work of the Departmental Group was unilaterally broken off. Discussion at the Council meeting held at CCS headquarters at Battleby in October was in closed session. The Director (Scotland) was given responsibility for coordinating a review of the position and evolving a new strategy for the area, but under the close control of the Council and the Chief Scientist Directorate (NCC Minutes November 1986). The matter had been taken altogether out of the hands of the Scottish Committee. Thus the report made to it in May 1987 said merely that the case for non-afforestation of peatlands was proceeding, that presentations were being made to English and Scottish Ministers, and that members would be given an opportunity to 'view the new package in due course'.

What lay behind all this secrecy came out soon enough. A glossy publication outdoing all NCC's previous efforts was launched in London in June 1986 in a blaze of publicity. Entitled *Birds, Bogs and Forestry*, it was embellished with numerous photographs, diagrams and tables. However, on closer examination the data displayed turned out to be stronger on birds than on bogs, and the publication appeared in its true light, as a polemical piece designed to marshal public opinion and stop forestry in its tracks. In this it met with early success. The conservation movement was delighted with the NCC's sudden aggressiveness. DoE Ministers took up the cause. Even before the launch, the Forestry Commission had agreed to refer to NCC all forestry applications in Caithness and Sutherland, not merely those affecting SSSIs.

But the effect in Scotland was different. The Deputy Chairman of HIDB had spoken at the launch, attacking NCC's decision to hold it in London rather than in Scotland – a decision which came to be regretted within NCC itself (Marren 1993). Highland Regional Council, and opinion in Scotland generally, were violently hostile, and the Scottish Minister responsible declined to view the NCC presentation. The Scottish Office called a meeting with officials of DoE, FC and the Chief Scientist Directorate in order to query various aspects of the scientific case. The Scottish Committee members were incensed at receiving copies of *Birds, Bogs and Forestry* only the day before the launch, with no opportunity to study, let alone defend, its contents (Scottish Committee Minutes September

1987). It was clear to them that they were not trusted.

Later developments were in a lower key. Responsibility for handling negotiations was returned to the Director (Scotland). Highland Regional Council agreed to chair a working party to examine land use options in Caithness and Sutherland, and secured the cooperation of virtually all parties. The Secretary of State for Scotland, while rejecting the call for a moratorium on forestry, accepted that a case for protection existed over approximately half the unafforested peatland area of 350,000 ha, and invited NCC to notify new SSSIs accordingly (January 1988). Belatedly, in March 1988, NCC published a full account of the peatland resources of the area, which commanded a much more complete scientific consensus. But the task of surveying and notifying the vast area of the flows imposed an enormous burden in terms of both personnel and finance, as subsequent events were to prove. The whole affair had dealt a fatal blow to the concept of the SSSI as the instrument of choice for protection of the nature conservation interest in Scotland, as Morton Boyd had foreseen several years earlier.

Glen Lochay

In October 1986 John Cameron, a noted farmer and landowner, submitted an application for forestry grant in respect of 640 ha on Glenlochay Estate, which he had recently acquired. The afforestation was to be in seven blocks, three of which were wholly within SSSIs. The application was opposed by numerous objectors, on scenic as well as nature conservation grounds. It went to the FC's Regional Advisory Committee in July 1987, and shortly thereafter the Commission refused the application on nature conservation grounds alone. It was open to the FC to invite the applicant to resubmit a modified scheme in respect of the area falling outside the SSSIs, but it did not do so (NCC Minutes March 1988). In terms of the financial guidelines under the 1981 Act, NCC was *prima facie* liable to pay compensation in respect of the entire frustrated development: but it contended that its liability should extend only to the SSSI portion. The feeling within NCC was that the FC was helping the applicant to make a killing out of a project which included agricultural intensification as well as forestry.

After lengthy proceedings before the District Valuer, Cameron was awarded about £700,000 in compensation by the Lands Tribunal in 1991. Taking account of fees and expenses, NCC was out of pocket to the tune of just under £1m. Throughout its progress the case aroused intense feeling on both sides, the landowning interest alleging that NCC had brought the trouble upon itself by its high–handed approach in the first place. A more widespread concern, however, was that in this and other cases the public purse was being raided for large sums in compensation for grant payable, though not actually paid, by another agency – when all the time there might never have been an intention to carry out the work at all. One professional adviser was quoted as defending himself against criticism for formulating a grant application along those lines by the contention that he could have been sued for professional negligence if he had not done so. At any rate the loophole was closed, in the case of forestry, by a Ministerial decision in May 1989 that the grant element would in future be excluded from the valuation of management agreement payments under the 1981 Act where grant had been refused on nature conservation grounds. But the case added to a growing resentment against the principle of paying so-called management grants for doing nothing, and also an anxiety about the cost in respect of forestry grant applications lodged before the rules were changed (Adams 1986).

NCC reorganisation

All these varied grounds of dissatisfaction were much in evidence in Scotland when the announcement of NCC's dismemberment broke in July 1989. The account of this event falls within the story of the NCC Council itself, but certain Scottish aspects are worth noting separately.

The Scottish Office followed up Ridley's announcement very quickly with a consultation document entitled 'Scotland's Natural Heritage', seeking comments on proposals for implementing the next stage of the Scottish reorganisation. Scottish members of NCC asked that the Committee for Scotland should be allowed to respond on its own account, but this request was refused (NCC Minutes, July 1989). Accordingly the first opportunity for the Committee to comment came at its ordinary meeting in September 1989. Not unexpectedly, the Committee was on balance in favour of the reorganisation, and enthusiastically so for the opportunity to combine policies and functions with CCS in a single, identifiably Scottish, agency.

Doubts were still expressed about the scientific capability of the new body, its financial backing, and the ability of the Scottish Office to stand back when conservation arguments outweighed those in favour of development. But these were regarded as matters on which reassurances could readily be given by the Government (Minutes, September 1989).

The Committee for Scotland did not let the grass grow under its feet so far as reorganisation was concerned. Already at its September 1989 meeting it had before it a submission on the corporate plan 1990-1995 which named as one of the key issues 'anticipation of legislative changes establishing a Scottish NCC and proposed subsequent merger with CCS'. The submission included a paper calling for a switch from protective designation to the support of schemes, mainly promoted by the Department of Agriculture, which gave farmers and others the opportunity to participate voluntarily in conservation measures – an emphasis which must at that time have been regarded in Peterborough as heretical.

Also in September 1989 the Scottish Office circulated a draft circular on Indicative Forestry Strategies [already discussed in Chapter 2]. The points to remark here are that the Scottish Headquarters immediately took responsibility for responding to the draft circular (duly clearing their lines with the NCC Director–General) and that, while making trenchant criticism of some of the contents of the circular, they gave it a thoroughly warm welcome – in contrast to NCC's half–hearted attitude towards the Highland Regional Council's Working Party on Caithness and Sutherland which had pioneered the 'indicative strategy' approach two years earlier. It is interesting to note at this point (though somewhat out of date order) that the next progress statement on the peatlands of Caithness and Sutherland (December 1990) was made to the Scottish Committee and not to the Council, which 2½ years before had refused to trust the Committee even with the knowledge of NCC policy on the issue. All these are indications of the increasing self-confidence of the Committee for Scotland and its headquarters staff.

It has already been shown how in July 1989 the NCC Council refused to let the Committee for Scotland comment on the Scottish Office consultation document 'Scotland's Natural Heritage'. By February 1990, when the House of Lords sub–committee under Lord Carver visited Edinburgh for the purpose of taking evidence, there was no question of muzzling the Scottish Committee or filtering its voice through that of the Council. Several past and present members of the Committee appeared before the Carver sub–committee and gave powerful advocacy to the notion of an independent Scottish agency. There was equally plain speaking at a conference hosted by the Royal Society of Edinburgh on 26 February, when the Society tabled proposals for a science base integrated with Scottish universities and institutes (J Balfour, pers. com.).

Natural Heritage (Scotland) Bill

No sooner had the Environmental Protection Bill received Royal Assent in November 1990 than the Natural Heritage (Scotland) Bill was introduced. This was much more than a machinery Bill, for it needed to spell out not merely the amalgamation of the Scottish end of NCC with the CCS but the scope of the new responsibilities to be laid upon the combined body named Scottish Natural Heritage. Clause 3 of the Bill proved to be of particular interest, requiring SNH in the discharge of its functions to take account of a bewildering variety of factors bearing upon the Scottish environment. A duty laid upon public bodies to take account of other interests was by no means a novelty, but the range of interests named in this case was altogether exceptional. Scottish Natural Heritage was already being cast in the role of an umbrella countryside agency – about as far removed from the narrow, single–minded scope of NCC as could be imagined. But, since the nature conservation provisions still remain in force in Great Britain as a whole, and SNH is the chosen instrument for their discharge in Scotland, Section 4 of the Act is as specific as the rest of the Act – eg the provisions regarding development projects and natural heritage areas – is open-ended.

Nature Conservancy Council for Scotland

On 1 April 1991 NCC ceased to exist and the three country agencies, along with the Joint Nature Coordinating Committee, came into being. In Scotland, however, the successor could be no more than a caretaker body until SNH became operative. But the caretaker – NCCS – proved to be anything but a 'mark–time' cipher. Its Chairman, Magnus Magnusson, had been designated over a year previously and had been involved in vigorous dialogue within the NCC Council, of which he was also a member. And so, immediately NCCS came on the scene, it launched itself with a publication which reads more like a prospectus for SNH than the report of a mere holding company. Advantage was taken from the start of new delegation provisions in the 1990 Act which permitted the great majority of decision-making to be carried out at the level of the four Scottish Regions, each headed by a public figure of note. Centralisation, it seemed, had been banished for good.

Nevertheless the transitional year was a fraught one for those at the centre. A great deal of unfinished business had to be concluded so that affairs could be tidily handed over to SNH on the due date. While operational matters remained with NCCS, the building up of a new organisation – with all that that involved in the way of recruitment of scientific staff and the integration of existing staff and premises from NCC and CCS – was assigned to a shadow SNH working from a different office and headed by the SNH Director-designate, Roger Crofts. But of course most of these decisions had to be taken jointly between NCCS and the shadow organisation, which made heavy demands on the patience of both of them.

Meanwhile Magnusson was not content to sit tight on SNH policies until he had the backing of the Natural Heritage Act. He judged that there was such lingering suspicion of the reorganisation, among the landowning interest on the one hand and the voluntary and 'green' sector on the other, that it was up to him to spell out clearly from the start the policies which SNH, under his leadership, could be expected to adopt. In this he had the overt support of Scottish Office Ministers. These policies were closely in line with those that had been under development by the NCC Committee for Scotland during the few months of *glasnost* which it enjoyed at the end of its life. At their heart was a concern that nature conservation should cease to be a self-contained crusade, wilfully pushing all other considerations aside (on the basis, argued in *Nature Conservation in Great Britain*, that there was little left to compromise about), and should take its place alongside other interests, seeking to understand their point of view and to gain their sympathy – with the aid of finance, if necessary.

This approach commended itself to the landowners. It was less warmly received by the conservation movement, but they had to admit that the hard-edged NCC line had not worked and they were prepared to give the embryonic SNH the benefit of the doubt.

As this volume is not concerned with the performance of SNH, its account of official nature conservation in Scotland must end at April 1992, when NCCS ceased to exist. It is relevant, however, to note that since then the site–related nature conservation problems have been greatly overshadowed by more general issues – whether of agricultural or forestry policy, deer management, or visitor pressure on sensitive habitat. The new thrust of Scottish nature conservation policy outlined in the preceding paragraph has therefore, so far, been shown to be appropriate.

The record of official nature conservation in Scotland is not just a repeat on a smaller scale of the record of NC/NCC in relation to Great Britain as a whole. There is an additional strand, represented by the increasing centralisation of the GB body and the consequent unwillingness to let things be done differently in Scotland, or to take account of different conditions prevailing there. The tensions thus created played a significant part in the eventual break-up of NCC.

7

ORGANISATION AND EFFECTIVENESS

Organisation of NC/NCC

Throughout its existence NC/NCC retained a remarkably constant form of organisation. Below the Council there were territorial committees for England, Scotland and Wales, with a variable number of functional committees dealing with, among other things, science policy and birds. The 'officer' organisation was less structured in the early days. The 'Scottish Headquarters' was one of the features from the start, its fine situation being particularly noted, as well as the energy of its first Director, Dr John Berry (Stamp 1969). As often happens with GB bodies, no need was seen initially for a Director for England – indeed no such appointment was made until NCC came into existence in 1973. The NC research stations in England came directly under the London headquarters, whereas in Scotland and Wales the territorial Directors were responsible for both research and conservation. For the latter purpose Scotland was divided into three regions, increasing to four in 1973. It is interesting to note that in 1952 the London staff numbered 35, as against fifteen in Edinburgh, with six outposted to the Scottish regions.

By 1975 (the date of its first Annual Report) NCC had effectively lost its research function, and with it a large proportion of its staff: but even so its personnel had grown to 451. The complement in 1978 was 551, and 689 in 1986 (1977–78 and 1985–86 Annual Reports). At 31 March 1991 the full-time staff numbered 855 (1990–91 Annual Report), including around 245 in Scotland. (Table 4 and Figure 7 in Part IV show the rate of staff increase, in relation to those of CCS and CCEW.) The main growth points were in the post-1973 Chief Scientist Team, where in the words of Sir William Wilkinson, the last NCC Chairman, 'a strong, internal science base was rebuilt'; and post-1981 Act, in the regions, where massive recruitment took place in order to carry out the fieldwork demanded in connection with 'renotification' of SSSIs. By the end of the 1980s, moreover, a very significant build-up had occurred at NCC Headquarters by way of a 'Policy, Planning and Services' Division handling personnel, finance, forward planning, publicity and international matters.

The structure of NCC during its final phase is shown in Figure 5 below, derived from the Corporate Plan 1986–1991: What it does not bring out is that one or two specialist units (latterly, those for Mountain & Moorland and Afforestation Ecology) of the Chief Scientist Directorate were 'out-housed' in Edinburgh, presumably so that they could interact with other scientists and administrators coming under the authority of the Director (Scotland). It is doubtful whether this intention was ever realised (J M Boyd, pers. com.).

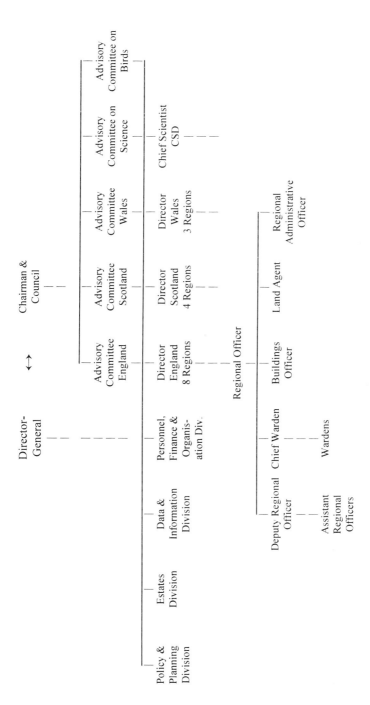

Figure 5:   NCC structure at 31 July 1986

Source: NCC Corporate Plan 1986-1991

Organisation of NCCS/SNH

It is of interest to investigate briefly the structure in Scotland following the dismantling of NCC, because of the light which this sheds on the pre-1991 situation.

Figure 6: SNH Executive Organisation Structure (at October 1993)

Chief Executive-----------Secretariat

NW Region	NE Region	SW Region	SE Region	Res. & Advisory Services Director-ate	Resources Director-ate	Policy Director-ate	Communi-cations Director-ate
Regional admin	Regional admin	Regional admin	Regional admin	Uplands & peatlands	Inform. systems	Corporate planning	Press & PR
Advisory services	Advisory services	Advisory services	Advisory services	Agric & woodland	CIR unit	Strategic issues	Public-ations & info.
Land man-agement	Communi-cations	Land man-agement	Land man-agement	Aquatic environ-ment	Common services	Sustain-ability & special proj.	Graphics
Caithness & Sutherland	Land man-agement	Argyll & Bute	Tayside	Internatnl & bio-diversity	Corporate Planning		Carto-graphic services
Ross, Crom. & Inverness	Strathspey	Mid-Strathclyde	Borders & Lothian	Earth Science	Finance		Education & training
Lochaber Skye & Lochalsh	N Isles	Dumfries & Galloway	Fife & Central	Designated areas & sites	Personnel		Display centre
W Isles	E Grampian			Recreation & access			Design advisory services
				Environ-mental audit			
				Landscape & recreation			
				Adminis-tration			

Source: SNH Research & Advisory Services Directorate

It was one of the main points of contention in the debate about the dismemberment of NCC to what extent a Scottish agency could function on its own, without the back-up of the Chief Scientist Directorate. Once it had been accepted that the split-up was going to happen, attention was focused on the scale and function of the JNCC and, conversely, the extent to which the scientific capability within NCCS/SNH would have to be 'beefed up'. This was one of the principal items within the remit of a study commissioned by NCC from consultants PE International in 1990, subsequently reviewed by a working group in the Department of the Environment. The latter came up with a range of options, the most generous of which would have boosted the complement in Scotland by no less than 106 staff. Following further consideration by the Joint Steering Group, the Scottish level was fixed at 335, 50 fewer than the 'maximalist' option. For comparison, the others were: Wales 205, England 635, JNCC 51. But this was not the last word, because the approved staff complement with which NCCS started its life was 385 – 140 more than the NCC in Scotland. Thus there was a big recruiting job to be done, mainly of scientists, but also of a variety of administrative officers needed to discharge central functions previously carried out at Peterborough.

What lay behind this staff increase was not simply the need to equip NCCS with the equivalent back-up to that provided by GB Headquarters. Over and above that, NCCS took a deliberate decision to delegate the great bulk of day-to-day work to the four regions, each headed not merely by a regional officer but by a regional board. Accordingly each region needed an enlarged team, comprising scientific, land management and administrative expertise. The officer in charge was no longer automatically a scientist, because administrative skills took precedence. In initiating this change (which had to be supported by the Scottish Office in view of the resource implications) Magnusson and his chief executive, John Francis, were obviously looking forward to the structure that would be needed to sustain not merely NCCS but SNH, with its additional burden of countryside functions to discharge. The Countryside Commission for Scotland had had no regional outposts, but it seemed inescapable that, if countryside and nature conservation were to be carried out in an integrated fashion, the regional model should prevail for both functions.

The model developed by NCCS was adopted by SNH (see Fig. 6). There is a certain structural resemblance between Figures 5 and 6, which may serve as a warning that, however firm SNH's current commitment to delegation may be, there is not a great deal standing in the way of its reverting to a centralised mode of operation.

Efficiency

In considering efficiency, the concern is with measuring the relationship of means to ends – of resources to achievements – not of estimating the value of the end-product. Measuring is a not inappropriate term to use, because without numerical yardsticks it is almost impossible to judge the efficiency of an organisation (Simon 1957, Williams and Anderson 1975).

There is little point, however, in probing the efficiency of NCC before the 1980s, because so few useful quantitative data are available. A House of Commons Estimates Committee looked at the work of the NC in 1957 (HC 255) and pronounced it 'not extravagant'. They commented that wisdom and commonsense were necessary in the selection of projects on a limited budget, with the implication that the Conservancy's choice seemed to them a wise one. But the Committee had nothing much to go on. The Annual Reports down the years have the expected tables of statistics – income and expenditure, numbers and ar-

Parliamentary and other Committees of Enquiry

The principle of Parliamentary scrutiny is a straightforward one. Any body which Parliament has legislated into existence and pays for is open to further enquiry at any time, not just on the narrow question of funding but on a principle of broad accountability. The operation of this principle, as has been observed in the context of the FC, is rather hit-or-miss, depending on the other claims on Parliament's attention, on the Parliamentary vehicles ie committees which happen to exist, and on the perceptiveness and energy of their Chairmen.

Reference has already been made to the Report of the Select Committee on Estimates of 1957 (HC 255). This Committee, although the most circumscribed of all in its terms of reference, has always felt free to construe its quest for value for money in a wide sense. And so, apart from finding the NC 'not extravagant', the Committee commented favourably on the applied value of the work being done in, for example, the fields of water conservation, soils and burning/grazing. What they were referring to, evidently, was applied research (that which ultimately passed to NERC) rather than the NC's conservation work.

It might have been expected that opportunities would have been found for appraisal of the work of NC/NCC in the reports of the inquiries which preceded the creation of NERC in 1965 and of NCC in 1973. This however did not happen. The Committee of Enquiry into the Organisation of Civil Science, which reported in October 1963 (Cmnd 2171), was wholly taken up with the principle of research councils and their structure. To the Committee the NC was just an awkward piece of the administrative machine which had to be fitted in somewhere: its record, and the conditions for its future effectiveness, were not considered in their own right. Likewise the odd cluster of reports out of which emerged the Nature Conservancy Council Act 1973 (the tripartite Cmnd 4814 of November 1971, and Cmnd 5046 of July 1972) were entitled *A Framework for Government Research and Development* and were dominated by the thinking of Lord Rothschild and the introduction of the customer/contractor principle. Again, it was because NC fitted awkwardly into the Government research framework that it was taken out of NERC, not so much out of concern about its functioning within NERC.[1] It is true that there had been an enquiry of a sort in 1971–72 into the hiving off of the NC, under the chairmanship of Dr C E Lucas of the Scottish Fisheries Research Laboratory: but this only happened because of pressure from *within* NC for hiving-off, which the enquiry found against (Sheail 1992).

Indeed we look in vain through the whole gamut of committee reports, whether Parliamentary or otherwise, for any measured judgment on NC/NCC, right on to the end of its life. For example, NAO, reporting in 1986 to the HC Committee on Public Accounts (PAC), merely noted that 'NCC is developing long-term policies within the framework of this document [*Nature Conservation in Great Britain*]... Detailed aims and objectives are laid down in the annual corporate plan' (1985–86 HC 534). This was a far cry from NAO's (and the PAC's) handling of the FC during the same year, which went deeply into the achievements and failures of the Commission. Representatives of NCC were constantly on the stand before Parliamentary committees, especially throughout the 1980s: successive NCC annual reports bear witness to this. But it was never NCC itself that was in the spotlight – it might be agriculture, or forestry, or even the working of the Wildlife and Countryside Act 1981, but not the working of NCC. This is an oddity which will be discussed further, in connection with the views of the Government and of environmental writers.

The second report of the House of Lords sub-committee on Science and Technology (the Carver Report, 1990 HL 33–I) was the last possible occasion for an authoritative outside verdict of this kind. But the committee sidestepped the issue. It declined to take up a position on the merits of reorganising the NCC. The nearest it came to delivering a judgment can be found in paras 3.18 and 3.21. The first of these says: '...the argument that nature conservation depends on acceptability to local people...has been used *convincingly* [author's emphasis] to suggest that nature conservation which appears to be dictated remotely from Peterborough...does not work'. In the second, the committee 'take this opportunity to praise the admirable work done by the NCC for conservation generally in Great Britain. Whatever local ·difficulties there may have been, the NCC has achieved a great deal'. This balanced and ultra-cautious expression of opinion takes us very little forward.

The Government

In a sense, central government's evaluation of NC/NCC was the strangest of all. The changes of 1965 and 1973 did not, as has been seen, imply any official criticism – or indeed any value-judgment of the organisation at all. Apart from one or two Ministerial comments, delivered in private, the posture of DoE as sponsor Department appears to have been one of non-committal silence – or perhaps tacit approval – right up to the point, in July 1989, when the sentence of dismemberment was passed.

A chance exchange during a 1984 hearing of a House of Lords select committee may throw some light upon this policy of silence. In the course of an enquiry into Agriculture and the Environment, Lord Stanley asked Martin Holdgate (now DoE's Chief Scientist): '...do you take for granted, for gospel, what the NCC tells you – or are you monitoring it scientifically?'(HL 272 – II, 22 Feb 1984). The reply was to the effect that DoE was certainly not monitoring NCC's work scientifically; that the Secretary of State had to answer for the funding of NCC and therefore for its being 'well organised and operating within lines laid down for the proper conduct of affairs'; but that Parliament had given NCC unfettered discretion in matters of scientific judgment, and in that sense DoE had simply to rely on NCC to discharge its own responsibility. Later on in the same enquiry, when NCC was being questioned about communication with DoE, its Chief Scientist admitted that NCC could 'only give rather a limited amount to liaison' even with the direct sponsor Division of that Department, because of other pressures (ibid., 16 May 1984). The impression strongly conveyed is one of permanent stand-off between the two bodies, based on a certain interpretation of their constitutional relationship.

If this was the understanding at the official level, it was not always shared by Ministers. Heseltine in 1981 was prepared to challenge NCC's staffing and spending levels, and he made it clear that his concern was not merely with good housekeeping. Why should not conservation be a revenue-producing activity? Why should NCC bother to survey SSSIs that were not actively threatened? Why should it own land? Why was its relationship with voluntary bodies closer than with agricultural and landowning interests? That these were not merely rhetorical questions was shown by Heseltine's pointed insistence on receiving answers before giving further consideration to NCC's bid for additional funds.

It appears that Heseltine's attention was diverted before he was able to press home these basic policy issues. Nevertheless Ministers kept on raising points of this kind, albeit sporadically. In 1985 NCC felt the need to produce a paper, aimed at Ministers and senior civil servants, entitled 'Why SSSI? – the rationale behind the selection of SSSIs'. It is interesting that in this document NCC did not seek to shelter behind the statutory independence of its scientific judgment, but was prepared to defend its selection of SSSIs from first principles. William Waldegrave, who was at that time the Minister with day-to-day responsibility for nature conservation, appears to have accepted the SSSI rationale: but in 1986 he made other criticisms of a broad policy nature, though in more moderate terms than his predecessor.

The same political pressures recurred in another form – a 'financial management and performance review' of NCC, the report of which arrived at NCC Headquarters in May 1987. This was not, as the NCC Council appears to have believed, a form of examination designed especially for its discomfort: rather, it was a routine to which all Government agencies were periodically subjected, under the general aegis of Sir Leo Pliatzky, a Treasury civil servant, reporting directly to the Prime Minister. Its main recommendation was for the division of NCC into a Nature Reserve Service (run as a kind of business) and a conservation advisory service. It also attacked the choice of members of the country advisory committees, calling for a greater injection of 'countrymen' as against scientists. The Council was able to enlist DoE's support in resisting the most overtly political of the proposals. Its main complaint was that there were 90 recommendations altogether, and though most were non-controversial the sheer effort of responding to them detracted from NCC's overall efficiency.

To sum up the evidence, such as there is, of the view formed by government of NCC's effectiveness – it has to be said that, from 1980 onwards, relations were generally rather distant, sometimes strained: but at no time was NCC given notice of such extreme dissatisfaction with its performance as to register a threat to its corporate existence.

Environmental writers

The constituency of environmental writers cannot be sharply distinguished from that of other environmental interests, because many writers have a foot in more than one camp. Tansley, Fraser Darling, Nicholson, Stamp, Sheail, Moore and Mabey are examples of writers who at some time or another were part of official nature conservation. Likewise those who have been active in conservation pressure groups are very much conditioned to pick up the pen in a polemical way, for example Lowe, MacEwen, Green, Rose and Pye-Smith. However, this does not make irrelevant the study of these writers in so far as they express a judgment on NC/NCC's performance. When writing on their own account they may be presumed to be expressing personal views rather than acting as mouthpiece for the interests with which they were associated: and this is borne out by the variety of opinions and prescriptions they offer.

Nevertheless, in one important respect virtually all come together and present a solid, unbroken front. This is in refusing to subject NC/NCC to sustained examination or criticism. In this there is a striking similarity with the behaviour of Parliamentary Select Committees as noted earlier in this chapter. It is as if all these writers were saying: This agency is doing its best in a 'no win' situation, with all the forces of darkness pitted against it – the last thing we want to do is to knock it, whatever the weaknesses we may see in it. And so what tends to come under fire is the Government, or Parliament, or the EC/EU, or the farming lobby, or whatever may have stood in the way of NC/NCC delivering the goods.

The first and most consistent area of criticism is that of the choice of members of the NCC Council. They are widely thought (notwithstanding the view of the Pliatzky review of 1987) to have been heavily weighted towards the countryman – ie landowning/forestry/sporting interest. Rose and Pye-Smith (1984) in particular are not afraid to name names. Sir Ralph Verney (Chairman NCC 1980–83) is characterised as a large farmer and one who did not hesitate to destroy a SSSI by afforestation; Dr Jean Balfour (member 1973–79) as the President of the Royal Scottish Forestry Society and 'a large absentee landlady in Sutherland'; Lord Dulverton (SAC member 1973–81) as a member of the Home Grown Timber Advisory Committee. As a result, say Rose and Pye-Smith, NCC slid into decline from the moment of its independent existence: it failed to confront afforestation and intensive agriculture, and became, along with the Countryside Commission, the Government's 'toothless watchdog' – a phrase borrowed from Shoard (1980).

Similar charges were made, in more restrained language, by Adams (1986) and Lowe et al. (1986). Of course, this is only indirectly a criticism of NCC, because the responsibility for appointments to the Council lay with the government of the day.[2]

Second, NCC is alleged to have let down the conservation movement crucially by its posture in relation to the provisions of the Wildlife and Countryside Bill and of the financial guidelines under the Act. Lowe et al. (1986) speak of a widening rift between the voluntary groups and the conservation agencies as the Bill progressed. Adams (1986) attributes the NCC's compliance with the Government's ever–changing proposals to a fear of seeming heavy-handed (in relation to farming and forestry interests), while the conservation movement generally seethed with indignation at the excessive payments which the Act, and in particular the terms of the financial guidelines, made possible. The Council for the Protection of Rural England joined in this latter criticism, calling the code of practice and the guidelines 'expensive and administratively burdensome'. The reasons for NCC's supportive attitude to the Act have been discussed previously; but whatever the motive, it is common ground that NCC – perhaps for the first time – was in a position to influence the fate of a piece of controversial legislation, and chose (wrongly, in the eyes of these commentators) to stand behind it.

A less hectic but more fundamental ground of complaint has surfaced in recent years. It was first voiced by Green (1981), who dared to ask if the scientific emphasis in NCC's terms of reference had not been overplayed. Pye-Smith and Hall (1987) went further, by denouncing NCC as 'the apotheosis of scientific conservatism', and questioning whether the scientific arguments had been effective in preserving nature. Once more, the criticism of NCC is oblique, because it strikes primarily at the legislative framework within NCC was required to operate.

Finally, NCC stands accused of holding itself aloof from landscape conservation. Again, it was Green (1981) who first brought this charge. He drew attention to the strength of the executive powers conferred on NC from the start, as against the weakness of the 1949 National Park provisions and, later, those of the Countryside Act 1968. Accordingly, joint working with CCEW was more a theoretical than a practical exercise: NCC had always been more interested in ploughing its own furrow. Moore (1987) cautiously avoided calling for a merger of NCC with the Countryside Commissions, but denounced the machinery of government as ill–adapted to deal with conservation.

NCC

In considering NCC's appraisal of its own performance it is unnecessary to go back beyond *Nature Conservation in Great Britain*. This is so because self-criticism was not a prominent feature of the earlier NCC or of its predecessor, and also because the 1984 publication is a thorough compendium of all that went before.

Nevertheless, *Nature Conservation in Great Britain* is not a very satisfactory self-audit of the work of NCC. The reason is that the responsibility borne by NCC itself is not clearly identified. Where there is blame, it falls upon the Government, the nation, or 'conservationists'. Equally, where there is credit, it is usually assigned to 'the nature conservation movement'.

Thus one looks in vain through the document for a clear NCC judgment on its own effectiveness. Such a judgment can be arrived at only by inference from a general reading of Chapters 11–14 (Successes, Failures, Conclusions and Reconsideration of Rationale), and from reading retrospectively from Chapter 15 (Future Objectives and Strategy).

It would appear that NCC gave itself some credit for the greater responsiveness of government departments and agencies to nature conservation (11.2.3), and for the asserted fact that Britain 'is now a world leader in conservation technology' (11.8.1). On the debit side, NCC seemed to accept blame for a failure in survey (12.6.1), which led to a gross under–estimation of the effects of agriculture and forestry (12.3.2). Slowness in organising a computerised data base was attributed specifically to NC/NCC (12.6.3).

An important concession was made in para 13.3. While some of the failures registered in Chapter 12 were laid at the door of 'unfavourable government decisions', it was allowed 'that government policy largely mirrors public demand'. Thus conservationists were to blame for not having demonstrated their cause with better effect. As the only source of official conservation advice to government, NCC itself must be in the target area for this admission. Linked with this was the confession of a disastrous lack of cohesion in the total effort of the nature conservation movement (13.3) and a corresponding resolve to seek a new coordination and unity within the movement (13.5). This may be translatable into a resolve on the part of NCC to lead the movement, not to be pushed from behind (14.4.3 and 14.4.4).

The final paragraph of the document (16.1) spoke about 'playing a hard yet clean game for our side' (the nature conservationists). This was a phrase queried at the drafting stage by Mabey, who saw the future not in closing nature conservationist ranks but in seeking to establish wider links and a better understanding with interests which might, on the face of it, not have very much in common with NCC. Mabey lost that argument. Even where it came to discussing integration with the landscape interest, *Nature Conservation in Great Britain* retained its stand-off posture. The furthest it would go was to recommend that the nature conservation bodies should examine, with the Countryside Commissions and the National Trusts, ways of developing 'a more satisfactory functional interface' between wildlife and amenity conservation (15.11.2).

Nature Conservation in Great Britain, with its demarcation of nine (or ten) subject areas and objectives, opened up the way for systematic monitoring by NCC of its own performance. This was part of what corporate planning was supposed to achieve: and no doubt the annual submission of an updated plan, with a detailed account of performance targets, achievements and costed objectives and sub–objectives, was a *sine qua non* for the commitment of future funding by DoE. Yet NCC does not appear to have used the corporate plan in a whole-hearted way as a check on its overall effectiveness or the balance of its activities. The subject areas of 1984 remained in place right to the end, with site safeguard still swallowing up half the total budget in 1990-91, and conservation in the wider environment a mere nine per cent. In none of the later corporate plans or annual reports was there so much as a word about the excessive centralisation which so galvanised the Council into action in the final months before its dismemberment was announced.

The Scottish perception

In summarising how NC/NCC's performance has been viewed in Scotland it may be salutary to recall the grounds on which the Ritchie Committee of 1947 considered that the Scottish Wild Life Service which they recommended should be run almost as a separate entity. These were i) that the terrain, the type and distribution of wildlife, and the significance of economic factors were different in Scotland from the rest of Britain; ii) that Scotland had its own institutions, both legal and administrative – especially the Scottish Office, with which the Wild Life Service would have to work closely; and iii) that conservation needed the whole-hearted backing of the Scottish people, which was most likely to be forthcoming if the Service were visibly centred in Edinburgh. If the Committee was correct, then the perceived effectiveness of NC/NCC in Scotland would be likely to depend to a great extent on how well devolved its administration turned out to be.

The 1971–72 Select Committee on Scottish Affairs was wholly composed of Scottish MPs. In its report on Land Resource Use it showed none of the sensitivities of the Ritchie Committee. It rejected the idea of bringing the NC into a Scottish Department of Rural Affairs, and instead called for the Conservancy (whose work came in for high praise) to be given increased powers in Scotland. In doing so it went against the advice of Fraser Darling, who had told the Select Committee: 'One is always a little bit afraid of giving anybody greater authority. In a small country like Scotland – this is the beauty of Scotland – we have only got 5 million people, we all know each other and we can work together without any great show of authority'. But his was about the only voice urging caution in this respect. In all the evidence submitted to the Select Committee from NFUS, the Landowners Federation, the Crofters Commission, the Highlands and Islands Development Board and the Department of Agriculture there was little mention of the NC, but what there was was entirely favourable.

By the end of the decade, with the creation of NCC and the appointment of Sir David Serpell as its chairman, a great change had taken place. There was strong pressure from within NCC for greater delegation to Scotland, which was successfully resisted. Five years further on, that pressure had almost reached boiling point, as testified by the minutes of the Scottish Advisory Committee and Morton Boyd's valedictory paper. Boyd argued that sustainable development should be the watchword in Scotland, rather than out-and-out preservation; that the procedures of NCC in SSSI notification were bound to cause widespread al-ienation of local communities, especially in the Highlands, and were 'being chal-lenged aggressively by Government agencies, local authorities and others in an attempt to curb NCC's activities, allied with resentment over the lack of demo-cratic control of NCC's powers'. If nature conservation were to reflect the value–judgments of the whole community, it had to take account of the distinc-tive physical, economic, social, legal and resource-development frameworks of the environment in which it was practised. There was a risk, with the inflexible application of the 1981 Act throughout Britain, that its success in Scotland could be jeopardised. Boyd also noted that NCC had failed to develop strong publicity and educational functions, relying instead on the voluntary bodies. Both sides – NCC and the voluntary bodies – would enjoy better public relations if they re-cruited local people for local posts.

In his paper Boyd was not merely speaking for himself: he was reporting the much more extreme perception of NCC held by a variety of people in Scotland in the mid-1980s. His assessment was also uncannily reminiscent of the warning note implicit in the Ritchie Committee's stipulations reproduced at the beginning of this chapter.

Boyd's warnings were echoed a year later in a surprising quarter. A paper en-titled 'Nature conservation in rural development: the need for new thinking about rural sector policies' was published by NCC itself (*Focus on Nature Conservation* No. 18, 1986). It was the work of Alan Mowle, a young NCC offi-cer with seven years' experience of service in Scotland. The paper had a wide scope, ending up by tentatively arguing for 'regional rural agencies' managed jointly by central and local government, and implementing land use and rural development policies within a single budget. Its particular interest here is the section on Conservation. In it Mowle appraised the 1981 Act and the site desig-nation provisions in particular. Site safeguard, he said, might be the only weapon to meet a direct and immediate threat: but this was only winning the skirmish, which was quite another thing than winning the battle, let alone winning the war.

In the long term, moreover, a lasting peace had to be negotiated throughout the whole of the countryside. Thus in Britain's Less Favoured Areas at least, site safeguard had serious limitations in the long-term context. This might be inter-preted as a covert message from Scotland that NCC's preoccupation with special sites was dangerously blinkered.

The next piece of evidence to be considered is the SDD consultation paper *Scotland's Natural Heritage* of July 1989. Although its arguments in favour of reorganisation have been generally ridiculed as thin and unconvincing, it has to be borne in mind that the document was bending over backwards to avoid direct criticism of NCC: so its strictures have to be decoded. In essence, the case it made for separate Scottish administration was the same as that of Ritchie, Boyd and Mowle: that Scotland was different from England, that Scottish affairs needed to be considered in an integrated fashion, and that NCC failed to recog-nise these requirements.

The debates in Parliament on the Environmental Protection and Natural

Heritage Bills scarcely add to the evidence about Scottish assessments of NCC. The Opposition started by trying to score party political points, but it soon became obvious that the support of Scottish Members for both Bills was bi-partisan. More informative were the Scottish hearings of the Carver Committee in February 1990. The Committee heard witnesses from a variety of sources, including the Royal Society of Edinburgh, the Scottish Wildlife Trust, Scottish Wildlife and Countryside Link, the National Trust for Scotland, and CCS. While the institutions were understandably cautious in their written evidence, individual spokesmen – often distinguished scientists in their own right – were prepared to come out into the open and testify to serious failings on the part of NCC to 'deliver nature conservation acceptably' in Scotland (HL 1989–90 33–II).

It is still alleged (see eg Marren 1993) that the break-up of NCC was achieved largely by a conspiracy between Scottish Office Ministers and their landowning constituents, and had little backing from informed Scottish opinion. The latter part of this contention cannot be supported, on the evidence cited above. While in the late 1980s there was, perhaps, no concerted criticism of NCC's performance in Scottish scientific and conservation circles (to parallel the groundswell of popular discontent which had been building up for some time, in the Highlands and Islands especially), a number of thinking people, both within and outwith the counsels of NCC, had come to the conclusion that NCC's approach to nature conservation in Scotland was unwise and dangerous.[3]

The elements in the Scottish discontent with NCC's performance are not easy to pin down. Undoubtedly there was a strand of nationalistic resentment, but why this should have developed in the 1980s rather than in the mid-1970s – when Scottish nationalism had its heyday – is difficult to explain. Perhaps it had something to do with the development of foci for environmental and conservation interest in Scotland, a matter which will be touched on in the next chapter.

Conclusions on effectiveness

A neat summing-up of views on NCC's effectiveness is not possible. Everything depends on the viewpoint from which NCC was being observed. Conservationists saw it as weak and unduly deferential to government and vested interests (see next chapter): land users, on the other hand, accused the organisation of doctrinaire thinking, undue interference and high–handedness. If there is agreement on one thing, it is that NCC failed to get its objectives across to the outside world, and to commend its policies to the parties who were affected by them.

NOTES

1. Sheail (1992), quoting from the NERC Council minutes of September 1971, records substantial agreement that the NC was 'a very uncomfortable partner for NERC'. This need not, however, be taken as a criticism of the ethos or effectiveness of the NC.

2. Appointments to NCC's Advisory Committees were made by the Council, but subject to the approval of 'the Secretary of State'.

3. Marren (1993) writes off the Scottish members of the NCC Council as on the whole

disloyal, and the Scottish Committee as totally so. He attributes this to the packing of both bodies by Ministers with members sympathetic to their point of view. Hornsby (pers. com.) paints a more complex picture. The author, from his personal knowledge of the individuals concerned, is convinced that the Scottish members' welcome for the Government's proposals was spontaneous and, indeed, inevitable.

Loch Monar hills, Ross and Cromarty
(access controlled through Glen Strathfarrar NNR)

8

THE CONSERVATION CLIENT GROUP

The term client group has been explained previously: it is of course a very vague and flexible definition, taking on a different quality with whichever sector of public life is under review. But as in other sectors, the nature conservation client group shows a characteristic dual aspect: on the one hand, the quiet domestic function of running some activity, usually local; and the campaigning fervour of the lobby or ginger group, whether locally or nationally expressed.

There is often a question whether the client group has brought the public agency into being, or has been brought into being, or at any rate into cohesion, by the existence of the agency. In the case of nature conservation in Britain – as with forestry – the first of these alternatives appears to be the correct one. Sheail (1976), Allen (1978) and Lowe (1983) have chronicled the growth of the wildlife societies which have been active since the late nineteenth century and which can claim, with justice, to have spearheaded the great movement of the 1940s that gave rise to national parks and the Nature Conservancy. And yet the Conservancy, once established, went on its own way with scarcely an acknowledgment of its debt to, or interdependence with, the voluntary societies. Not until 1961 did the Conservancy get round to organising itself to give consistent support to the voluntary bodies.

The explanation of the NC's apparent insensitivity may lie in the fact that the conservation movement over the years has proved unusually volatile. Without much doubt, the societies in the 1950s were in the doldrums, almost a nonentity. Membership of the RSPB in 1959 was 8100, having scarcely increased since the Second World War (*Nature Conservation in Great Britain* 1984). Hays (1987) has traced the rise in the US of environmental concern from about 1962 onwards. The movement crossed the Atlantic and burgeoned, so that – to take the RSPB again as a pointer – membership had grown to 66,000 by 1970 and to 850,000 by 1993.

Composition of the client group

A client group does not necessarily define itself – and in this field certain bodies change their names and orientations with bewildering freedom. However NCC did a useful job in *Nature Conservation in Great Britain* in classifying what it oddly defined as 'non-governmental organisations for nature conservation' (NGOs). The RSPB stands on its own by virtue of its size and influence. Then there are the nature conservation trusts, with the umbrella organ the Royal Society for Nature Conservation, and over 180,000 members throughout UK. Next come the specialist NGOs, often academic, with particular interests in botany, ornithology, woodlands, or ecology as such. Finally are described the broad spectrum NGOs – whether liaison-type bodies like Wildlife Link which are still clearly nature-oriented, or those concerned with wider environmental issues, such as the National Trusts, CoEnCo (now the Environment Council), Friends of the Earth, and Greenpeace.

The conservation trusts merit a fuller description, as they are at the core of 'official' nature conservation's clientele. There are around 50 trusts, based for the most part on English counties: the Scottish Wildlife Trust covers the whole of Scotland. Almost invariably they started out in the late 1950s or early 1960s, through local enthusiasts seeking to acquire or lease land in their vicinity for nature reserve purposes. Their *raison d'être* is to manage these reserves but, as pointed out by Bull (1989), they have acquired other functions as well. He found that the English counties with the highest per capita trust membership were also those with the highest rates of in-migration, and came to the conclusion, also reached by Connell (1978) and Newby (1985), that trust members are typically newcomers to the countryside who are keen to see the local amenities preserved. Thus there are strong links with local authorities and, in many cases, a standing arrangement by which the trusts see and comment on all planning applications.

So far as NCC and its successors are concerned, trusts are the vital link with the grassroots of nature conservation. In a typical year in the 1980s, out of approximately £1m available for land purchase grants, NCC would pay out one or two large sums to the big organisations such as RSPB, but the majority of grant awards would go to individual county trusts – along with help with their staffing and organisation. Bull went so far as to call them 'the local arm of the NCC', emphasising their role as local watchdog and also, through their membership of the Royal Society for Nature Conservation, as a strong ally in lobbying central government.

The client group as a lobby

The voluntary bodies have all along been outspoken on local issues. Their importance on the national scene, however, developed only in the late 1970s and the 1980s. In 1976 the Society for the Promotion of Nature Reserves received a royal charter, in recognition of its significance as an umbrella organisation, and changed its name to the Royal Society for Nature Conservation soon afterwards. It is to this period – when the RSPB was also experiencing phenomenal growth – that we can trace the campaign for new conservation legislation which led to the passing of the 1981 Act (*Nature Conservation in Great Britain*). There was an attempt by NCC to fend off the NGOs' pressure for stronger protection of SSSIs, but it was eventually compelled to ride on the wave which the voluntary bodies had created. It may have been partly his experiences in connection with the Wildlife and Countryside Bill that led Heseltine to demand, in November 1981, that NCC rein in these troublesome allies, with (as he saw it) their snooping and confrontational ways.

The relationship with the NGOs was a continual source of awkwardness to NCC. It saw the need, which was continually being urged on it by Ministers, to build bridges with the main land users – Government Departments, local authorities, FC, and farming and landowning organisations – but it felt that it could not desert the voluntary organisations who as it saw it were more ideologically correct, even if their tongues were rough. As a member of NCC staff once put it to the author: 'You may think we are extreme, but you should hear our clientele!'

The way out which NCC devised was to coin the expression 'the nature conservation movement', which featured prominently in *Nature Conservation in Great Britain*. The section on Future Strategy contained no section dedicated to the NGOs, but two of its themes – Resources for Conservation and The Distribution of Effort – were largely about NCC's relationships with the voluntary sector. The conservation movement was portrayed as having a dual personality. With its statutory duties, its responsibility to Parliament, and its expertise, NCC was 'ideally placed to give leadership to the whole movement'. The NGOs had 'a greater political freedom as a lobby and a larger potential capacity for action in various fields – survey, management, education and publicity'. The different strengths of the partners must be utilised. Thus NCC might do less (in the executive sense) but increasingly become the avenue for distributing funds to the NGOs.

The client group during the final years

In line with this new approach, the corporate plan for 1985–1990 stated that NCC would discuss with the NGOs how far they could play a greater role in the management of nature reserves; assist with survey and monitoring of the wider countryside; further conservation education; and publicise the importance of nature conservation. Extra funding would be needed to prime the NGO pump, though in the end the exercise was expected to be cost–effective. Finance for these purposes were indeed increased in the succeeding two financial years, but not to the extent projected; and the bold new initiative did not live up to its early promise. Indeed the 1986–1991 corporate plan put the emphasis not on the voluntary bodies but on 'those who live and work in the countryside'.

It is a reasonable inference that this change of direction – towards the agricultural and landed interests and away from the NGOs – owed a great deal to the influence of the new DoE Ministerial team which took over in October 1986. Small wonder that among the many strictures which Derek Ratcliffe delivered in his valedictory message (June 1989) was the following:

> Our political masters…allow a promotional role, together with closely enmeshed relationships with respective private sectors, in the case of interests such as agriculture and forestry. I fail to see why NCC cannot be allowed an entirely analogous role and relationship with our private sector. Yet we are not at present regarded by the voluntary organisations as giving conspicuous leadership to the nature conservation movement, which was one of the intentions agreed in 1984.

If the NGOs felt themselves let down during the second half of the 1980s, they did not allow themselves the luxury of washing their hands of NCC when the sentence of dissolution fell on it in July 1989. On the contrary, they rallied to its defence with energy and singleness of purpose. It may well have been the Government's recognition of the strength of the conservation lobby that moved them to act without prior consultation with anyone – though of course that lack of consultation became a further stick for the NGOs to pick up and beat the Government with. The NGOs' consistent and vigorous opposition was a source of comfort to the beleaguered staff at Peterborough; and they were among the most effective exponents of the NCC case before the Carver sub–committee. But there was one serious weakness in the NGOs' evidence to the committee. They felt unable to take up any posture other than outright denunciation of the

Government's proposals – at a time when NCC would have been prepared to settle for a compromise solution (T Hornsby, pers. com.). Thus the relationship between NCC and its client group remained uneasy to the very end.

The client group in Scotland

In his 1985 paper, Morton Boyd pointed out that the membership of the voluntary bodies in Scotland was relatively very weak. At a time when the NGOs south of the Border were experiencing unprecedented growth, recruitment in Scotland remained stubbornly low. For example, in 1983 the RSPB had 22,000 Scottish members, as against 450,000 for Great Britain; the Association for the Preservation of Rural Scotland had a membership of 400, as against 30,000 and 3,500 for its English and Welsh counterparts; and the Scottish Wildlife Trust numbered under 7,000, compared with 150,000 in Trusts in England and Wales (NCC Corporate Plan 1985–1990). The Scottish Wildlife Trust, in commenting on Nature Conservation in Great Britain, put their finger on the practical implications of this situation when they said: 'We draw particular attention to the imbalance in Britain between SE England and NW Scotland, since much of the public support for conservation lies at the opposite corner of Britain to this major wildlife resource'. Looking at the problem the other way, SWT might have said (with no more than a hint of exaggeration) that the more the South–East of England became agitated over conservation issues in Scotland, the stronger became the Scottish anti-conservation lobby, and the harder it became to recruit to the Scottish conservation cause. Sir William Wilkinson was misreading the Scottish situation when he wrote: 'In Scotland...attitudes to nature conservation have been less supportive. The voluntary movement is less numerous and it has become convenient for some to blame a Great Britain body, with its main headquarters in Peterborough, for the impact of...national legislation' (NCC 1990–91 Annual Report).

It is not the case that interest in natural history is markedly less, or of more recent origin, in Scotland than elsewhere in the United Kingdom. *Who's Who in the Environment, Scotland* (The Environment Council 1993) lists at least 30 bodies concerned with nature, most of them unique to Scotland and some of ancient foundation. What marks off the Scottish approach from that south of the Border is its different orientation. It tends to be generalist rather than specialist, seeking to integrate rather than to dissect. As Boyd put it, the conservation movement in 1985 needed to be brought together as an integrated whole if it was to meet the needs and special characteristics of the Highlands and Islands, about which he was particularly concerned. Wildlife legislation had to be applied with an eye to the support of human as well as natural communities, and respect for wildlife had to be engendered as a valued component of, rather than as a constraint upon, the business of everyday living. The implication of Boyd's message was that the propaganda of the big Great Britain voluntary societies, with their single-minded emphasis on species preservation, was having a negative impact on communities which were themselves threatened with extinction.

Boyd's theme was taken up when representatives of the Scottish conservation interest gave evidence to the Carver subcommittee in 1990. There was strong condemnation of the way in which the break-up of NCC had been announced, and suspicion of the Government's motives. Yet the prevailing view among those that gave evidence was that the devolution of nature conservation to Scotland offered the opportunity of a wider, less confrontational approach to land use, and a partnership with other agencies and bodies which had been treated hitherto as inevitable enemies.

A striking illustration of this new look among voluntary organisations came with the publication by Scottish Wildlife and Countryside Link of *State of the Scottish Environment 1991*. This was an all-encompassing review of the Scottish scene, with sections on the atmosphere, soil and water resources, agriculture, forestry, minerals, energy and recreation, as well as the more conventional chapters on natural habitats and species. Showing a deep concern for the Scottish environment, its authors (Dargie and Briggs) nevertheless eschewed a campaigning approach in favour of fairness and objectivity. Commenting on the publication, the Scottish officer of the World Wide Fund for Nature, another NGO, said that it deserved to play a part in the agenda of the new agency SNH – whose inheritance came from NCC, but which would, it was hoped, be able to take a much broader resource management view than NCC had done (*Scotsman*, 2 December 1991).

Thus SNH took over its new and enhanced role with a renewal of goodwill from its nature conservation client group. Whether this proves to be a honeymoon phenomenon, or the reflection of a more stable relationship than that enjoyed by NCC with its client group, remains still to be seen.

Beinn Eighe NNR, Ross & Cromarty

IV

COUNTRYSIDE

9

COUNTRYSIDE COMMISSION FOR SCOTLAND

The story of CCS is shorter and simpler than the accounts of the other two agencies being examined. It has had a briefer time-span than either the FC or the NC/NCC, and its remit has been exclusively Scottish from the start. However, the reality is more complex than might appear on the surface. The history of the countryside movement in Scotland stretches back to the 1930s, at least 30 years before 1968 when CCS was established. Moreover, the movement was never a purely Scottish affair: it began with a strong GB emphasis, and the interactions have continued across the border ever since.

It is important to clarify what is to be understood by the term 'countryside' in this context. The word is an expansive one, better equipped with connotation than with precise meaning. In the Great Britain setting – and the concept occurs scarcely anywhere else – countryside policy has had four distinct but inter-related strands. These are i) access by the public; ii) development of facilities for public enjoyment; iii) protection of scenic, scientific and cultural values; and iv) the economic use and welfare of the countryside and its inhabitants. All four elements have been observable in the British countryside movement down the years, though the emphasis and the interpretation given to each has varied widely. Each of them assumes that it knows what the countryside is, without actually defining it. Attempts to import a fifth strand, prominent in North American thinking – the concept of wilderness – have made little headway in view of the continuous history of human occupation in this country.

The years up to 1949

Enthusiasm for natural beauty and for the delights of the countryside was, of course, well developed in this country by the early nineteenth century, under the influence of Wordsworth and Scott in particular. In those days, however, it was largely thought of as the prerogative of the leisured class of society, in particular the moneyed tourists, and of the improving lairds and sporting landowners. The countryside movement may be regarded as making its appearance, at least in embryo, with the expression of the daring notion that the enjoyment of the countryside belonged to everyone.

An early manifestation of this was the foundation in 1843 of the Scottish Rights of Way Society and its successful prosecution of a series of lawsuits vindicating public rights of passage across the Grampians. Even bolder were the repeated (although vain) attempts, in the closing years of the nineteenth century, by the Liberal James Bryce (a lawyer with an Aberdeenshire constit-uency) to bring in a Bill giving universal access to mountainous areas (Stephenson 1989).

The movement in this country was stirred by the National Park successes in the US, but gained no popular support until the late 1920s. Suddenly, the creation of national parks, both north and south of the Border, became a 'cause', attracting all-party political support (Smout 1991). In 1929 Ramsay Macdonald appointed the Addison Committee to pursue the idea. It ran into the sand, however, in the atmosphere of economic crisis which dominated the 1930s (Sheail 1976). Likewise a revived Access to Mountains Bill, which appeared to command general approval, was emasculated by the landowning interests in the House of Lords to the extent that by the time it reached the statute book in 1939 all the outdoor interests had repudiated it.

The countryside movement revived again in the wartime and post–war reconstruction era, when town and country planning, nature conservation, agriculture and forestry all profited from the awakening of the national conscience to the need to build a new Britain (Cherry 1975). A remarkable series of Government-sponsored reports contributed to this result. The first of these was the work of an individual, John Dower, who reported single-handed to the Minister of Housing and Local Government on not merely the concept but also the delimitation of national parks in England and Wales (1945 Cmd 6628). It may be worth quoting Dower's definition of a national park in relation to Great Britain: 'an extensive area of beautiful and relatively wild country in which, for the nation's benefit and by appropriate national decision and action, (a) the characteristic landscape beauty is strictly preserved, (b) access and facilities for public open-air enjoyment are amply provided, (c) wild life and buildings and places of architectural and historic interest are suitably protected, while (d) established farming use is effectively maintained'. Dower's report prepared the ground for the work of the Hobhouse Committee (1945–47), which took a wider look at countryside issues in England and Wales and – along with the report of the Wild Life Conservation Special Committee under Huxley – became the general framework for the National Parks and Access to the Countryside Act 1949.

Meanwhile north of the border developments had followed a parallel course, with some interesting variations. The background was different in Scotland, with its 'Highland problem', its powerful landowning lobby, and its relatively weak amenity and access interest groups. These factors were all destined to haunt the national park movement and, indeed, to affect the form in which CCS emerged 25 years later. A Scottish Council on National Parks was formed in 1942. It is said to have owed its origin and influence to concern over hydro-electric development, coupled with a widespread apprehension of the role and aspirations of the FC, which had declared several National Forest Parks in Scotland and was at that time bidding to become in effect the national park authority in Scotland (Cherry 1975; Sheail 1981). The Council's early submissions to the Scottish Office were rebuffed: but the Secretary of State, Tom Johnston, quickly saw which way the wind was blowing and in January 1944 appointed a Committee under Sir Douglas Ramsay (an active participant in the Council) to advise on the selection of a smallish number of National Parks in Scotland. Later, in February 1946, Ramsay was asked to chair a full-blown Scottish National Parks Committee with wider terms of reference including administration and financing, and with cross-membership with the Scottish Wild Life Conservation Committee set up at the same time.

The Ramsay Committee reported in 1947 (Cmd 7235). It adopted the Dower concept of a national park, but gave much more explicit emphasis to the princi-

Meanwhile, however, an important initiative had been launched south of the border which was destined to have decisive effects in Scotland. Max Nicholson, Director of the NC, had taken the lead in arranging a conference in 1963 entitled 'The Countryside in 1970' (the year fixed as European Conservation Year), and had secured the patronage of HRH the Duke of Edinburgh as its chairman. If the 1963 event turned out rather an indecisive affair (marked, so far as Scotland was concerned, by an intemperate outburst by the SLF chairman against national parks), Nicholson was not discouraged. He redoubled his efforts to make the next stage in the preparation for 1970 a significant one. In this he was successful. Twelve study groups, with terms of reference ranging from the training and qualifications of planners to the preservation of natural and historic treasures, presented an impressive dossier of in–depth reports on their specialties to the next conference held in November 1965.

For the purposes of this volume, the most significant of the study groups were those numbered 5 and 9. Group 5 (Review of Legislation) recommended that the National Parks Commission should be reconstituted with countrywide [sc. England and Wales] responsibilities for conservation of landscape and the development of recreation; and that a nationwide wardens' service should be established. Group 9 (Countryside: Planning and Development in Scotland) wrestled with the national park issue yet again. The outcome was an acceptance that the concept of National Parks had been very limiting because of the dangers of overuse of park areas, and of ignoring other, very important countryside. The major factor was not the label but the concept of coordinated attention to the problems and opportunities of particular areas.

Group 9 also looked at the various agencies in Scotland to which unified administration could be assigned. Individual local authorities were ruled out by virtue of their small size and resources. Groupings of local authorities had proved a source more of local rivalry than of achievement, and the prospect of a new structure of enlarged local authorities seemed remote. The Scottish Office itself had shown 'initiative and drive' in dealing with countryside matters: but it was inappropriate for an organ of central government to be made responsible for action at a local level, particularly in view of the Secretary of State's appellate role in planning matters. The conclusion to which the Group was driven, therefore, was to recommend an *ad hoc* Countryside Commission – bringing Scotland into closer analogy with the arrangements proposed for England and Wales by Study Group 5. In doing so they 'were deeply aware of the temptation for a committee such as theirs, faced with a particular problem…to recommend an *ad hoc* body'. They were quite clear, however, that the problem was one of the highest order of magnitude and therefore that it merited a tailor–made solution.

As to the role of the Countryside Commission, the Group assumed that whatever was to be done for national park areas would now be done, or directed, by the new agency. It would not usurp the functions of the Forestry Commission, or the Department of Agriculture, or the planning authorities, but they would be required to consult the Commission on forward plans. Nor would it in the ordinary course make grants to local authorities at its own hand: it would recommend the making of grants by the Secretary of State. Its role would be not so much executive as policy-forming and advisory, on both the conservation and the recreational sides.

As with the other two agencies considered in this project (FC and NC/NCC), the interest groups struck at exactly the right time. During the run-up to the May

1965 General Election, Labour had caught the vibrations which energised the 'Countryside in 1970' movement, and had promised an enhanced National Parks Commission for England and Wales. Scotland, said the manifesto, must have a comparable authority. The Scottish Council for National Parks capitalised on this undertaking and demanded of the new Labour government full-blown national parks and statutory control of the countryside. But, not for the first (or the last) time, the government once in office saw things in a different light and attempted to backtrack.

The clinching factor, according to Cherry (1975), was the November 1965 conference. The Minister for Land and Natural Resources had undertaken to re-port to the Conference his proposals for countryside legislation in England and Wales. The Secretary of State for Scotland was 'bounced' into similar action, and so the Scottish announcement was made in Parliament on 17 November 1965.

The terms of the announcement were spare and uninformative. A Country-side Commission for Scotland was to be established, with a responsibility both to conserve scenic beauty and also to develop recreation and tourism. It would not supplant but supplement existing agencies, such as HIDB, the FC, the NC, local authorities and voluntary bodies: and it would be supported by adequate Exchequer funding. There followed consultation with the countryside interests, which welcomed the proposals, and with the local authority associations, which maintained their opposition. The Home Affairs Committee of the Cabinet proved a tougher nut to crack (Cherry, 1975). The Secretary of State (William Ross) had to confront or persuade colleagues who were suspicious of any deviation from the pattern envisaged for England and Wales, and in particular of a body poten-tially duplicating the work of other agencies, and spending public money at its own hand. As a result, the executive powers of the proposed Commission were whittled to the bone.

By an odd twist of fortune, Scotland achieved a place for its countryside legislation ahead of England and Wales. It therefore fell to Scottish Ministers to steer through Parliament the new statutory provisions regarding the concept of countryside, its conservation and enhancement, access, public paths, country parks and so on, which were intended to be common throughout Great Britain. Accordingly it was difficult to accept amendments, however worthy, during the passage of the Scottish Bill, because they would have either diverged from exist-ing England and Wales legislation, or else tied the hands of the Whitehall legis-lators in the following Session. Fortunately, the Bill had an easy ride through both Houses, and it reached the statute book in October 1967.

Countryside (Scotland) Act 1967

Considering its limited purposes, the Act is surprisingly long and involved. Much of its bulk, however, is taken up with provisions about such matters as ac-cess, public paths and rights of way which tend to be hedged about with legal complications. The sections dealing with the Countryside Commission are brief and straightforward. The Commission was to have a maximum of fourteen members, to be appointed by the Secretary of State, and to represent local authority, countryside and other interests in such proportions as he saw fit. Its duties were a) to keep under review matters affecting facilities for the enjoyment of the countryside, the conservation and enhancement of its natural beauty and amenity, and public access; b) to consult with local authorities and others over such matters; c) to encourage and coordinate the implementation of practical measures; and d) to advise the Government on matters affecting the countryside. In carrying out its duties it was to have regard to the need to promote 'the balanced economic and social development of the countryside'. The vexed question as to what constitutes the countryside was to be settled once and for all by the Secretary of State drawing up detailed maps which, for all practical purposes, were to categorise as countryside everything that was not built-up.

The powers of the Commission were to be mainly of an enabling or auxiliary nature – to engage in cooperative action, to educate and inform the public, to charge for services, and to hold land. Powers to act entrepreneurially were strictly limited – in effect to Section 5, which provided for 'development projects' of an innovative or demonstration character to be undertaken by the Commission itself, but only with the specific approval of the Secretary of State. Grant aid to local authorities was to be handled by the Scottish Office, with the Commission acting in an advisory capacity.

The Commission was to be responsible for grant aid to the private sector, but only with the consent of the Secretary of State and where in all the circumstances it was 'preferable that the project should be carried out by a person other than a public body' (Section 7). The Commission's role in planning matters was to be purely advisory, though in areas of special planning control (Section 9) the local authority might be placed under an obligation to refer planning applications to the Commission – their final disposal, however, resting with the Secretary of State. All these limitations were imposed in order to calm the fears of the local authorities that the Commission would constitute an intermediate layer of administration between themselves and the Secretary of State.

1968–1985

The period from 1968 to 1985 is not a clear–cut epoch in CCS history. It has been chosen because it coincides with the tenure of office of the Commission's first Director, John Foster, who must be regarded as having given CCS its initial orientation. Foster, a Scotsman, had spent a number of years as Chief Officer of the Peak Park Planning Board, accepting a reduction in salary on his appointment to CCS. The Commission took office on 1 April 1968, five months after the parent Act became law. The part–time Chairman was John McWilliam, prominent in local government circles as Convener of Fife County Council. Most of the other thirteen members (the maximum number under the Act) were drawn from the local authority, landed interest and countryside sources. However, the Secretary of State used his own prerogative under section 1(4)(c) of the Act to make some imaginative appointments – a retired Director of Education, the Deputy Chairman–elect of the newly formed HIDB, and a noted town planner.

The Commission did not begin its life with a flourish of trumpets. By July 1969, when its first Annual Report (priced at 2/6d or 12½p), was published, it had acquired an emblem – an unassuming blue circle enclosing two back-to-back letter Cs. It is interesting that the two cardinal points in the instructions to the design consultant were to avoid 'a) a strong representational symbol (such as a thistle, bird or animal, or mountain peak); and b) the overworked country-side colour of green'. Whether deliberately or otherwise, the SNH emblem adopted every single one of these forbidden elements.

The 1968 report records 'a modest start' on the Commission's various statutory responsibilities, at a time of national financial stringency. By the end of the year the staff totalled eleven, operating from temporary headquarters in Perth. But already the Commission had identified three key tasks for itself: i) classification of the scenic resources of Scotland; ii) encouragement to local authorities to work up systematic programmes for recreation and conservation within their areas (with grant under Section 67 as the incentive); and iii) development of facilities for the interpretation of the countryside both to its own residents and to visitors. It was this last activity which was chosen as the Scottish theme for European Conservation Year 1970, for which CCS volunteered itself as Great Britain coordinator.

The following two years (1969 and 1970) saw the Commission consolidate its administrative base, with the staff complement increasing to 25 and permanent headquarters being acquired at Battleby, near Perth. While the references in the Annual Reports wax eloquent in praise of the strategic situation and opportunities for development of this 'country house' site, there were misgivings in some quarters over its relative isolation and remoteness from other administrative centres. The Commission had been established as a free-standing body, in contrast with its counterpart south of the border, where the staff were, in effect, civil servants.

Among the issues occupying the minds of Commissioners in the early years were relationships with other statutory bodies, in particular the Scottish Tourist Board, HIDB, and the NC (which had recently become absorbed into NERC). The Commission resisted a proposal by the Conservancy's Scottish Chairman that a circular should be issued to local authorities defining the roles of the two bodies. This would immediately raise the question: what of the relations with all the other bodies? However, CCS had to agree to an acknowledgment that the powers and duties conferred upon it by the 1967 Act were without prejudice to the existing functions of the NC relating to the scientific aspects of natural beauty. The Commission took note with some concern of the doubt expressed in the Report of the Wheatley Commission on Local Government in Scotland (1969 Cmnd 4150) whether, following local government reorganisation, there would be any need for a Countryside Commission at all. It hastened to reassure itself that many functions under the 1967 Act could not be discharged by any new local authority structure, however large.

The work of CCS expanded rapidly in these early years, though in terms more of breadth than of depth. Research – on which the Commission set great store – had mainly to be commissioned from outside agencies because of its own limited staff resources. Development of Commission policy on conservation and the use of the countryside rested on the back burner, ostensibly because it had to await the outcome of research still in progress. Casework – in the form of advice on town and country planning questions and on grants to local authorities – became a heavy burden and was already giving rise to concern that neither Government nor local authorities were paying enough attention to the Commission's function or to its advice on particular issues. These could be interpreted as signs of frustration on the part of CCS at the want of an executive role.

Others, however, were not slow in urging the Commission to launch out in an executive direction, using its powers under Section 5 of the 1967 Act to promote development projects. During the Committee stage of the Bill, MPs had seen this provision as enabling CCS to pioneer such projects as marinas, weekend villages, caravan parks and heliports on high mountains.

The Commission, reconsidering these suggestions in October 1969, was advised by its staff to reject all of them as 'non-starters or even abhorrent', and to think instead merely of a demonstration and training centre for countryside facilities. Such a centre was in fact quickly established at Battleby itself (though not, as it happened, as a Section 5 project). But once again MPs – this time during a Scottish Grand Committee debate on the CCS report for 1970 (HC 1970–71 Standing Committees VI 15.7.71) – showed themselves anxious to see a more adventurous use of Section 5. The staff were instructed to dig up some possible projects, but again came forward with very cautious suggestions.

Land Resource Use

Later in 1971 CCS was in the spotlight of the Commons Select Committee on Scottish Affairs, whose inquiry into Land Resource Use has already been noted. Representatives of the Commission were among the very first witnesses to be interviewed by the Select Committee, and it was evident that high expectations were entertained of the new agency.

Questioning was consistently directed at the extent to which CCS was prepared to use its muscle in order to achieve the desired results in the countryside, whether by way of promoting, or opposing, new developments. But every time the Commission's response was guarded (HC 1971–72 511 – iii). It saw its role as heavily circumscribed by the terms of the 1967 Act. It had little to do with rural land uses – and in any case there were no significant conflicts with the Department of Agriculture or the FC, although consultation on new planting would be appreciated. Rural depopulation was a matter of concern, but not really for the Commission. The agency was prepared to speak out where required, for example at public inquiries, but preferred to work by quiet diplomacy.

In the end, the Select Committee decided to accept the Commission's own assessment of its role and priorities. The Committee's idea of a Land Use Council for Scotland, if it had been implemented, would of course have had profound implications for the future of a Countryside Commission which placed all the emphasis, so far as its own role was concerned, on coordination rather than leadership. But the Land Use Council never saw the light of day.

One of the topics on which the Select Committee had pressed CCS during its hearing of evidence was that of national parks. Specifically, the Committee wanted to know whether CCS favoured parks with *ad hoc* administration, joint committees of local authorities, or direct local authority control. This question put CCS on the spot, with the Chairman coming out in favour of direct control and financing through the new regional councils proposed by the Wheatley Commission, while his fellow-Commissioner (Parnell) and the Director (Foster) argued for *ad hoc* park authorities. Later, CCS undertook to reflect further and to submit a separate memorandum on the subject.

In the end, the CCS paper (HC 1971–72 511 – v) neatly sidestepped the straight question posed by the Select Committee. It widened the national park issue to embrace the notion of a park system for Scotland – a phrase which became a kind of watchword of the Commission for the next two decades. The argument started from the premise that the main weakness in countryside management in Scotland was not the absence of national parks but the uncoordinated nature of the existing landscape designations. These included: at the national scale – NPDAs, National Forest Parks, NNRs and some of the NTS mountain areas; and, at the more local scale – Areas of Great Landscape Value, regional and country parks, and green belts. What was required was a classification of countryside resources so as to provide the basis for a hierarchy of landscape protection as well as of landscape management. Statutory designation of the most important areas under Section 9 of the 1967 Act would be a start towards adequate protection. But active management – power to acquire and develop land and to manage it for conservation or recreational purposes – was also needed: and where a landscape area straddled local authority boundaries 'unified administration through a joint body would be essential'. To ensure uniform standards, the park *system* should be matched by a comprehensive park *service*.

The Select Committee had no hesitation in giving its blessing to the CCS approach, which it recommended should be accorded high priority by the new Land Use Council proposed by the Committee (HC 1971–72 511–i). In its response the Government rejected the Land Use Council, but indicated openness to CCS' further ideas on the park system. As regards the future of CCS as an institution, the Government saw the prospect of a new local government structure as likely to relieve the Commission of some of its burden, and undertook to keep the level of staff and resources under continuous review (Cmnd 5428, September 1973).

A new Chairman

Meanwhile the Commission had experienced its first internal shake-up since its establishment. With the advent of a Conservative government in 1971 it was inevitable that public appointments would be reassessed, and Sir John (as he now was) McWilliam's chairmanship of CCS was not renewed after his first term ended in February 1972. He was replaced by Mrs Jean Balfour, a landowner and local authority member – also from Fife – with scientific interests and training (she was to be appointed to the newly-formed NCC a year later). Some changes in style and organisation were to follow. A formal appointment of Vice-Chairman was introduced, and the two-monthly cycle of Commission meetings, with intermediate meetings of functional committees, was discarded in favour of a monthly cycle, with no delegation of functions except to a small Chairman's Committee with powers to handle urgent or sensitive business.

This of course put an additional strain on the Commission meetings, which had to cover a wide range of subject–matter and casework.

The park system

While CCS did not feel unduly threatened by the new administration, it was clear that many of the initiatives which had been given a receptive hearing under a Labour government were in danger of slipping in the more *laissez faire* atmosphere which now prevailed. It was up to the Commission to make the running, in particular on the park system. But on this there was a wide variety of views within the Commission. The staff, and some members, favoured a *dirigiste* model with heavy intervention from central government, especially in the constitution and running of areas of national significance. Others, especially those with local authority background, found it hard to accept that *ad hoc* administration should be advocated just at the time when local government was being reformed to take on greater responsibilities. Extended meetings were held throughout 1972, 1973 and 1974 at which Commission thinking gradually crystallised. Perhaps the most formative influence was a series of consultations held over the winter of 1973–74 with various statutory and other bodies – NCC, CCEW, the FC, HIDB, Scottish Tourist Board, Scottish Sports Council, Crofters Commission, NTS and SLF. Some of these bodies – NCC in particular – felt directly threatened by the plans for *ad hoc* park authorities. But the message that came across most forcibly was that the public would not stomach the bypassing of the local democratic processes, particularly in the town and country planning context.

What emerged finally, in the shape of the memorandum 'A Park System for Scotland' (November 1974), was a much diluted set of proposals. National Parks as such were abandoned. The park system was to be geared towards the development and control of recreation, leaving the conservation of landscape to other mechanisms (in particular, the designation of ASPC under Section 9 of the 1967 Act). Within the system, the only kind of park to be designated by the Secretary of State and governed by an *ad hoc* authority would be the 'special' park, satisfying what was clearly seen as a national recreational need. Even so, it would be constituted as to two-thirds from local authority members, with one-third nominated to represent the national interest. Exchequer grant, at a higher level than the 75 per cent normally applying to countryside provision, should be available both for the provision of visitor facilities and for the negotiation of management, access and footpath agreements.

It is only necessary to add, by·way of rounding off the park system saga, that the November 1974 memorandum did not arouse either fierce hostility on the one hand or great enthusiasm on the other. Subject to certain safeguards (letter to SDD dated 19 September 1975), COSLA accepted its main proposals. Although a Labour government had again come into power, it was more concerned with urban than rural affairs and it was not eager to spend money – as the Secretary of State's response (HC 29 March 1976) made clear. The CCS memorandum moved into the ambit of working parties from which emerged, much later, various provisions amending the 1967 Act in minor respects. Parts of the Report were implemented – eg the recommendations for urban parks and (much later) regional parks. But once again the national park ideal in Scotland had been submerged – this time for a further fifteen years – and with it the prospect of the Commission becoming a major executive agency.

A time of reappraisal

There is no indication that CCS took the sidelining of 'A Park System for Scotland' as a severe disappointment. A great deal of effort and nervous energy, however, had been invested in it: and perhaps the Commission felt that the more bread-and-butter side of its work had suffered in consequence. At all events, 1975 saw a return to self-examination and review of CCS activities as a whole – aided by the first of numerous staff inspections instituted by SDD as sponsor Department. Commissioners demanded of the staff, for the first time, a statement of aims and objectives. This was subjected to a certain amount of criticism and redrafting, and finally approved in October 1975. It listed five main objectives, which may be shortly described as review, planning advice, countryside projects, education, and research and development. The following paragraphs summarise some of the initiatives which emerged from this period of reappraisal.

Recreation strategy: It was logical that the process of redefining objectives should begin with an assessment of the various strands of past Commission activity. Research had claimed a fair share of resources and had yielded useful background information on such diverse matters as the condition of Highland beaches, the distribution of second homes in Scotland, and the potential for 'special' parks. It was now time, in the Commission's judgment, to take a more comprehensive view of the demand for and supply of 'countryside recreational facilities' and the ways of managing the anticipated pressures. In cooperation with other agencies, a database on tourism and recreation was commissioned: and the new regional councils were put under pressure to draw up strategies for tourism and recreation within their areas. The Commission had been disappointed that its earlier drive to set up countryside committees in each of the major authorities had met with only moderate success, and had finally been sabotaged by the recommendation of the Paterson Committee (on management and organisation within the new authorities) that countryside matters should be handled by more broadly–based Leisure and Recreation Committees. The recreation strategy was a device for reclaiming this lost ground.

The new authorities, however, beset on all sides by demands for surveys, regional reports and structure plans, found the attentions of CCS less than welcome. The only factor which continued to give the Commission some clout was the persistence of *ad hoc* grant at 75 per cent for countryside projects.

Rangers: Another theme taken up by CCS at this period – perhaps as a means of stamping its authority on the new local government system – was the need to create a nation-wide ranger service. Ranger appointments, in Speyside and Glen Nevis, had been among the Commission's first exercises of its powers under Section 5 of the 1967 Act to promote experimental projects. In a graphic report on his two-year stint in Glen Nevis, the Project Officer described his role – as perceived by the public – as something between that of a rural litter collector, a car mechanic and a professional weather forecaster. Staff now sought to raise the status of the local authority ranger by establishing a common (CCS) emblem, a uniform, and membership of a common corps – always with the incentive of the 75 per cent countryside grant for approved expenditure. The Commissioners agreed, with the proviso that 'all reference to the Commission should be deleted from the design samples to be used for discussion purposes with employing authorities'.

Long-distance routes: The 1967 Act – more in order to preserve uniformity with England and Wales than from any overt Scottish anxiety on the matter – had made provision, in Sections 39 to 42, for the creation of long-distance routes. The West Highland Way, for which the Secretary of State gave approval in 1974, was the first such route in Scotland. In 1975 the staff put forward a series of papers arguing for the extension of the network and, in particular, for a Grampian Way between Elgin and Blair Atholl, traversing the Cairngorms via the Lairig Ghru. In the process of consultation objections were voiced on three main grounds: first, that the declaration of a long-distance route would debase a precious wilderness environment; second, that it would expose ill-equipped walkers to real danger; and third, that the demand for such routes had been exaggerated anyway. In response the staff argued that the Cairngorms were heavily trafficked already; that an element of risk in some long-distance routes was acceptable; that many letters had been received, especially from south of the border, seeking signposted routes, accompanied by published guides, so as to gain greater enjoyment from the Scottish countryside; and that the objectors were really a small minority of elitists. Further consultations showed that the staff had underestimated the opposition to the Lairig Ghru route, which was almost total. The Grampian Way was therefore abandoned in favour of a low-level Speyside Way.

The West Highland Way eventually materialised in 1980, and from the start was well patronised (unlike the 212-mile Southern Upland Way, opened in 1984). The very popularity of the route, however, brought problems of maintenance, and in some cases hardened the attitudes of farmers and landowners – leading to a degree of threat to the public access for which the routes were created in the first place (Blunden and Curry 1990, Paterson 1992).

Vehicle tracks: A related topic which came to light in the mid-1970s was that of 'Land Rover' tracks in the Scottish hills. A letter from the Scottish Countryside Activities Council drew attention to the proliferation of such tracks – for forestry, agriculture or, more often, sporting purposes – which tended to be intrusive, ill-designed and badly constructed. The initial staff response was fairly complacent. While agreeing that there might be a problem, they doubted whether it was a serious one so far as the interests of the Commission were concerned: indeed tracks could be advantageous to some hill–walkers. The answer might lie in disseminating advice to track constructors, and in offering direct grant or management agreements to provide an incentive for a better standard of construction. Simply bringing vehicle tracks within planning control was not a solution. The Commission took a rather more serious view of the problem, but had no new solution to offer, other than consulting SLF. A report and code of practice on track construction was commissioned from NERC, which submitted a draft towards the end of 1975. Thereafter a protracted series of consultations took place, so that the report was not published until July 1978. Even then, nothing much happened. In a letter dated 1 December 1978, SLF took exception to the Commission's modest proposals for bringing agricultural and forestry tracks within the scope of planning control in sensitive areas, and for making it clear that tracks for sporting use were not permitted development. The Commission found the SLF arguments on the latter point persuasive, and decided to pursue the issue of vehicle tracks only in the context of sensitive landscape areas.

Areas of Special Planning Control (ASPC): The use to be made of Section 9 of the 1967 Act (providing for the designation of areas in which planning applications would have to be vetted by CCS) exercised the Commission's mind for many years. To a limited extent, CCS was already involved in planning matters in the five NPDAs established in 1948: but when the national park debate came to the forefront in the early 1970s the Commission became more and more convinced that Section 9 was the method of choice for regulating development in the most important landscape areas. In the face of evident Government reluctance to meet the Commission's demand on this point, staff drew attention to the fact that Section 9 could be applied to recreational as well as landscape areas, and that a start might be made by way of designating as an ASPC the area of the proposed Pentland Hills Regional Park. This duly came to pass on 16 May 1975, the day that the new local government structure became operative. The designation was not a success. The Commission became involved in a good deal of trivial casework of an urban rather than a countryside character: for example, the summary for the last quarter of 1979 mentions planning applications for a new window at the Hillend Ski Centre and for four houses in Balerno, on neither of which CCS had any observations. Without protest, the Commission agreed to the sponsor Department's proposal, notified to local authorities in October 1979, to wind up the arrangements for both ASPCs and NPDAs. The Commission's solitary venture into executive planning control came to an end in August 1980.

There was a *quid pro quo*, however. Since the publication of the park system proposals in 1974, the Department had been trying to steer the Commission's main thrust away from the designation of parks as such and towards the protection of landscape. The interest of CCS in landscape classification fitted in well with this. In 1978 the Commission published *Scotland's Scenic Heritage* – a large volume identifying and describing 40 areas of outstanding landscape, thereafter entitled National Scenic Areas (NSAs). The arrangement now proposed by the Department, and accepted by CCS and the local authorities, was that planning applications within certain specified categories affecting NSAs which an authority was minded to approve had to be notified to the Commission – and to the Secretary of State if the Commission's advice were not accepted. The categories of development in question were fairly restricted. They included schemes for five or more houses, buildings over 12 metres high, roadworks costing more than £100,000, and vehicle tracks above 300m altitude. By mid-1982, just under two years after the new procedure had come into force, 58 planning applications had been notified to CCS, of which only thirteen were allowed to go ahead without modification. The procedure was working: but there was concern whether the criteria for notification were strict enough, and whether local authorities were vigilant enough in checking developments – especially vehicle tracks – that were undertaken without the benefit of planning permission.

North Sea oil and gas: Development of oil and gas reserves was building up to a climax in the mid-1970s, and CCS was heavily involved in the drafting of planning guidelines and in casework related to on–shore installations. However, the Commission tended to be marginalised when such projects reached the point of decision – partly because of its rural image but mainly because the need for platform sites, for example, was deemed to be so urgent in the national interest as to justify riding roughshod over environmental objections. In connection with Portavadie on Loch Fyne (a particularly ill-chosen site, where the environmental damage was extreme, although no platform was ever built), the CCS submission was to the effect that 'a site there would only be accepted by the Commission if it was established at the public local enquiry that the Government's assessment of the need for five additional platform designs was substantiated'. The NSA notification procedure gave CCS considerably more leverage in regard to oil platform sites: unfortunately, the great wave of site development was over by the time the procedure was introduced.

Country parks: Section 48 of the 1967 Act provided for country parks to be created 'in relation to major concentrations of population', for the enjoyment of the countryside or open-air recreation. The concept was already a familiar one south of the border: the report of CCEW for 1969–70 notes a number of long-standing country parks recognised by the Commission, as well as new parks brought into existence with the aid of grant from the Commission. But in Scotland by the end of 1974 only three country parks were in existence. Staff were asked to explain, and to suggest how matters might be improved. Their answer was that registration was made to sound too complex and difficult, and authorities were in fact providing the relevant facilities without calling them country parks. So the solution lay in calling for a simple statement of objectives, but at the same time giving notice that priority in grant awards would go to projects which had first been registered as country parks. The recipe was adopted, and country parks began to blossom: twenty-one had been registered by 1980. Indeed there was some concern that too large a share of CCS resources was being devoted to country parks: but after a review of the whole situation it was decided not to impose a moratorium. A major factor in the decision was that, in terms of cost/benefit, country parks rated highly among the Commission's investments, especially during a period when unemployment was rising and incomes were under stress (1980 Annual Report).

Countryside around towns: CCS was aware from the start that its remit extended to 98 per cent of the Scottish land surface, not just to the areas of high scenic attractiveness. In the early years, however, the only input to the urban fringe and the industrial wasteland of central Scotland had been by way of assistance with country parks. The heading 'The countryside around [or near] towns' did not make its appearance in Commission reports until 1975, when it was announced that a situation report on Scottish green belts had been received from a consultant, and that another study of priorities for research and experiment had been commissioned from the Dartington Institute (at a cost of £2475). By mid-1977 the report of this study had been received and discussed with central belt local authorities and government agencies. The priorities which emerged were modest indeed – a survey of visitor use of Strathclyde Country Park, development of farm open days, and a demonstration project to renovate the Union Canal for recreational purposes. But by the following spring two much more significant initiatives had come forward. One was a proposal by Fife Regional Council to improve and open up to public access a wide stretch of countryside around the Lomond Hills. The other, resulting from discussions between local authorities and the FC, was aimed at enhancing a blighted area of 150 square miles centred on the Slamannan plateau, mainly by tree planting (1978 and 1979 Annual Reports).

Thereafter the countryside around towns tended to be downgraded on the Commission's agenda, although individual projects still went on. It was not until 1985 that the Dartington Institute was recommissioned to update the 1975 report – this time with more lasting consequences.

Public policy: During the second half of the 1970s the Commission was exercised about a number of items of policy which were on the agenda of government. Nearest to the Commission's heart was the question of new countryside legislation, and a long shopping list, embracing everything from national parks to powers to employ rangers on long-distance routes, was drawn up for discussion with SDD. The Government showed little inclination to authorise legislation on any matters beyond what could be safely entrusted to a Private Member, and regretfully the Commission accepted this. The resultant Bill, sponsored by Lord Hughes, lapsed on the dissolution of Parliament in 1979. The incoming Government proved to be a little more cooperative, and although CCS had to be content once again with a Private Member's measure, Mr Peter Fraser's Bill had a wider scope. The most significant changes brought about in the Countryside (Scotland) Act 1981 were the formal recognition of regional parks, and the power conferred on CCS to make grants to local authorities on its own account, no longer as a mere agent of the Department.

Outside its own field, CCS played an active role in discussions on taxation changes as they applied to forestry and landholding. The Commission took a strongly supportive line towards private forestry (1976 Annual Report): as regards measures to redistribute wealth through fiscal means it professed neutrality, but was anxious to offer itself as a recipient of scenic land should it fall into the public domain (1979 Annual Report). In this context CCS had been acting since 1975 as adviser to the Treasury on the exemption of scenic land from capital taxation, on condition that a degree of public access was guaranteed. But neither the Labour nor the Conservative government showed any inclination to countenance the Commission's holding land on its own account.

Devolution exercised the Commission's mind strenuously throughout the period of Labour rule. The main issue for CCS soon emerged through the success of NCC in having nature conservation treated as a wholly reserved subject, while countryside matters were devolved – nothwithstanding that all the statutes hitherto had treated natural beauty and amenity as the basis for both nature and scenic conservation. The publication of the Scotland Bill in 1977 raised hopes that conservation in all its aspects would be a responsibility of the Scottish Assembly (1977 Annual Report). However, a letter from a Scottish Office Minister made it plain that the extent of the Assembly's responsibility with regard to nature conservation would be to give effect to advice from NCC. The Countryside Commission should be satisfied with the assurance that its own lines of communication with the Assembly would be clear and unimpeded: and it should work out a commonsense demarcation with NCC in the new circumstances. As it turned out, all the anxieties over the Bill dissolved with the failure of the Scotland and Wales Acts to be passed into law – and the subsequent election of a Conservative government flatly opposed to devolution in any form. But the incident had highlighted the artificiality of keeping nature and scenic conservation in separate compartments.

Review

A brief review of the Commission's achievements by 1984 may be useful at this point. Dr Jean Balfour's long reign as Chairman had ended in 1982. The Annual Report for that year paid eloquent tribute to her expertise and commitment to the work of the Commission. She had been something approaching an executive chairman, which may have inhibited the staff, and in particular the Director, from showing the initiative and drive that might have been expected of them. Much useful work had been done, in terms not only of physical developments on the ground but also of understanding of the factors affecting the Scottish countryside and its recreational use. But the attempts at formulating and expressing policy had not met with success – partly because of the Commission's low profile and lack of political clout, partly because it appeared to be over-influenced in its choice of targets by thinking south of the Border. As with NCC, there was much emphasis on classification and designation of particular pieces of land, while the rising threats to the Scottish countryside in general – from intensive agriculture and afforestation – went unremarked.

1985–1992

A new look

The new Chairman of the Commission, who had taken office in 1983, was David Nickson, an English industrialist. He had come to the Secretary of State's notice because of his drive, his ready acclimatisation to the Scottish scene, his environmental interests – and his political affiliations. His style was different from that of his predecessor's. He was a relaxed and distinctly non-executive Chairman, leaving the Director (Foster) to make the running. Foster, however, had only two years to go before retirement and found it difficult to take up the opportunities thus presented.

Changes began to show: subtly at first, more markedly as time went on. From the start, however, Nickson made it clear that he wished CCS's horizons to be broadened. The Chairman's monthly reports to the Commission of his own activities displayed a balance of interest towards the less glamorous countryside, and also a willingness to use his contacts within industry and government to increase the Commission's influence. An early change of emphasis can be detected in the attitude towards traditional land uses. Whereas the Annual Report for 1982 had stated that CCS conservation policy must 'recognise the importance of providing for wise and progressive land use for productive and profitable forms of agriculture and forestry', the Report for 1983 pointed to a risk of complacency within farming and forestry circles, and 'an assumption that the Scottish countryside can accept any amount of change where this can be justified on the simple contention that the economics of the industry… require changes of use'. By the time of the 1984 Annual Report the tone was sharper: '…it is small wonder that we should seek to play a prominent role and become more involved in the decision-making process on farming and forestry practices in Scotland'.

Without doubt the Commission's more interventionist approach owed something to the initiative of its sister Commission south of the Border. In 1978 CCEW had published a comprehensive study, carried out by ITE, entitled *Upland land use in England and Wales*. The steering committee which guided its compilation included representation from CCS as well as FC and NCC. Following this preparatory piece of fieldwork, CCEW promoted in 1983 what it called the Uplands Debate, reviewing on a broad front public policies towards land above 800 feet or within the Less Favoured Areas (LFA) as defined under EC regulations. Since over 80 per cent of Scotland was within the LFA it might be supposed that CCS would have wished to extend the Debate to cover the whole of Great Britain, especially as the staff considered that 'the nature of issues in the uplands are not all that different north and south of the border'. However, the scale of the factors involved was thought to be different, and the social and economic problems in Scotland more difficult, and well outside the capacity of CCS to head up an inquiry. Above all, with the demise in 1980 of the Standing Committee on Rural Land Use (SCRLU) there was now no forum in which the main actors in the Scottish land use debate – DAFS and the FC – could be brought into constructive dialogue. Accordingly the only action which the Commission was prompted to pursue was to ask about the possibility of reviving the Standing Committee. Somewhat to the Commission's surprise, its plea met with a positive response: early in 1985 the Secretary of State set up a Departmental Group on the Countryside, with a remit which was wider than that of SCRLU.

It took two further initiatives from south of the Border to force CCS to abandon finally its low profile posture. The genesis of *Nature Conservation in Great Britain* (NCGB) has already been described. It first came to CCS' notice in 1983, when an early draft, produced by NCC's Chief Scientist, Derek Ratcliffe, was circulated for comments. NCC was at that time overwhelmed by what it had come to see as the unfair consequences of the Wildlife and Countryside Act 1981, and called on the two Countryside Commissions to join with it in denouncing current farming and forestry policies. The Scottish Commission, which had been only marginally affected by the 1981 Act, reacted with alarm. Staff reminded the members that 'in the past this Commission has adopted policies in relation to land–using interests which sought to work with them and to influence and modify change rather than to confront it'. In the end CCS declined to be quoted as endorsing even the much softer terms of the final draft of NCGB, and agreed only to send a letter of qualified support.

The other initiative, resulting in NCC's *Nature Conservation and Afforestation*, has already been discussed. Again, the receipt by CCS of the first consultation draft in September 1985 caused some consternation. While the value of most of the NCC recommendations was conceded, the critique of past forestry policy and practice was considered by CCS staff to be 'partisan, equivocal and in places misleading'. Once more, NCC paid enough heed to the comments of consultees to enable the Commission to give *Nature Conservation and Afforestation* its general support. But this time CCS did better. Alongside its consideration of the NCC draft the Commission had been gestating its own internal appraisal of forestry policy. Thinking had moved a long way since 1978, when staff, in reviewing FC's *The Wood Production Outlook in Britain*, had tamely recommended agreement in principle to a 'substantially increased planting programme' which it should be possible to carry out 'without significant damage to the scenic heritage of Scotland'. Now, in 1985, the staff complement included a forestry specialist whose contribution enabled the Commission to speak with authority. With the prospect of NCC's publication, CCS was emboldened to turn its internal discussion document into a public statement. Accordingly, *Forestry in Scotland: a Policy Paper* appeared in May 1986, just failing to beat the publication date of *Nature Conservation and Afforestation*. The CCS document has already been summarised.

Meanwhile a new Director had taken post. Michael Taylor, who had been Chief Executive of the Lake District Planning Board since 1978, was appointed in November 1984 after interview of a large number of short-listed candidates by a panel consisting of the Chairman, the Vice-Chairman and two Commissioners. The appointment did not take effect until August 1985, so that Taylor – although not released from his previous job until June 1985 – had the better part of a year to familiarise himself with the Commission's work.

Management crisis

The new Director had been in post only a month when CCS had its first taste of the management climate which was steadily working its way through the Civil Service at that time. The Commission was required to submit, by June 1986, a 5–year corporate plan showing its proposals for the use of resources on various assumptions about the level of grant-in-aid, together with the means of measur-

ment of popular mountain areas, and the countryside around towns. It may be helpful to select two or three of these major issues preoccupying the Commission during the late 1980s, by way of illustrating its approach to such problems.

Countryside around towns: The modest response of the Commission during the 1970s to the challenge presented by the blighted areas of central Scotland has already been highlighted. In 1985 the CCS conscience stirred again, to the extent of re-commissioning the Dartington Institute to review conditions in the urban fringe in the mid-1980s. The Institute's report, published in early 1987, laid emphasis on the need to tackle derelict areas in a comprehensive way, through projects such as the Central Scotland Woodlands Project and the Clyde–Calders Urban Fringe project (a local authority initiative already supported by CCS). This time the Commission did not leave the report to gather dust, but used it as the text for a series of meetings with 'all the appropriate local authorities and national agencies' with a view to extending action to virtually all the priority areas (1987 Annual Report). The kind of action needed was unglamorous, expensive and daunting in its complexity. Large stretches of derelict land might need to be reclaimed; access routes over many different ownerships would have to be negotiated and constructed; volunteers and unemployed would have to be recruited, trained and motivated. All this involved straining at the statutory limitations on CCS powers in a way that would not have been countenanced by an earlier generation of Commissioners and staff. And, it has to be admitted, the results even of successful schemes were not always very visible on the ground, so great was (and is) the scale of industrial and urban squalor that had to be contended with. By 1987, over one-fifth of the CCS grant budget was being committed to the Countryside around Towns, a sizeable part of it going to the private sector (1987 Annual Report).

When reviewing the Corporate Strategy in 1989, staff drew attention to the fact that the Countryside around Towns programme area did not adequately distinguish between urban fringe and degraded areas on the one hand and on the other the more attractive parts of Central Belt countryside. They proposed that a sub-programme should be created specifically for the run-down areas which would enjoy budget priority and within which higher grant rates would apply. This was agreed, but staff were warned not to extend the number of projects beyond what the Commission could afford. In the corresponding exercise the following year, Commissioners decided to increase the provision from total budget committed to the Countryside around Towns from twenty per cent to well over 30 per cent; to use performance indicators not just as a routine management device but as a means of assessing, and rewarding with additional grant, projects which were working well; and to establish a forum within which project staff could exchange ideas and discuss funding and other problems. All this indicated a degree of commitment to an inconspicuous and unrewarding side of the Commission's work which would not have been forthcoming ten or even five years earlier.

It was not an overstatement to refer to the Countryside around Towns initiatives as 'the Commission's principal achievement of the 1980s' (1991– 92 Annual Report).

National Parks: It has been noted how the Commission's bid in the mid-1970s for a parks hierarchy in Scotland – with something like the English National

Park as the top tier – was thwarted. The aspiration did not go away, however, and it was rekindled in CCS staff at every international conservation forum where the absence of national parks in Scotland, virtually alone in the civilised world, was deemed a national reproach. An attempt to get national park legislation by the back door had been made in 1982, so as to provide for a statutory authority for a Loch Lomond Park. The Secretary of State pointed out however that the recently introduced Act of 1981 provided for regional park authorities, and invited CCS to pursue that line of approach. This it reluctantly did.

In 1987 Highland Regional Council (HRC), in the course of updating its structure plan, showed an interest in the concept of national heritage parks. This was good news for CCS, since HRC had been hitherto one of the chief sceptics. Although discussion at the Commission's June meeting showed that members were not at one on the value of, or the objectives to be sought in, national park designation, it was agreed that further talks should be set up with Highland and Grampian Regional Councils regarding the Cairngorm area in particular. However, HRC appeared to lose interest and the matter went into abeyance.

Eighteen months later the subject was again on the agenda. Lord James Douglas-Hamilton, at that time the junior Minister for the Environment at the Scottish Office, was well known for his individual style and persistence in following out his own ideas, not simply those of his officials or of the Party machine. He took up the national park cause personally and discussed it with CCS. The outcome was a formal request in February 1989 'to study management arrangements for popular mountain areas such as the Cairngorms, taking into consideration the case for arrangements on national park lines in Scotland'. The paper setting out procedure for the review was at the same time eager and cautious, because it had to recognise that there were divided views within the Commission.

The deadline for completion of the mountain areas review was the end of 1989. This was somewhat unrealistic if the job were to be done properly and in particular if outside consultation were to be more than a formality.

An advisory panel chaired by the CCS Deputy Chairman allowed the outlook of a variety of other interests to be brought to bear. Public meetings were held in six centres in the Highlands; a major seminar was held in the Lake District; visits were paid (in company with HRC) to France and Germany; and a consultation leaflet attracted responses from a wide range of organisations and individuals.

December 1989 found the Commission only at the point of beginning to draw its thoughts together, on the basis of a first draft of the report prepared by staff. Some members were still unconvinced that a national park type approach was required: the necessary political will to manage sensitive areas under pressure 'might be generated if sufficient resources were made available to a local authority'. However, this was a minority view. By a considerable margin, Commissioners voted for the title 'national park' in preference to alternatives such as 'national heritage area'. Oddly enough, this decision was queried by members of CCEW at a joint seminar held at Aviemore in June 1990. In England and Wales, they argued, national parks were 'the most precious areas': in Scotland, designation was proposed for 'precious areas most under threat'.

The report *The Mountain Areas of Scotland: Conservation and Management* was published in September 1990. It had been preceded, by a few days, by a letter in the correspondence columns of the *Scotsman* from the Assistant Director (Communications) of the Commission. The letter attacked the 'increasingly solitary' anti-park faction and defended the record of the English National Parks against 'scaremongering tactics'. The opposition to national parks, however, showed up as fairly substantial as soon as *Mountain Areas* was published, and included SLF and NFUS. It also included Adam Watson, a member of the Commission and an expert on the Cairngorms.

The report did not pull its punches, either in criticising existing management of mountain areas or in putting forward definite recommendations. In three out of the four National Parks which it advocated (for the Cairngorms, Loch Lomond and Glen Coe) independent planning boards were proposed, much on the English model but, it was implied, with local representation drawn rather more from community organisations and less from elected councillors. Grant should be paid at 85 per cent, and local authorities precepted for the rest.

The Government's response to the report was not quite what CCS might have wished. The Commission was, in effect, told to go out and do the consultation all over again, treating the *Mountain Areas* report as a kind of green paper. This time, the volume of comment was doubled, in spite of the fact that the report cost £10 to buy. The period for consultation had to be extended, and 28 meetings were held with interested parties and organisations. In summarising the comments for the benefit of Commissioners, staff admitted that some consultees had regarded the report as a blueprint, rather than as a concept document: perhaps this might have been made clearer from the start. *The Mountain Areas of Scotland: a Report on Public Consultation*, published in February 1991, illustrated the difficulty facing staff, deeply committed to a particular cause, in doing justice to a variety of contrary evidence. The space given in the document to reporting comments was considerably exceeded by that devoted to discussion and defence of the CCS position. While 'strenuous efforts had been made to be fair and even-handed in compiling the report', the overall finding was that 'no arguments had been advanced which overturned the Commission's recommendations'. Virtually the only concession made was to recognise 'the very strong local opposition to a national park in Wester Ross'.

The Scottish Office Environment Department (SOEnD – SDD under a new name) had asked to see, not only the summary of responses, but copies of all the individual responses. It was clear from a fairly early stage that the Department was uneasy about the trend of the Commission's consideration. As far back as March 1990 the Department's assessor, after echoing the concern of Commissioners that the draft of the original Mountain Areas report then under consideration did not make it clear why the national park solution was the only one available or how it would work, gave a warning that he would find it difficult to recommend Ministers to accept the report unless these defects were addressed. It may have been because of continuing concern on this point that the assessor, during consideration of the final draft of the public consultation document early in 1991, tabled a paper on Natural Heritage Areas (NHAs). The Natural Heritage (Scotland) Bill was at that time going through Parliament, and NHAs represented a new concept which would be introduced into the Bill via a new clause.

Devil's Point, Lairig Ghru, Cairngorms

Commissioners took exception to the sudden emergence of the NHA concept, which clearly overlapped with their own national park proposals. The assessor, however, saw a number of advantages in NHAs over national parks. It was not until September 1991 that CCS received the Secretary of State's formal response to the Mountain Areas exercise, by which time the Natural Heritage Bill had become law – and the Department's assessor had become the first Director of Scottish Natural Heritage. The response was full and courteous in tone: but as far as national parks were concerned it was firm. The Government considered that the Commission's consultation process had failed to establish 'the essential degree of commitment to the proposals as they stand' in the local areas for which parks had been proposed. It was not clear 'how the proposed structures...drawn broadly from the system operating in England and Wales, would resolve the problems identified in Scotland'. The Government had therefore decided not to take forward the Commission's proposals at this stage, though not ruling out some form of national park mechanism in the future. Working parties were being set up to look at the options for both the Cairngorm and Loch Lomond areas: SNH would be in a position to advise on the situation in Glen Coe and Wester Ross. The new agency would also be expected to make use of the NHA machinery to deal with some of the management problems which the Mountain Areas reports had addressed.

The Commission reacted to the Secretary of State's letter with dignity. The Chairman wrote on 3 October 1991 expressing the Commission's pained acceptance of the decision about national parks, while stressing that the problems existed and would not go away. So ended the long saga of the CCS involvement with the national park issue, although not the issue itself.

Skiing extension at Cairngorm: In terms of complexity and time-scale this issue is at the opposite pole from the one just discussed. It is selected for consideration because it throws light on the political (with a small *p*) role and sensitivity of the Commission. The issue came before the Commission in the autumn of 1987 by way of a renewed proposal by the Cairngorm Chairlift Company to extend downhill facilities westward into Lurchers Gully in order to meet the rapidly increasing demand from the skiing public in the Aviemore area. It was not necessary at the meeting in question to reach any kind of decision, but the mere tabling of the matter revealed a wide variety of points of view coupled with a recognition that on issues of this kind, where conservation and development were in direct conflict, CCS was very much on public trial.

The Commission decided to set up its own internal study group to assess the impact of the proposed development – on the appearance and 'wilderness quality' of the Northern Corries and their hinterland, on the skiing potential of the area and further afield, and on other forms of recreation.

In the course of the study Commissioners visited the area, took evidence from public and voluntary bodies, and commissioned an independent analysis of the landscape (1988 Annual Report). By this time HRC had adopted the extension proposals in its structure plan review, so that the issue was bound to come to the Secretary of State, and the CCS view would be an essential input to his decision.

It was in October 1988 that the Commission finally made up its mind. The issue was keenly debated, and the majority against the development wafer-thin. But even more tense was the process of drafting the statement in which the CCS decision was to be expressed. It evoked a paper from one of the minority pointing out that, in the choice between economic development and visual amenity, the Commission had a delicate balancing act to perform and that it should not be afraid to present both sides of the case. In the end, the statement (December 1988) failed to satisfy members on either side of the argument. It had been expanded to emphasise the Commission's support for skiing in general and its desire to find room for its expansion, as well as the need to diversify activities within the Glen More area. But it presented the Commission's decision on the issue itself as more clear-cut than it actually had been.

The Secretary of State's decision, announced only in June 1990, was to refuse permission for the skiing extension. Probably the convergent advice of the two major environmental agencies – CCS and NCC – was a major factor in his decision. Each of the agencies, however, had mounted a separate, and expensive, exercise in support of its advice; and it may have occurred to the Secretary of State that a joint submission by the two would have been preferable.

Scottish Natural Heritage

The developments underlying the break-up of NCC, leading to its amalgamation in Scotland with CCS, have been outlined previously. The move took CCS by surprise. Relations with NCC had never been particularly close: they were at their strongest in the technical field, through the joint sponsorship by the two agencies of the National Countryside Monitoring Scheme (1985–91), an over-elaborate and largely abortive project. In September 1987, after HRC, on Government invitation, had convened a working party on forestry and land use in Caithness and Sutherland, CCS set up its own mini-inquiry, summoning representatives of NCC to give evidence along with Fountain Forestry. In April 1988, SDD drew attention to the differing approach of CCS and NCC towards afforestation, which the Vice-Chairman explained as arising from their divergent basic interests.

Nevertheless, on the issue of the NCC/CCS merger, CCS quickly took up a point of view supportive of the Government's position, from which it never wavered. Its chief argument was based on 'holism' – a concept which it claimed to have embraced from the start, in seeking to secure integrated rural development along with conservation. Thus within Scotland it made sense to look at nature and scenic conservation together. Not only that, but the Government should take the opportunity to consider a wider integration of agencies, including those responsible for the cultural heritage, for forestry and for red deer.

In the CCS view a merged agency (with NCC) would have, on balance, a number of advantages. It would be able to capitalise on the CCS approach of enablement and consensus, as against the NCC's 'more autocratic stance'. A unified view could be taken of countryside designations, and a one-door entry point would be offered for advice and assistance on conservation matters. There could be greater input into tourism, leisure provision, and public access. Resources would be larger (something like 300 staff in total, compared with the CCS complement of 58), and the benefits of NCC's regional organisation could be extended to countryside operations. Battleby looked like an ideal centre for the conjoint agency.

These were all Scottish issues, and they were rehearsed in the Commission's response to the Scottish Office consultation paper 'Scotland's Natural Heritage' (July 1989). The biggest threat to a successful outcome, from the CCS point of view, came from outside, in the shape of the determination of NCC to retain a strong 'umbrella' science and policy unit for Great Britain as a whole. The Secretary of State assured the CCS Chairman, however, that if his objective of 'a properly integrated merged body' for Scotland were to be compromised by the NCC manoeuvres, then CCS would continue as a separate independent body. In the event, the recommendations of the Carver Committee in March 1990 (1989–90 HL 33–I) just saved the day. The Committee found in favour of a strong Joint Nature Conservation Committee, with a remit extending to countryside and landscape conservation: but it should derive its funds, a proportion of its staff and the majority of its members from the constituent countries.

The Carver Committee also considered that 'amalgamation of the Countryside Commission and the NCC in England would be logical'. This was discussed at a joint meeting of CCS and CCEW – the first such meeting for many years – held at Aviemore in June 1990. Members of both Commissions were concerned at 'the possibility that scientific interest, in the merged agencies, would prevail on account of its claim for objectivity'. The Chairman of CCEW concluded that, for this reason, he was against a merger with NCC (England). His wishes prevailed. When the Environmental Protection Bill became law in November 1990 it provided for the break-up of NCC among the three countries, and for a separate Countryside Council for Wales, but for no further legislative changes south of the border.

The Commission certainly had no intention of being cast in the role of poor relation *vis-à-vis* the new NCC (Scotland). It was planned that the two outgoing agencies should make their separate proposals to the Department for the initial corporate strategy of the new joint agency SNH. The current corporate strategy of NCC was, in the opinion of CCS, unduly complex, and it proposed headings for the joint strategy very little different from its own current headings. In the end a compromise set of headings was arrived at. The Commission welcomed the proposal to constitute regional boards of SNH and to delegate substantial executive powers to each.

In April 1991 SNH came into existence under its Chairman, Magnus Magnusson, who had been designated the previous year and had already interacted positively with CCS. In May came the announcement of Roger Crofts' appointment as Chief Executive of the new agency, following the recommendation of an independent board. Crofts had been the Departmental assessor on the Commission for two years, and had found himself in vigorous dialogue with Commissioners on several occasions. He continued to serve in that capacity until his SNH appointment took effect.

The remainder of 1991 was fully taken up with joint meetings at staff and Board member level, aided by a considerable cross-membership among the several Boards concerned. On the agenda were mainly the thousand and one problems of creating a new structure and fitting existing and new staff into it – the projected SNH complement having risen to 500 by this time, of whom a mere 70 were CCS employees at the final count.

But this did not prevent CCS from continuing, up to the last, to discharge its own policy and executive duties. The Annual Report for 1991–92 gives ample testimony to the volume of business transacted and to the determination of Commissioners to keep up the momentum on all fronts. This was true in particular of access policy, on which no fewer than six research projects had been put in hand since January 1991. An advisory group, comprising representatives of all the main land-using and recreational interests, also laboured throughout 1991 to produce a policy statement and a consultative document. The drafts concerned went through intensive scrutiny during the Commission's final meetings, always in the direction of making consultation more open-ended. But there remained a strong implication that the current status of access to the countryside was not satisfactory and needed to be made more universal and less problematic. This was particularly so in a 'Commission's Opinion' which was passed on to SNH as the advice of CCS on the subject of public access.

The final chapter on the access question remains to be written. However, the SNH consultation document *Enjoying the Outdoors* which emerged in December 1992 was a pale shadow of the draft which CCS handed over at the beginning of that year. In their responses to *Enjoying the Outdoors*, Roger Carr (by now Chairman of the Ramblers' Association) and Foster, ex-Director of CCS, both made the point that the document had failed to acknowledge and build upon the tradition of free access to the Scottish hills, and that a statutory right of access was now the only way forward (*Scotsman*, 13 February 1993). Thus the final gesture from the Commission was the most uninhibited of all – but it had been left too late to have any real impact.

Summary

Compared with the other agencies reviewed, CCS had a short and uneventful history. It was a low-key, small-scale enterprise, which had a measure of achievement in terms of grass-roots projects without ever fulfilling the expectations entertained about it at the start. Towards the end of its life, when it began to grapple, not unsuccessfully, with some of the big issues of principle in Scottish land use, it had to deal with a Government which took a somewhat doctrinaire position on these issues – and which, in the end, decided to wind up the Commission for reasons which had little to do with the performance of CCS itself.

NOTES

1. An Addendum to the Ramsay report, signed by eight of its members (and evidently not dissented from by the rest), illustrates the freedom with which the Committee interpreted the National Park concept. The Addendum took the form of suggestions for the development of the Glen Affric area (which at that time was the subject of a hydro-electric constructional scheme). It envisaged the opening up of the area by new or improved roads and bridle paths; development of accommodation in the form of small hotels, youth hostels, camping sites, mountain huts etc; provision of games and sports facilities and guide services; and the promotion of rural industries based on indigenous resources. Villages, mainly occupied (it would seem) by National Park and forestry employees, would boost the population of the area to around 2000.

10

ORGANISATION AND EFFECTIVENESS

Organisation

The Countryside Commission for Scotland remained a small and compact organisation throughout its life. From the start it was headed by the equivalent of a Grade 5 officer in civil service terms: attempts were made in the 1970s and 1980s to enhance the grading to Grade 4 or Grade 3, but these were unsuccessful. The hierarchy was extremely simple. Reporting to the Director were four heads of branches: the Secretary and three Assistant Directors, responsible for Planning and Research, Resource Management and Projects, and Information and Education. Committees of Commissioners were formed to match the staff structure (1969 Annual Report) but were disbanded in 1972.

There was no territorial structure: the Commission operated solely from its headquarters – for much the greatest part of its life, Battleby. Planning officers alone held regional responsibilities, but they had no regional outposts. The Select Committee on Scottish Affairs, in its report on Land Resource Use, proposed that CCS staff should be seconded to each of the new authorities following local government reform, and that the Commission should be manned up to that end (1971–72 HC 511–i). Nothing came of this: the Government merely undertook to keep the Commission's complement under close watch (1973 Cmnd 5428).

As it turned out, the Government's close watch generally meant a downwards pressure on staffing. In 1979, when the complement was 62, the Commission applied for an increase of no fewer than 31, or 50 per cent. The staff inspection which followed came to the conclusion that nineteen of these new posts were justified at once and that the case for an additional five posts should be considered later. But a week or two later the Department announced a general freeze on staffing, and the extra posts never materialised. Indeed nine years afterwards there were only 48 full-time staff in post (1988 Annual Report). The shortfall had to be made good by such devices as temporary staff working on contract (Annual Reports for 1976 onwards).

The steady level of CCS staffing contrasted somewhat with that of CCEW, and markedly with that of NCC, whose complement was on a steady upward curve throughout most of its life (see Table 4 and Figure 7). The contrast is partly explained by the fact that Parliament put relatively few additional statutory responsibilities upon CCS over the years. But for the most part it was due to a combination of Scottish Office parsimony and the Commission's lack of clout. Even in 1988 a staff inspection recommended a net reduction of one post, to which CCS responded mildly to the effect that 'the expanding range of activity in the Commission's work can only be achieved with a modest increase in overall staffing' (1988 Annual Report).

Table 4 : Staffing[ab] of Countryside Agencies

	'75	'76	'77	'78	'79	'80	'81	'82	'83	'84	'85	'86	'87	'88	'89	'90	'91
CCS	55	59	59	59	63	63	58	58	58	58	58	58	53	53	53	57	68
CCEW	[100][c]					125	108	102	91	96	100	115	120	128	155	170	183
NCC	451	488	515	557	650	650	535	559	552	550	577	689	758	783	770	792	855

Source: Annual Reports

NOTES

a The figures given are wherever possible the numbers of permanent staff in post during the year in question. Sometimes this figure is not available, because the agency has supplied only the authorised complement for the year (ie ignoring vacancies).

b In addition to permanent staff, it was a common practice with each of the agencies to employ temporary staff, either to handle specific short–term projects or, on occasion, to evade the limit imposed by way of the authorised complement. Information about the numbers of temporary staff is sketchy in the case of CCEW and NCC: but in 1978 NCC employed as many as 62 additional staff in this way (11% of complement), and in 1978 CCEW employed an additional 20 staff (16% of complement).

c For several years – 1973 to 1979 – CCEW appears to have published no details at all of the numbers of staff employed. The estimate of 100 for 1975 is derived by interpolation from the 1972 figure of 93 staff and the 1980 figure of 125 staff.

Figure 7: Percentage variation in staffing of Countryside Agencies

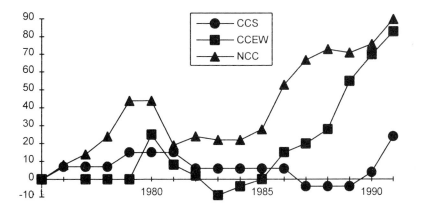

(1975 = 100)
Source: Table 4

Changes in staff structure were fairly minor until near the end of the Commission's life. A separate post of Deputy Director was created in 1973, and

the Commission under statute'.

A wind of change, however, was beginning to blow, ever so gently at first. 'With the assistance of records now maintained on the Commission's microcomputer', it was possible by 1983 to show the number of planning and countryside grant cases disposed of annually. 'Despite some hypothetical expectation of a falling casework load due to the recession and other factors...the totals...over the past five years have remained remarkably stable, thereby confirming the continuing appropriateness of the level of staff resources allocated to these activities. During the coming year, selected other activities will be examined in a similar way'. This *ex post facto* style of justification was not destined to continue for much longer.

March 1985 saw a relaxed and friendly meeting between the Chairman and the Secretary of State, with not a word spoken about economy or efficiency. In September, however, came the intimation that from now on the Commission would be required to submit an annually updated corporate plan in order to support its claim on public funds. The trauma attending the Commission's response to this demand has been noted in the previous chapter. It was not a case of a black hole being suddenly revealed in CCS administration, but rather of an overall tightening up of procedures on business management lines which hit the Commission particularly hard because of the light rein on which it had been held all along (in regard to everything except staffing).

Nevertheless, the shortcomings were there for all to see, including Commissioners themselves. The Chairman personally asked SDD to resume the lapsed practice of sending an assessor to attend all Commission meetings, 'in order to provide for improved liaison and understanding'. In the absence of suitable expertise within CCS, financial advice was imported from the Department, first on a consultancy basis and later on full secondment. A new appraisal system had to be set up, 'coupled to the introduction of key result areas for staff as a means of assessing "how well we are doing".' And, in the end, the senior management had to go.

The new corporate plan differed from the old aims and objectives document as chalk from cheese. The programme areas were regrouped to reflect the main fields of activity and expenditure, with read-outs of staff costs, and key performance indicators. By 1988 expenditure within each of the seven programme areas (NSAs, regional parks, country parks, countryside around towns, wider countryside, long-distance routes, and central functions) was open to analysis under seventeen different heads, and options could be shown instantly for switching around expenditure within given totals, or on assumptions about increased or constrained overall resources. Commissioners responded well to the altered management style, though they were sceptical of attempts to quantify environmental improvement.

The Scottish Office began to take a very favourable view of CCS efficiency, as it was evidenced by the successive editions of the Corporate Plan and associated performance report. The Treasury persisted in finding fault with these documents, but it became increasingly clear that their comments were superficial and routine, relating more to the ideology of privatisation and sponsorship than to the statutory purposes of the Commission. Meanwhile the commitment of CCS to monitoring its own performance continued. By 1991 Commissioners were provided with several hundred indicators, most of them including unit costs over a series of years, and so designed as to feed into the SNH corporate strategy. But the staff were realistic enough to remind Commissioners how 'crude and incomplete' was the picture provided by performance indicators, which served as no more than pointers towards closer scrutiny of the programme area concerned.

Effectiveness

In earlier chapters it has been fairly easy to assess the effectiveness of the agency concerned as seen through the eyes of outside observers: Parliamentary committees, the sponsor department of state, environmental writers and so on. With CCS it is harder to build up a picture, because the commentators are fewer. This is partly, of course, a result of CCS being a Scottish agency, with a smaller constituency. But that cannot be the whole story, since agencies like HIDB/HIE, the Crofters Commission and RDC have attracted their full share of outside attention and comment. There seems to be something about the CCS statutory remit and approach to its task that deflects attention from the body itself.

In this section, an attempt will nevertheless be made to distil what outside commentators have said, or thought, about the effectiveness of CCS as an agency. This may call for more reading between the lines than has been necessary with the FC or NCC.

Parliamentary and other committees of enquiry

The first outside commentary on the Commission came very early and was somewhat ominous. The report of the Royal Commission on Local Government in Scotland (1969 Cmnd 4150) cast doubt on the very *raison d'être* of CCS, calling for the whole position under the Countryside (Scotland) Act 1967 to be reviewed once a new larger local government structure had been introduced. It was not the need for the powers that was being questioned but the need for a separate agency.

These doubts were echoed in a Scottish Grand Committee debate in July 1971 on the Annual Reports of CCS and the equally fledgling Scottish Tourist Board. John P Mackintosh, for the Opposition, was puzzled about what the Commission had been set up to do. If it was to substitute for the existing local authorities, with their generally limited resources, why was it not getting on with development projects under Section 5 where there was a crying need for them? The Secretary of State, in replying, played to local government sensitivities by deprecating the use of the 'big stick' by CCS, and emphasising that its role was one of persuading, facilitating and working with local authorities.

Hard on the heels of this debate came the enquiry of the HC Select Committee into Land Resource Use in Scotland. Giving evidence in December 1971, CCS was pressed on the question how far it would be prepared to speak out or take action where other bodies, in particular local authorities and the FC, were failing in their duty towards the countryside. The Commission was on the whole defensive and played down the extent of conflict in the countryside (HC 1971–72 51–i & ii). The Select Committee accepted most of CCS's specific ideas, for example on constructing a hierarchy of landscape protection and on the setting up of local authority countryside committees. But the Committee was clearly not happy with the restricted interpretation which CCS placed upon its own role. In its report it urged a 'broad view of countryside problems', and recommended that NC and CCS should be given a more significant role in the enforcement of Section 66 of the 1967 Act, which placed a vague duty on public bodies to respect the countryside (HC 1971–72 511–i). The Government ignored this recommendation in their response (1973 Cmnd 5428), apparently to the relief of CCS (1973 Annual Report).

Almost contemporary with the Scottish Land Resource Use enquiry was that of the Lords Select Committee on Sport and Leisure – although its report proved to be, appropriately, a much more leisurely production, appearing in late 1973 (1972–73 HL 84). The Committee pronounced both Countryside Commissions to be 'too weak', by which it meant restricted in staffing and financial powers, especially in comparison with the Sports Councils.

This seems to have been the last time that CCS came under significant notice in any Parliamentary enquiry. The Commission appeared before a number of Committees in the 1970s and the 1980s: its influential evidence to the Commons Agriculture Committee in 1989 has already been noted. But all these enquiries were into other topics than the Scottish countryside and its statutory custodian. Even the Lords Committee on Science and Technology (the Carver Committee), in its report of March 1990 which more or less determined the final shape of conservation arrangements in Scotland, made no specific recommendation with regard to CCS. The Commission appears not to have attained to the critical mass needed to attract Parliamentary scrutiny, either of its finances or of its policies.

The Government

In the previous chapter a good deal was made of SDD's pressure on CCS in 1985–86, leading to a clean sweep of the top management and the imposition of a whole new financial and administrative regime. Undoubtedly this reflected a severe verdict by the sponsor department on the way that the Commission was being run at the time. But the scope of the Department's criticism must not be exaggerated. It was a management intervention, not a policy one. Ministers were not involved, and there was no purge of Board members – as occurred more than once in the annals of the FC and NCC. Moreover, the events of 1985–86 form an isolated chapter in the relations between CCS and Government. Overall, the handling of the Commission by the Department was as low-key as was the image cultivated by the Commission itself.

This cannot automatically be taken to mean that the sponsor was satisfied, let alone enthusiastic, about the performance of its protégé. In the early days Ministers were not slow to heap praise on the Commission. As time went on and the public profile of CCS sank almost to vanishing point, such encomia ceased to be called for and were not given.

The acid test of the esteem in which CCS was held must be the response of Government to Commission requests or proposals. On this the record speaks for itself. The 1973 recommendation of the House of Lords Select Committee, that CCS should be given power to grant-aid local authorities in its own right, was shelved, and came into effect only in 1982. The Park System report (1974) was put on hold and was never more than partially implemented. Scant regard was paid to the Commission's very pertinent representations on devolution from 1976 onwards. The Department failed to implement the findings of its own staff inspection of CCS in 1979 and, far from enhancing the complement, brought it down. Legislative proposals submitted by the Commission in 1978 did not reach the statute book until 1981 – and then only by courtesy of a Private Member's Bill. The CCS memorandum 'Forestry in Scotland' (1986) was not even given the courtesy of a Government response at the time, although many of its recommendations were quietly adopted. The Commission had to apply formally for a response, and this was not received until February 1989. Finally the Commission's sustained bid for national parks, which seemed initially to have the backing of Ministers, was turned down politely but firmly in October 1991.

At the same time it has to be recognised that in the final quinquennium CCS began to earn the respect of the Scottish Office. This showed itself in two ways. First, the Commission's reaction to the very heavy management pressure from the Department was positive and came to be appreciated and even admired. This had practical results. For the first time, the Department accepted the CCS bid for increased staff costs. Second, Ministers and civil servants began to pay attention to what the Commission said and to value their interaction with Commissioners and staff. This is difficult to document, but it shows up in the Commission's minutes, in terms of the frequent interchanges involving the Departmental assessor during the final three or four years. In June 1988 the Secretary of SDD took part in a full afternoon's seminar on the Corporate Strategy, and at the end expressed 'general support for the work of the Commission', singling out for special mention its contribution in the fields of forestry, fish farming, and countryside around towns.

The Commission

Unlike the NCC, the Commission never conducted a full-scale audit of its own effectiveness. This does not mean that CCS was not self-conscious about its image and performance. Its ancillary role and lack of executive functions in fact made it acutely sensitive from the start. The very first Annual Report expressed surprise that the Commission had been allowed to come into existence at all, at a time of financial stringency. In the second Report, for 1969, it was felt necessary to counter the suggestion that local government reform as envisaged by the Wheatley Commission might diminish the Commission's own responsibilities. This was against the background of a possible doubt 'in the minds of some...whether the Commission will be needed at all'.

In its very first engagement with the Commons Select Committee in 1971 the Commission was forced to defend itself. 'It has been said that we are a body without teeth, but we are more than that. We are now coming to the end of our fourth year and I think we have a fair record behind us' (HC 1971–72 51–i). The support given by the Select Committee's report came as a great relief to CCS (1972 Annual Report). Thereafter, the Commission settled down to its day-to-day tasks with less evidence of nervousness and self-criticism, blaming its lack of achievement mainly on the seemingly never-ending national economic crises which constrained its finances.

In fact it was not until 1986 that CCS publicly indulged in any fresh stocktaking exercise. This was not a Commission initiative but was enforced by the Department, with dramatic effects. It altered the pattern of future activity, but it left behind no appraisal of the past:

> Throughout 1986 we have been taking a close and critical look at our past work and achievements...The results of our efforts are now set out in our Strategy and Programme...We can perhaps take some satisfaction from what we regard as

being a substantial record of achievement since the Commission began its work in 1968 (1986 Annual Report).

And that is all – apart from the admission that 'we have recognised the need to adopt a more public stance in order to generate increased public awareness and debate about countryside issues'. It is the same story right up to the end. The very last paragraph of the Annual Report for 1991–92 is the nearest we come to a reflection by CCS on its own performance:

> This, the final CCS Annual Report, has allowed an opportunity to look back over the twenty four years of the Commission…Inevitably there have been failures and disappointments, but these have been more than outweighed by the successes…The Commission has over its 24 years spent some £75 million at today's prices – an average of £3.1 million per year…Whether or not that represents good value for money, and what might have been achieved by CCS had there been more resources available to it, present a challenge to any biographer wishing to write up the Commission's history and to analyse its contribution to the well being of the Scottish countryside.

If ever there was an appeal to make bricks without straw, this is it!

Other commentators

Because of CCS's chronic unwillingness to raise its head above the parapet, it is very difficult to find any kind of spread of writings even taking notice of the Commission's existence, let alone expressing an opinion on its effectiveness. Almost everything that follows, therefore, will be based on inference rather than evidence. We must be content to pick up such scraps as can be found.

Local authorities: The Commission was specifically set up to act as a handmaid to local government, and the attitude of local authorities towards the agency is or ought to be an important field of study. The problem is that occasions seldom arose for authorities, either singly or collectively, to make their views on the Commission known. The Commission was early recognised as a source of funds, and therefore not as an object of criticism. The perception may have been, however, that the Commission was a soft touch, as a dispenser of advice and grants: the thing to do was to ignore the advice and accept the grants (R Fairley, pers.comm.). This was certainly the case as regards country parks in the early days, and it appears to have been true also of countryside rangers. A policy review was ordered in June 1989 (CCS(89)53) because of the escalating costs of ranger services, and a report by the consultants PIEDA was delivered in January 1990. It emerged that the Commission was being milked by the inadequately supervised excesses of appointing authorities, encouraged by the 75 per cent (subsequently reduced to 60 per cent) rate of grant. A new, tougher regime imposed on ranger appointments was accepted without much protest.

Landowners: It has already been noted how SLF exercised what seemed like an unreasonable degree of influence over the Commission's thinking on the subject of vehicle tracks during the 1970s. The influence may have had something to do with the high proportion of landowning members introduced on to the Commission during the Heath government, but it certainly persisted after the proportion was reduced. It appears, at any rate, that SLF tended to regard the Commission as a punch bag, unable to stand up to even modest pressure. On the subject of public access – one of the founding articles in the CCS charter – debate was virtually absent until the very end of the Commission's life, and the Federation's influence may be seen in this. In the early days CCS was persuaded that the only avenue to improved access was through formal paid agreements with landowners.

Even in 1990 SLF was able, in an uncompromising statement of its own position, to quote a 1987 CCS Guide on Access to the Scottish Countryside giving a one–sided and deferential interpretation of the law of trespass.

NCC: Relations between the Commission and NC/NCC have been discussed at various points in the previous chapter. At the start, liaison with the NC's Scottish Committee could hardly have been closer. In 1968 the two bodies agreed to joint consultations on developments furthering their respective interests, on forestry and on conservation education. Papers and minutes would be exchanged, and assessors from one body would attend the meetings of the other. But in 1974 everything suddenly changed. The newly formed NCC announced without explanation that reciprocal assessorships were to cease. In 1977, when the NCC Chairman paid a formal visit to CCS, it was as if the two bodies had never previously met.

Relations, although re-established, were on a much more distant basis than before. It is not clear whether this represented a revised value-judgment by NCC on its sister agency, or was simply a manifestation of NCC's single-minded attitude to interests other than its own.

International. In sharp contrast to these rather downbeat indications of regard on the domestic front was the reputation enjoyed by CCS abroad. From the beginning the Commission sought to build up its image by accepting responsibility for coordinating Scotland's contribution to international events, in particular European Conservation Year (1970), the World Heritage Convention (1986 onwards) and the European Year of the Environment (1987).

In the autumn of 1978 both the Director and the Secretary were abroad, the one attending the IUCN Congress in Turkmenia, the other studying the Adirondack Park in USA. Other officers acquired an international reputation for their contributions in the fields of conservation education and scenic evaluation. These efforts may have enhanced the standing of the Commission south of the Border and further afield. It is doubtful if they did much for the CCS image at home.

Summary

The evidence cited may convey the impression that CCS earned generally low marks for effectiveness. This is probably unfair. What has to be borne in mind is the wide scope of the Commission's remit, coupled with the small scale of CCS operations and finance. This combination did not allow the Commission to make a big impact, in its own right, on the problems of the Scottish countryside – which was hardly the Commission's fault. However, CCS may be fairly criticised for failing to perceive and capitalise upon a potential role as coordinator and energiser of other agencies.

11

THE COUNTRYSIDE CLIENT GROUP

In analysing the other agencies it has been fairly easy to identify and describe a client group for the agency in question. With CCS there is an immediate problem – the term client group seems to have lost its obvious meaning, and it is necessary to get down at once to closer analysis and definition.

A starting point might be: who or what were the driving forces in getting CCS off the ground in the first place? The answer must surely be found in the membership of Study Group 9 of the Second 'Countryside in 1970' Conference in 1965, which produced the virtual blueprint of the Commission. But this merely deepens the mystery, for the members of the study group were not drawn from fiery campaigning organisations but from the Scottish establishment – public bodies such as FC, STB and the Association of County Councils, interest groups such as SLF, NFUS and the Scottish Council for Physical Recreation, and the universities. Not one of these constituting bodies proved in after years to be an ardent supporter of CCS or of the countryside cause.

The reality was that CCS was not established to serve a definite cause but to fill a gap. This is evident from its multiple objectives and its ancillary role. So it lacked from the start the backing of a clearly defined clientele and, when a clientele emerged, it was of a diffused and highly disparate character.

The 'clients'

In its first Annual Report (for 1968) the Commission noted as one its first tasks that of establishing relations with the many bodies which had been 'shouldering the burden of responsibility for countryside interests'. It divided these into four groups: government departments and agencies, local authorities, national non-governmental organisations (NGOs) representing recreational, natural history and amenity interests, and local NGOs covering the same field. The Annual Report went on: 'if any justification were needed for the introduction of another government agency, it is for the purpose of co-ordinating these views and opinions, and providing an opportunity for discussion and meeting of minds'. If this was the Commission's hope, it was to be sadly disappointed. For a number of years, the Annual Reports optimistically included a section headed 'Liaison with other bodies'. But by 1971 the bodies mentioned had shrunk to the public sector, and thereafter the liaison in question was more often than not at a national or international level.

The client group of an environmental agency will normally serve three functions: i) to receive and apply the agency's grant-aid; ii) to act as a consultative medium and a support when the agency needs to mobilise opinions; and iii) to keep the agency up to the mark as to the needs of particular sectors and as regards its overall effectiveness. These may be called respectively the beneficiary, the forum and the gadfly functions. With CCS the functions became separated, and the last of them sank into almost total atrophy.

The beneficiary role was at first monopolised by the local authorities, which were not much interested in the other functions. The private sector received no grants at all during the first three years, and it was 1976 before the grant total exceeded £50,000 – while annual payments to local authorities were averaging ten times that amount. Once grant aid to the private sector had reached a reasonable level (by the early 1980s), it became evident that it was going predominantly to certain categories. These were private landowners, NTS, the Scottish Youth Hostels Association, volunteer conservation projects, countryside trusts and community councils. While these were no doubt worthy beneficiaries, they did not to any degree discharge the forum or gadfly functions. The bodies which were emerging as opinion–formers – Friends of the Earth, the Ramblers' Association Scotland, the Scottish Wild Land Group, the various articulate local groups such as the Campaign for the Border Hills, the North East Mountain Trust and Save the Cairngorms Campaign – were either not in the business of spending public money or were suspicious of it.

Relations with clients

It appears to have been 1987 before the Commission first formally met one of these campaigning organisations. This was the Scottish Wildlife and Countryside Link (SWCL) – an umbrella NGO covering eighteen (now 28) conservation and recreation bodies, and with the unusual distinction of having received funding from the Scottish Office. The two delegations exchanged details of their memberships and objectives, commenting on the difficulty caused by the coincidence in both their constitutions of a responsibility for wildlife and countryside, and for conservation and recreation. The Commission Chairman said that CCS 'was committed to improving relationships with the NGOs', and looked forward to a further meeting 'at a later date'. It is not clear whether the meeting ever took place: but it is reported that subsequently relations with SWCL at the working level became closer (J Mackay and R Aitken, pers. comm.).

It is true, of course, that CCS hosted many conferences, at Battleby and elsewhere, which countryside organisations were invited to attend and on occasions address. Yet these were invariably on a fixed agenda: they therefore served the purpose of a forum but not the gadfly function. They were also overborne, especially in the early days, by representation from landowning, farming, local authority and Governmental interests. In the matter of research, too, the Commission always insisted on setting the agenda, but without the benefit of a consultative forum. Although a significant proportion of CCS annual expenditure went on research – usually between five and ten per cent – the idea of a research advisory committee or of peer group appraisal of projects seems never to have been entertained. (There was a Countryside Recreation Research Advisory Group in which CCS participated, along with CCEW and the Sports Councils: but this was confined to recreational matters, and was essentially for coordinating purposes, not for appraisal).

Towards the end of the Commission's life there was a marked improvement in the quality of dialogue opened up between CCS and its clients. The Countryside around Towns Forum (1989) was an example of this. Another was the belated commitment, in 1991, to providing management support for Scottish Conservation Projects – the principal organisation for training volunteers and leaders in countryside skills. Until then, assistance had been given only on a pump-priming basis to particular projects (1991–92 Annual Report). The same principle was used to support Countryside Trusts – a form of partnership between the public and private sectors designed to channel funds and voluntary effort into environmental improvement and recreation (1990 Annual Report).

Perhaps the most striking example of the Commission's changing attitude towards its clientele may be seen in the contrast between the handling of the two 'parks' consultations, in 1973–74 and 1989–91 respectively. The first exercise was carried out in considerable secrecy. The only clue the public received was to the effect that CCS was reviewing the ways in which outstanding landscape was protected and the suitability of differing types of countryside for varying degrees of intensity of recreational use (1972 and 1973 Annual Reports). Actual consultation on the CCS proposals was confined to a small number of statutory or representative bodies: CCEW, STB, Scottish Sports Council, the FC, HIDB, the Crofters Commission, NCC, SLF and NTS. The document that emerged (A Park System for Scotland, December 1974) was confusing as to its own status: it read as though it had been intended as a report to the Secretary of State to enable him to consult local authorities, but he had instructed its publication as a means of 'wider consideration by representative organisations and by the public at large'. The demand for the published document took CCS by surprise (1975 Annual Report). The comments received were considered, digested for the benefit of Commissioners, and passed on to the Secretary of State: no public account was given of what they amounted to, except that they generally favoured the CCS proposals.

The other consultation process (on the Mountain Areas reports) has already been mentioned. At the start of the exercise a specific invitation to comment was sent to 86 'organisations representing land-use interests in the Scottish countryside', but the written response was far greater. This, and the attendance at public meetings held during the early part of 1990, must have caused CCS to rewrite any list that it may have held of its known clientele. But it all paled into insignificance beside the effects of the second phase consultation ordered by the Scottish Office, which was packed into the four-month period September–December 1990. Not only were over 230 responses received but 28 meetings were held, half of them involving the public; and there were repeated complaints that 'the Commission did not consult widely enough with local interests in those areas that might be most affected by its proposals'. The list of environmental bodies, mostly local, taking an interest in the proposals lengthened again, and included a revived Scottish Council for National Parks. The agency must have trembled at the possibility of the Secretary of State's ordering a third round of consultation. The Commission's final comment was that 'it cannot be bad…to have stimulated such a lively debate…on an issue which few would dispute is of the utmost significance to the future of Scotland's countryside' (Report on Public Consultation, February 1991). It had been a hard, but salutary, learning process.

Ben Lawers, Perth & Kinross, showing path erosion

Conclusion

In spite of all the advances made in the final years, the author's view is that CCS finished up, as it had begun, without a clear clientele to interact with. Whereas it was found that NCC's liaison with its interest group was uneasy, it would have to be said that CCS's was virtually non-existent.

The reasons for this state of affairs have been probed in the paragraphs above. There is no single explanation. The lack of a strong executive role for CCS was one factor, as was its orientation towards the public sector. Other relevant considerations included the diffusion of countryside interests – particularly evident in Scotland – and the fissiparous tendencies of the countryside lobby (Lowe and Goyder 1983). Nor was there a pack leader to parallel the role played by RSPB in nature conservation. The emergence of umbrella groups like SWCL had, and continues to have, a potential for unifying the countryside movement, and also for bridging the artificial gap between scenic and nature conservation – greatly aided by the merging of CCS with NCC in Scotland. It remains to be seen whether this potential will be realised.

These are all factors external to CCS itself, for which it might reasonably decline to accept responsibility. But at least as significant as any of them was the Commission's chosen method of working. By adopting a low profile throughout most of its life CCS may have narrowed its contacts to those with which it felt most comfortable. But it was also selling short its potential clients, some of whom probably felt that the Commission was scarcely worth doing business with, while others were not even aware of its existence.

V

EVALUATION

Ben Nevis, Lochaber

12

THE RECORD OF THE AGENCIES IN SCOTLAND

This chapter evaluates the performance in Scotland of the three agencies under scrutiny; and considers what lessons emerge as regards the practice of 'government by agency'. The record of the agencies is reviewed, both individually and collectively, against the background of what are believed to have been the key land use issues in Scotland over the relevant period. It further aims at reaching an understanding of the reasons for the shortcomings that are perceived, and offers an alternative institutional framework in which the problems might be addressed.

It is worth saying, in the first place, that nothing has emerged to cast doubt on the basic rationale of the jobs which the three agencies were set up to perform. As regards *forestry*, it was a commonplace in the early years of this century that Great Britain was shamefully under-forested, that there had to be greater national self-sufficiency in timber, and that private enterprise could not compete with imports of the 'free gifts of nature' from forests abroad without a big input of public funds. In *nature conservation*, informed opinion in the post-Second World War period was justifiably exercised over the need for the better safeguarding of the natural resource – which could not be left to market forces to achieve, because there simply was no market. Similarly as regards the *countryside* functions, the work of the 'Countryside in 1970' movement had established beyond reasonable doubt that a pressing need existed for certain facilities and that the local authorities could not meet it. Moreover it has not been seriously argued that the country would be better off (or no worse off) if the agencies, and their functions, were simply to disappear. The jobs of the agencies may have changed over the years, but they have not become redundant.

In previous chapters the effectiveness of the agencies has been explored through the perceptions of various observers. These have included Government departments, Parliamentary committees, environmental writers, client groups, and the agencies themselves. The outcome is not decisive, and indeed could not be – not only because there is no kind of consensus, but because each of the observers has been gauging effectiveness against criteria which are often unstated and are almost always limited or flawed. Thus on the part of Government and Parliament there tends to be an over-emphasis on managerial or financial efficiency. An agency's self-assessment is found to be minimal, or defensive. Outside commentators are usually ranged either strongly in favour of the agency concerned, or strongly against: if in favour, they do not adequately question the agency's objectives; if against, they often fail to distinguish between imposed and self-chosen objectives, and between the choice of objectives and effectiveness in achieving them. And overall, there is some difficulty, in the case of the GB agencies, in getting a feel for the assessment of performance in Scottish terms.

It appears that we are not going to get nearer a satisfactory appraisal by collecting voices. A broader approach is needed. This may be found in the concept of stewardship, or accountable management.

The stewardship of the land use agencies

Stewardship is currently a popular term in environmental circles[1], invested with all sorts of moral overtones (UK Government 1990, Reed and Slaymaker 1992). But in its strict sense it is ethically fairly neutral, referring simply to the appropriate handling by a functionary of resources entrusted to him. It has two aspects, the one looking to the standard of care accorded to the resource, the other to the need to give an account to the party which has awarded the trusteeship. In the case of the land use agencies in Britain, trusteeship may be deemed to have been awarded jointly by government and Parliament, as proxy for the public interest.

As has been noted in Part I, agencies are useful for getting particular jobs done, but tend to be weak on public accountability. Governments have to think of ways of satisfying Parliament on this score, whether in the founding statute or subsequently. The conventional means in the nationalised industries has been through consultative councils, or in the case of private monopolies through watchdog bodies. Even the HIDB had its consultative council. With the land use agencies, no need was seen for such apparatus. It was deemed sufficient for each agency to give an account of its stewardship by presenting an annual report, including a financial statement, to Parliament.[2]

Looking at the statutory functions of the land use agencies (and leaving on one side their ancillary and enabling powers), the functions divide broadly into *executive* and *custodial*. The agencies' stewardship may be examined in relation to each of these two broad areas. The two overlap to some degree, of course. For example, within the FC, the Forest Enterprise's executive activity in planting trees has to meet the quality standards set by the Forestry Authority *qua* custodian.

Executive functions

The bulk of the agency's money is spent on executive functions, where efficiency can be tested and achievement quantified. They tend therefore to attract particular attention in official and Parliamentary quarters, and also from the client group. (Whether they are of the same interest to the general public is another question.) In the case of forestry, stewardship is assessed on criteria such as the area of new planting per annum, the average cost per hectare, the extent of new recreational provision, or the amount of grant aid dispensed to the private sector. With nature conservation, attention is paid to items such as the number and extent of new NNRs, or the number of SSSIs notified or renotified. With countryside, the focus is on such achievements as the number and cost of local authority and private sector projects financed, the number and extent of new regional or country parks, or the establishment of new ranger services.

It can safely be said that in the area of executive responsibilities the agencies have been under close scrutiny and on the whole have come out well. Statutory functions have been discharged conscientiously and with enthusiasm. As regards *forestry*, the FC's planting achievements have been impressive. The 1943 target of 2m ha of productive forest in GB was attained around 1980 – fully a decade ahead of schedule. The design standards of FC planting and felling have steadily improved over the years (Mattingly 1992). The proportion of land in Scotland under formal *nature conservation* designation – 10.5 per cent – is probably as high as anywhere in the world. Less striking but probably more significant is the 112,000 ha (1.5 per cent) of land designated as NNR and thus under positive (although variable) nature conservation management. *Countryside* projects, while not always eye-catching, are pervasive and on the whole useful. They include 36 country parks and four regional parks: besides, there are the 40 NSAs, covering thirteen per cent of the Scottish land area, in which more stringent landscape protection applies. All these statistics testify to dedicated effort and achievement on the part of the agencies, which very few of the commentators are inclined to gainsay.

Regrettably, however, the kind of scrutiny to which the discharge of executive functions has been exposed has not always been constructive. Valid questions have certainly been asked, from time to time, about the agencies' efficiency and effectiveness in the use of resources. But the emphasis of governments and of the House of Commons Public Accounts Committee on cutting Forest Enterprise unit costs, and on economies in consultation and supervision over private planting, contributed directly to much unsympathetic afforestation, particularly in Scotland. The SSSI provisions of the Wildlife and Countryside Act 1981 – not sought, although acquiesced in, by NCC – absorbed staff time and finance throughout the 1980s in an unhelpful direction. The activities of CCS were less closely scrutinised, but it is possible that its over-concentration on items like ranger services, long-distance routes and park designations stemmed from an anxiety to show visible results. The question to what extent the agencies should have resisted governmental pressures and asserted their own priorities is an interesting one and will be taken up later.

There is a certain difficulty in appraising the GB agencies' activities in Scotland because – as has already been noted – their records are poorly disaggregated. Overall, however, it has to be said that the agencies' performance, in terms of discharge of executive functions, has been of a high standard, even with the qualifications noted above. If they stood to be judged on the basis of executive functions alone they would pass with commendation.

Custodial functions

Custodial functions were also assigned to each of the three agencies from the start. In a way this is surprising, bearing in mind the overriding concern of government and Parliament to get an executive task done. But as time has gone on, the custodial role has emerged as the more fundamental and important, because it is not just the specific resources of money and manpower assigned to an agency for which it has to give account but the wider use of the national land resource over which it has been appointed (in a real sense) steward. Stewardship in this context means the agency's duty to keep under review the resource for which it is responsible – to see whether it is being deployed in the best interests of the nation and/or the more local community – and to take action accordingly.

It is clear that, particularly in regard to custodial functions, ethical issues do arise and must be faced. A land use agency has to decide, in the first place, its attitude to the 'moral high ground' notion that the natural environment has a claim to conservation in its own right, not just as it impinges on the perceptions and interests of humankind or, in the words of Stone (1972), as a mere 'collection of useful senseless objects' (Young 1982, O'Riordan 1983, Harrison 1993). This is a minority position, although it was embodied in the UN World Charter for Nature (1982)[3], and it has gained currency through the influence of writers such as Naess (1984, 1989) and Johnson (1991). Its logical weakness has been exposed by Hare (1989). Berry (1992) argues cogently that it is inconsistent with the notion of stewardship: and it is interesting that it was not espoused by such an ardent and mystical conservationist as Ansel Adams, who related his concept of wilderness preservation to 'the general, ultimate good of mankind' (Adams 1992). Nor, unsurprisingly, has any GB agency espoused it, although individuals connected with NC/NCC – eg Nicholson (1987) and Goodier (1990) – have come close to doing so.

Even if we are concerned only with custodianship as it respects the interests of people, land use agencies still have work to do in deciding, both in their general policy and in individual casework, how far they should have regard to the claims of posterity, of the long term as against the short term, of the few as against the many – on which Hare (1989) offers useful guidelines for rational moral judgments. Some would deny that these are moral issues and would categorise them as merely prudential – eg the behavioural ecologists of whom Heinen and Lowe (1992) may be taken as representative. They contend that human behaviour has evolved to sequester resources to meet essentially short-term goals and is poorly adapted to the longer-term perspective required to cope with current environmental threats. Sticks and carrots, coupled with education, are appropriate mechanisms for inducing the correct responses, but the mechanisms must be sensitively geared to the public's perception of the particular threat to be guarded against. This kind of analysis may have something to contribute to the practical handling of environmental problems, but there is no reason to regard it as displacing the ethical dimension. Moral categories have been firmly fixed in the environmental agenda for a long time now, and the public both understand and respond to them, even if imperfectly.

UK agencies, however, have sometimes argued that on such issues – whatever their private views might be – they have had to take a lead from government policy, and that until 1990 there were no clear moral signals from government. It has in fact been clear all along that governments looked to the agencies as their environmental conscience: conscience could of course be disobeyed, but there was never much hope of government taking a higher ethical stance than that of its statutory adviser and appointed custodian.

Two subsidiary duties, implicit in the custodial role, follow from what has been said above. The first is that of maintaining an information and research base, so that an environmental agency is well informed about the condition of its resource and able to make sound judgments with regard to it. It is not essential, of course, that the agency takes upon itself the whole burden of data collection, interpretation, and (where appropriate) prediction, provided that it is in a position to call upon the requisite body of knowledge when occasion arises. As pointed out by Goldsmith (1993), the extent and depth of biological monitoring in GB is without parallel elsewhere, and yet it by no means follows that it can all be put to practical use. It is the job of the agency, as the resource custodian and adviser of government, to ensure that it is in possession of the information relevant to its task.

The second duty is not so clearly laid out in the statutes, but it is no less important. It is that of having regard to the concerns and views of a wider community than the one which the agency specifically serves. Parliament has assumed – rightly or wrongly – that a land use agency needs no special bidding to keep in touch with its own client group. It has, however, increasingly over the last fifteen years put the agencies under obligation to pay heed to other land-use interests. The need to do this arises, no doubt, from the perception of the agencies as one-track organisations, at risk of isolation from the real world in which various categories of people have to make a living off the land. But there is an even broader context to this duty. It is incumbent on each agency, as the custodian of the national interest in a major land use, to keep the general public informed about its role and, even more important, to consult the public about its proposals.

The rationale of this duty is not quite the same as that of the obligation to have regard to other classes of land users. It stems from two sources: the inherent burden of custodianship, which must have regard to the general interest rather than sectional interests; and the agencies' status as appointed bodies, lacking democratic accountability and direct feedback. It is a duty which all agencies are in danger of ignoring – particularly when, as often happens, the public appears not to know or care too much about conservation values. But it is one which, in the long run, may have as much to do with an agency's success and even survival as any other.

It is in some ways easier to disaggregate geographically the performance of the GB agencies in a custodial than in an executive capacity. Particularly this is so as regards the two subsidiary duties just discussed. The steps taken by each agency to maintain a Scottish research/information base should be on public record, as should the efforts made to consult and inform the Scottish public.

Land use issues

It may be useful, by way of scene-setting, to consider what have been the main issues for the Scottish countryside over the period during which the three agencies have been operating together – ie from around 1970 – and where the custodial responsibilities of each fit into the picture.

This might seem so ambitious a project as to be worthy of a separate enquiry. Fortunately, however, it is not too difficult to reach general conclusions quickly, thanks to a remarkable series of fundamental reviews, of widely different kinds, carried out around the start of that period of which the following deserve mention: Fraser Darling (1955), Institute of Biology (1958), Scottish Council (Development and Industry) (1961), McVean and Ratcliffe (1962), Burnett (1964), British Association for the Advancement of Science (1964), Advisory Panel on the Highlands and Islands (1964), The Countryside in 1970 (Study Group 9) (1965), McVean and Lockie (1969), HC Select Committee on Land Resource Use (1971-72). These all – in different ways and to varying degrees – posted a warning that the problem area in the Scottish countryside (as against what might be the case south of the Border) was not the fifteen per cent in intensive agricultural use but the 70 per cent broadly described as upland. This is the zone on which, for different reasons, the interest of each of the three agencies has focused – the FC, as cheap land for afforestation; NCC, as the repository of most of the remaining natural or semi-natural habitat in Britain; CCS, as the location of outstanding landscapes, often under heavy visitor pressure.

The importance, and fragility, of this upland zone had been recognised long before 1970. It was the Department of Agriculture for Scotland that supported Darling's West Highland Survey just after the Second World War – and then delayed its publication for several years because of what it revealed. His thesis was that the problems of the uplands, which he characterised as a 'wet desert', had been exacerbated by centuries of exploitation and neglect. He saw the root problem as ecological – the systematic removal of those elements (deciduous forest, grazing cattle, and finally the native population) which helped to maintain fertility: and then the steady expansion of sheep and deer, whose effects in excessive numbers – with associated muirburn – were generally to reduce species variety to the minimum and to impoverish already poor soil.

> Reduced to basic ecological and chemical terms, we can see that a country of acid rocks, steep slopes and high rainfall is primarily by nature a cellulose-producing area; in short, timber. Any protein crop is secondary, eg a limited number of deer. But what has been attempted through two centuries, with continuing declining success, has been to draw a double protein crop, of mutton and wool, from a degraded vegetation overlying blanket peat on acid rocks. Such a proposition is not ecologically sound, nor is it good chemistry. **(Darling 1968)**

> To put it quite baldly, scenery is money, and the Highlands are throwing away their capital. **(Darling 1968)**

> The British uplands are not simply a stable and unpleasant habitat, they are getting worse. This continuous deterioration takes two forms i) the loss of the vegetation cover which is being washed down to the lowlands; and ii) changes in the remaining vegetation and soil in the direction of lower and less useful production, and less stability. **(Newbould 1958)**

> A well-farmed and thoroughly domesticated countryside and untouched, natural terrain with its vegetation and wildlife complexes intact can both be deeply satisfying. But an inherently infertile region devastated by deforestation and repeated burning, largely depopulated and then opened to heavy and uncontrolled sheep grazing is a distressing sight to anyone with some appreciation of ecological principles. This is the 'untouched wilderness' and 'rugged grandeur' which we are now being asked to 'sell' as a tourist attraction. **(McVean and Lockie 1969)**

Efforts were made in the earlier part of the twentieth century to relieve the burden of guilt for the past exploitation of the Scottish uplands, and of the Highlands in particular. They focused on the priority of holding or increasing population and employment through industrial development, aided by hydro-electricity, excavation of minerals, and coniferous afforestation (Sheail 1981, Boyd 1992). But by the 1960s it had become clear that these were not even palliatives, and that the basic questions of sustainability of the land economy and ecology had to be addressed.

The work of the 1971-72 House of Commons Select Committee on Land Resource Use, which has already been freely quoted from in this study, provides a useful summation of the thinking of the period. Almost all the authors cited above gave evidence to the Committee, as well as all the agencies and the Departments of State. Although Part II ('Rural') of the Committee's Report (HC 511-i) did not in terms confine itself to the uplands, only two or three pages out of 64 were devoted to what the Committee called 'better land', and almost all the recommendations had primary reference to the uplands.

Two preliminary points need to be made about the Committee's approach. First, it adopted without question the prevailing assumption that the countryside was to be regarded as a resource for productive use, rather than as an element of intrinsic value to be conserved for its natural features. This assumption was common property among the ecologists of the period (*cf* Cragg 1958, Sc Council [D & I] 1961, Darling *passim*). Second, the Committee did not accept uncritically the evidence of the conservationists, either on the impoverishment of the Scottish uplands or on the responsibility of sheep for the alleged deterioration. The evidence of the Hill Farming Research Organisation (HFRO) clearly weighed quite heavily with the Committee; although the Report was careful to point out that any improvement in soil or vegetation attributable to sheep would depend critically on the adoption of HFRO-recommended farming methods. Much the same applied to the charge that conifer planting had a neutral or deleterious effect on upland soils, on which the Committee declared itself not competent to pronounce.

Thus the Committee declined to endorse, in terms, the crisis in upland land use diagnosed by many of the conservation witnesses (not, interestingly enough, by the representatives of the conservation agencies). The verdict was not, however, a 'not guilty' but a 'not proven'. The Committee's comment on the situation as it found it – made quite strongly, and cogently – can be summarised as follows:

1. Better understanding was needed on a whole range of ecological and management issues: the effect of sheep grazing, muirburn, protection forestry, the interaction of deer with forestry and sheep, and so on.

2. Grant-aid to the uplands should be targeted, instead of being scattered at random – 'The several kinds of financial assistance cannot be monitored in their effect, because they have no individual objective in respect of land use nor are they related to an overall policy objective'.

3. Policies needed to be developed for multiple land use, instead of the single-minded pursuit of a number of different uses – 'There is no consideration of the benefit overall to the community in the uplands from so arranging forestry (and public support for it) and the other uses of land concerned – agriculture, wildlife, recreation – that together they produce benefits greater than those derived from the maximisation of any one of them'.

The Committee then went on to make specific recommendations about the role of NC/NCC and CCS in pursuing multiple land use, and about a Land Use Council to act as a central forum and arbiter for discussion of rural land use affairs and conflicts, supported by a professional Land Use Unit. The organisational recommendations, as we have seen, were rejected by the Government as a piece of superfluous bureaucracy (1973 Cmnd 5428). What is not so obvious is that the Government, by rejecting the mechanisms, in effect subverted a promising means of addressing the fairly self-evident defects which the Committee had diagnosed.

The post-1973 story is of how the basic questions were not addressed – how instead UK and EC agricultural policies (as well as fiscal and planning policies) combined to intensify pressure on Scottish hill land, and how an almost complete vacuum ensued on the question of an overview or guiding framework for natural resource management (Warren 1991, Wigan 1991, Adams 1993, Ramsay 1993). It has taken until the 1990s – in the context of the UK's belated response to the World Conservation Strategy – for the Government to take up the watch-word of sustainability, and to recognise that *laissez-faire* in this context is not acceptable. With a degree of complacency, the White Paper 'This Common In-heritance' (1990 Cm 1200) claimed that '…the Government's policies for the countryside are based both on sound stewardship of the heritage and on creating the conditions for a healthy and growing economy'.

The relevance for the present study of the early-1970s debate on the Scottish uplands calls for restatement at this point. The HC Select Committee highlighted the need for a policy and research framework for upland land use as the most pressing issue facing rural Scotland in the years ahead. The Government of the day disagreed. The Government could have been right, and the Committee wrong, for one or other of two reasons. The Committee might have mis-diag-nosed the situation as it was in 1972; or the problems which they (correctly) saw could have gone away or their nature could have changed beyond recognition. A first question, therefore – in which all three agencies should have had the keenest interest, in view of the key role which the Committee assigned to them – is whether the situation, and the problems, identified in 1972 with regard to the Scottish uplands remained relevant in the ensuing years and are recognisable to-day.

The current upland 'budget'

The most authoritative recent appraisal of the status of the uplands is that of Usher and Thompson (1988). Unfortunately it does not specifically address the Scottish situation (although most of the contributors had a Scottish perspective), and it is not sufficiently up-to-date to take account of the many changes in land use incentives which have affected the uplands in the last few years. More re-cent, but also more broad-brush, is the work of Dargie and Briggs (1991).[4]

Disappointingly, there is little in either review which confirms or refutes the judgments of the 1960s and 1970s, or witnesses to trends that might have taken place in the intervening decades. The overriding impression gained from both reviews is one of extreme reluctance to express a firm opinion about the man-agement of the uplands. In every sphere, we are told, a great deal more monitor-ing and research has to be done before we can be sure of the facts, let alone ad-vise on future policies. Gone is the robustness, whether in diagnosis or in pre-scription, which characterised the 1960s. No doubt some of this uncertainty is due to the changes which overtook both the agricultural and forestry regimes to-wards the close of the 1980s. Gimingham, (*in* Usher and Thompson), expresses the hope that these may provide the opportunity for taking the initiative in pro-moting ecological improvement, instead of having to react against changes im-posed from without. But it is disappointing that the fields in which the 1972 Re-port gave a clear call for continuous monitoring and research remain so fallow. Usher pinpoints the basic malaise:

> We…need more synthetic approaches… First, a better dialogue between the many research institutes and sponsors would hopefully lead to a more goal-orientated form of research. Second, desk studies are needed to review the literature, synthesize the present state of scientific knowledge and indicate the way ahead. It was a feature of the Edinburgh meeting [of which U & T is the record] that par-ticipants *started* [author's emphasis] to think laterally, becoming aware that other interest groups had already addressed similar problems in upland research and management.

Fortunately, Usher's appeal seems to be being heeded, on the evidence of such work as that of Gauld et al. (1991); Brown, Horsfield and Thompson (1993); and Brown, Birks and Thompson (1993).

It remains the case, however, that we are scarcely in any better position than was the Commons Select Committee in 1972 to pronounce definitively on the ecological status of the Scottish uplands (Mather 1992). We need to be reminded that the Committee's interest in this was not primarily scientific, but practical: it wished to be satisfied about the sustainability of the resource under the then current regimes. And as these regimes were arguably exploitative and extractive in concept, there were grounds for the Committee's scepticism over the effects of their persistence into the future, without the overall administrative and political supervision which the Committee demanded.

In spite of the disappointing progress made by the scientists, the answer to the question posed earlier – have the issues raised by the 1972 Committee remained relevant? – must be a resounding *Yes*. It is plain that the plea of the Committee for a concerted, action-oriented, research and policy framework for the Scottish uplands is even more relevant today than it was two decades ago. The fact that there is only beginning to be such a framework is not evidence that the urgency the Committee felt was misplaced. All it means is that the land use policies of the last twenty years – including some traumatic changes in policy – have not been guided by the kind of overview which would have been possible had the spirit of the Committee' s recommendations been heeded.

Role of the land use agencies

It is not, of course, contended that the three agencies were responsible for the failure, or the absence, of concerted land use policies for the Scottish uplands during the 1970s and 1980s. That responsibility must rest primarily on successive governments, by virtue both of their central policy role and of their enormous resource input via DAFS. As has already been emphasised, the agencies were and are actors on the stage, rather than directors. But in their custodial capacity all of them had weighty responsibilities, both statutory and moral. How these responsibilities were discharged, having particular regard to upland land use, will now be examined.

Forestry Commission

Statutory functions: The FC's custodial function is broadly spelled out in the 1967 Act – Section 1 (although this also covers the developmental function) and Part II. The power to make surveys is covered in Section 3. Recreational powers are consolidated in the Countryside (Scotland) Act 1967, Sections 58-60. The duty to achieve a 'reasonable balance' with other countryside interests (dating from 1985) is consolidated in Section 1(3A) of the Forestry Act 1967. There is no duty, in terms, to consult the general public. 'Public relations' appeared as a heading in the Commission's Annual Reports from 1977 onwards (although it always had more to do with the FC's relations with the media than with the general public): mysteriously, the heading disappeared in the Annual Report for 1991-92.

Environmental responsibility: The Commission's discharge of its custodial responsibility in Scotland may be examined from a number of directions. First, as forest enterprise it had from the start duties to society, by way of providing employment in needy areas and making its forests accessible to the public. Second, as forestry authority it had a general duty towards the country's forest estate – both to establish the facts about it and to oversee, for example, its state of silvicultural health, its quality of design and species mix. Third, again as forestry authority it was bound to consider the distribution of forestry throughout the country and its interaction with other land uses. On this aspect in particular it had a duty to inform and consult the public, in the first instance through Parliament but more locally as well. All these responsibilities were implicit in what became Section 1 of the 1967 Act, although it would be unrealistic to expect some of them to have figured very actively in the early days.

Duties to society: It has already been noted that the criteria for forestry policy are widely in dispute, and cannot all be satisfied together. Thus it is no surprise that the objective of providing employment in needy areas of Scotland has been fulfilled only patchily and with decreasing success, having been squeezed by other factors. The early notion of Forest Workers' Holdings – a preoccupation of Lord Lovat's – never took off in Scotland, and was probably a misconception from the start. Employment continued to feature as a forestry objective into the 1960s and 1970s – indeed as the main justification for continued afforestation in Scotland. But jobs in the forest kept on shrinking, through mechanisation, altered forestry practice, and above all the pressure to show positive financial returns. On the credit side, the FC, after 40 years of myopia towards the downstream implications of its planting programme, began in the 1960s to establish a partnership with the processing interests which has been successful in creating some local employment. In 1992, however, the total number of Scottish jobs in forestry and the wood-processing industries stood at under 15,000, still reducing at a rate of 1.5 per cent per annum (Forestry Facts and Figures 1991-92).

Access: Access to FC forests has been a bright star in the Commission's firmament from an early date. Scotland provided the lead, and kept it through the declaration of national forest parks, mainly in the 1930s and 1940s – at which time the FC was bidding to become the national park authority. Although the number of new parks has dwindled to a trickle, the tradition of providing access and facilities (mainly free) has persisted, and constitutes a definite plus in the public's perception of the FC today. Indeed, in the new climate which assigns specific worth to environmental benefits, the Commission have cashed in with a 1992 Bulletin *Valuing Informal Recreation on the FC Estate* which arrives at a total valuation per annum of at least £53 million, several times higher than the estimate of the NAO in 1986. Comparatively little of the 'consumer surplus', however, is contributed by Scottish forests: while the main reason for this is obviously the small population adjoining the forests, it may be significant that many of them are characterised as having high proportions of immature conifers and a high windthrow hazard classification.

The forest estate: This is concerned mainly with the FC's general responsibility for forestry (including private forestry) in terms of quality rather than quantity – although the two cannot be wholly separated. The lead-in is the Commission's duty to collect statistics which has been discharged by censuses in 1947-49, 1965-66 and 1981-82. That these censuses have been undertaken at widely separated intervals is understandable, given the immense burden of work which each represents. However, the Commission seems to have regarded them as something of an embarrassment and to have done virtually nothing with them. In particular, the FC has made no serious attempt to monitor forest ownership - a prerequisite, surely, of designing appropriate policy instruments for encouraging the right kind of private forestry.

Research: Throughout its life the FC sponsored a great volume of research, initially geared to its own needs *qua* Forestry Enterprise, but having useful spin-offs for forestry in general, both at home and abroad. The Northern Research Station at the Bush Estate outside Edinburgh ministered to Scottish needs from 1969 onwards, and interacted fruitfully with other stations on the Estate. However there was increasing dissatisfaction among scientists throughout the 1970s with the narrow focus and lack of direction of FC-sponsored research, a complaint taken up by the HL Science and Technology Committee in its Second Report (1979-80 381 I). In response, the Government appointed an FC-headed Forestry Research Coordinating Committee, which in turn came under criticism from the same HL Committee in 1988-89 for its lack of vision and restricted membership. A subsequent review of forestry research in Scotland carried out by Mason in 1990 found a lack of overall Scottish strategy, poor coordination, and inadequate transfer of technology to the private sector (*SF* 46). Although there appears to have been an improvement in recent years – no doubt in response to the criticisms of the Lords Committee and of Mason – the Commission's record in this field overall must be considered disappointing.

Forestry policies: Among FC initiatives pride of place should no doubt be given to the Broadleaves in Britain review, described in the Annual Report for 1985-86 as 'one of the most important and difficult exercises we have undertaken in recent years'. But perversely in the grant scheme which resulted assistance was given only for pure broadleaf planting and not mixtures, which made it virtually inapplicable in Scotland – and entirely so in the uplands. The same was true of the assistance for the regeneration of native Scots pine (in which the 1971-72 House of Commons Select Committee had shown an interest): it remained totally inadequate until 1990. As early as 1959 Steven and Carlisle, in a masterly survey, had pointed out that a high proportion of the native pinewoods of Scotland was in FC hands, and had offered a simple prescription for their preservation and enhancement, inviting the FC and the NC to take the lead. This was not followed up, and the pinewoods continued in steady decline (Goodier and Bunce 1977, Bain 1987). Grants for the management of private plantings in general, which the private sector had always regarded as essential to good-quality forestry, were discontinued in 1973 without any demur by the Commission, and again not restored until 1990.

Most seriously of all, the FC presided over the infiltration of Scottish private forestry by investment interests, from the early 1960s onwards with apparent approval and encouragement – no doubt because it contributed to the fulfilment of forestry 'targets'. The result was a progressive lowering of standards of design over the succeeding three decades, with some evidence of planting for tax benefits alone – ie in places where trees were unlikely to yield a commercial crop. The legacy is an enormous area of blanket Sitka spruce in the Southern Uplands, matched by a similar extent in parts of the Highlands. They cordon off – both visually and in terms of access – a good deal of fine landscape, and can only be regarded as a blot on the FC's custodial escutcheon. It appears to have been this kind of forestry which prompted the recommendations of the House of Commons Agriculture Committee's Report of 1989-90, many of which were given effect shortly afterwards.

Forest distribution: Finally, it is necessary to consider the FC's performance regarding the distribution of forestry in Scotland and its interaction with other land uses. At first, of course, the Commission simply took land wherever it could get it – it was the poor relation, and for years it failed to reach its own targets for acquisition and planting. Its objective was to build up a strategic reserve, and in that context, as Ryle (1969) comments: 'What did it matter [whether planting took place on bare land or on existing woodland]?...The objective would be equally well attained, so far as end-production was concerned, whichever class of land was the more quickly put to efficient use'. The Scottish public was in favour of forest expansion, and fairly indifferent as to where it took place and how it looked.

By the Second World War the FC had so far refined its objectives as to propose concentration in huge blocks in certain forest regions, such as the Moray Firth and the Borders. This objective again came unstuck because of the difficulty of getting hold of large stretches of agricultural land – accentuated this time by the protective attitude of the Department of Agriculture for Scotland. The Commission was thus being driven further 'up the hill' and northwards and westwards.

When at last hill land became easier to acquire – both by the FC and the private sector – it is little wonder that the Commission simply gave thanks and encouraged a free-for-all. It became public policy in 1963 that planting should be restricted in England (by considerations of economic advantage and landscape improvement) and concentrated in upland Scotland and Wales. In 1965 the era of cost-consciousness began, driving the Commissioners ever further away from any kind of sensitive locational strategy.

By 1973, however, when the HC Select Committee gave its Report on Land Resource Use in Scotland, voices were being raised in protest against the totally unplanned nature of afforestation and the failure even to contemplate the integration of agriculture and forestry. The Committee made the revolutionary proposal that changes of use should be adjudicated, in the first instance, by countryside committees of local authorities. The proposal was rejected: but the Government decided to bring in local authorities, in a modest way, by way of requiring the FC to consult them on amenity aspects of grant aid applications.

This marked the beginning of effective consultation on afforestation (as against agricultural clearance), which has grown to the point where 'indicative forestry strategies' are now an accepted part of the scene. It has to be said, however, that the changes were brought in against FC opposition. The Commission – perhaps because of the history rehearsed above of perpetual struggle for land – never took on board the reasonableness of submitting its plans for public discussion. Its attitude was far removed from that expressed in Westoby's (1989) aphorism that 'forestry is...about people, and how trees can serve people'. At the global level, there was a tendency to cling to planting targets set by government without consultation, which were in no way reconciled with regional strategies (Mather 1991, Kanowski and Potter 1993). At the local level, FC stuck to the notion that regional advisory committees heavily weighted with vested interests, and with a conciliating rather than a deliberative role, were an appropriate mechanism for settling disputed afforestation proposals. Its response to the Government's recent Citizen's Charter initiative was to prepare a charter for forestry grant applicants, but not one for those affected by afforestation plans.

The truth seems to be that the FC over the years developed a fear of openness and devolved decision-taking which was inconsistent with its custodial role. The initially promised delegation of both administration and executive decision to national and regional organs failed to be delivered. Devolution of FC functions to Scotland and Wales in the late 1970s was resisted, though behind the scenes. Even in 1993, the grant schemes remained *ad hoc*, monolithic and inflexible (Kanowski and Potter 1993).

The overall judgment on the FC as custodian over the period with which this study is concerned must be an unfavourable one. There are of course some very positive features, but the negative ones outweigh them. Some of these are found in forestry authorities in other countries (Hummel and Hilmi 1988, Mather 1993a), so the explanation may be in part structural. This will be discussed in a later section.

Nature Conservancy Council

There is a problem in identifying the official organ of nature conservation in Britain over the past 40 years, because – unlike the FC – it has changed its name and character several times during that time. Since the focus is on the period following the 1972 Report of the HC Select Committee on Scottish Land Resource Use, it will be convenient to concentrate on the era of the NCC, starting in 1973. In any case, as regards the custodial function there has been substantial continuity throughout the 40 years.

Statutory functions: The Act of 1973 conferred two important custodial duties upon NCC: those of advising Ministers on the development and implementation of 'policies for or affecting nature conservation in Great Britain'; and, in general, of providing advice and disseminating information about nature conservation. These were supported by powers to undertake research in support of its own functions (more limited than under the old NC, which was responsible for conservation and control of nature); and to make grants for any purpose 'conducive to nature conservation or the understanding thereof' [wording broadened by the Wildlife and Countryside Act 1981].

On the consultative side, NCC was obliged to appoint committees for England, Wales and Scotland to advise it on the discharge of its functions in each country. This was less specific than Article 10 of the 1949 Royal Charter, since the latter required the appointment of a Scottish Committee which could have been given an executive as well as an advisory role.

Environmental responsibility: It is important to be reminded, at the start, of the background to the change from the original NC function of conservation and control. The Conservancy, as stated in *Nature Conservation in Great Britain*, had something of the character of a research council in ecology, with the full panoply of research responsibilities, and a promotional role thrown in. During the period that the NC was part of NERC (1965-73), it became evident that the range of responsibilities was too wide. The solution that was adopted in the 1973 Act was therefore not unreasonable, and freed NCC to carry out its promotional

tive action instead of providing specialist advice (T Hornsby, pers. com.).

These would appear on the surface to be matters of internal concern only, of little interest to the outside world since the quantum of scientific work was at least sufficient to support NCC's custodial responsibilities. But there were wider implications. The balance of effort was skewed, for example towards birds in deference to RSPB pressures (J Balfour, pers. com.). Peer review of projects was inadequate (W E S Mutch, M Usher, pers.comm.). Survey work was skimped. Thus there could be no guarantee that the massive scientific effort was fully in support of NCC's functions, as the 1973 Act required: some of it could even have been counter-productive. This gave point to Mutch's contention, at the controversial 119th meeting of Council (July 1989), that land management, policy and science went together and that the gains from devolving nature conservation to Scotland – even with a smaller science base – outweighed the losses.

Consultation: There is a certain parallelism with the FC, in that in the run-up to the creation of both GB agencies there was an emphasis not merely on effective consultative machinery at the Scottish level but also on the delegation of executive functions. Although this was not delivered in the founding legislation, the Scottish Committee enjoyed a measure of *de facto* autonomy during the life of the NC. The basis for this disappeared in the 1973 Act, and delegation was progressively withdrawn throughout the 1970s and 1980s. The issue came to a head in constitutional terms during the devolution debate from 1975 to 1979, and in practical terms during the flow country episode of 1986-88. By this time NCC was verging on the monolithic – somewhat like the FC, except that (from a Scottish point of view) it did not have the saving grace of a national headquarters located in Scotland. It is true that in 1989, under the shadow of dissolution, the NCC Council rediscovered the virtue of federalism. But the situation had become explosive, and the break-up of NCC was both the manifestation and the release of the tension that had built up.

Determined delegation of executive functions is an essential safety valve for a Great Britain agency. But the custodial role demands more than this. Local communities, and the individual public, must be convinced that the agency is acting on their behalf. In its publication *The First Ten Years* (1959) the NC acknowledged this, without being able to suggest effective means of making conservation a national cause (as had been done successfully in US). The growing dependence on SSSIs as the medium of conservation did not help, because it put the onus of site selection solely on scientific judgment, and required no public consultation whatsoever – not even notification to those directly affected. It was understandable that NCC lost touch with the public, and awoke to the need for consultation only when the 1981 Act made consultation statutory. Even then, so far as the wider public was concerned, *Nature Conservation in Great Britain* (1984) said nothing about consultation but only about education and persuasion – mainly through the client group. Even the painful experience of SSSI declaration on Islay in 1986-87 did not persuade the Council that, where an entire community was affected, there had to be thorough and genuine negotiation with the public. By this time a considerable gulf had opened up between NCC's Scottish Committee and the Council, so that the Council failed even to consult the Committee.

The judgment on NCC's showing in regard to consultation and democratic involvement – as indeed on most aspects of its custodial role – must therefore be negative. It can be argued that in Scotland, by virtue of the high proportion (10.5 per cent) of land designated NNR or SSSI, NCC effectively discharged a custodial responsibility through the use of its executive powers. This argument has some force: but the fact remains that, in the regions where designations are most widespread, NCC failed in an essential part of the custodial role, namely to convince the inhabitants that designation, and even more the listing of potentially damaging operations, were meaningful and worthwhile.

Countryside Commission for Scotland

Statutory functions: To a greater degree than the other two agencies under consideration, CCS had the custodial function put at the head of its agenda. Section 3(a) of the Countryside (Scotland) Act 1967 required the Commission to keep under review the provision of facilities for enjoyment of the countryside, the conservation and enhancement of its natural beauty, and the need to secure access to it for informal recreation – all in the context of a 'due regard...for the balanced economic and social development of the countryside' :Section 1(2). Similarly the need to consult with elected and other bodies was given prominence, as well as the advisory function *vis-à-vis* government: Section 3(e). The Commission's executive role, in contrast, was somewhat constrained.

Environmental responsibility

A degree of ambivalence was built in to the CCS remit by virtue of the responsibility for improved facilities and access to the countryside, along with a duty to conserve and enhance its natural beauty. These had not been seen as in conflict in the 1940s, but experience in the English and Welsh National Parks in the intervening period had shown that there was no easy reconciliation (Blunden and Curry 1990). The succeeding paragraphs will look first at CCS' discharge of the developmental side of its review function, then at the conservation side, and finally at its efforts at reconciling the two.

Developmental: This is concerned with both facilities and access. For the most part the facilities that CCS had under review were the kinds of things which it enabled, or in exceptional cases provided, as part of its executive role. These were fairly non-controversial items like roadside facilities, visitor centres, youth hostels and country parks. On the overall provision CCS was probably entitled to express a good measure of satisfaction (1991-92 Annual Report). There were other facilities like skiing and beach provision in which CCS, on the whole, declined to become directly involved; it was probably right to do so. But there was a wider aspect to this, namely the planning of recreational provision, on which CCS took an early initiative through its promotion of Scottish Tourism and Recreation Planning Studies (STARPS) from about 1974 onwards. This made slow progress with local authorities, perhaps because it was over-technical and fussy. It was wound up in 1981, by which time it had influenced some regional strategies but had failed to achieve anything like national coverage.

The Commission took little part in the planning of major skiing provision, leaving the initiative with SDD and the Highland Regional Council. It made an ineffective showing at the public inquiry in 1981 into the extension of facilities at Cairngorm. Its performance at the second inquiry in 1988-89 was similarly uncertain.

FC were mentioned in Annual Reports from time to time, but mainly on casework. Agriculture was discussed only in a Great Britain context. In the FC, the same sectoral approach prevailed. It was not until 1978 that talks opened with DAFS and other interests on the integration of forestry and farming. In the 1980s the agencies started to take an interest in one another and in agriculture, but usually on a basis of confrontation rather than cooperation. And there was inadequate recognition on the part of the GB agencies of the opportunities for fruitful interaction at the Scottish level. The same of course was true of the Scottish Office, which must bear at least an equal share of the blame.

An alternative scenario

At this point it may be helpful to speculate a little, and to ask the question: In what ways might things be different today if there had been the looked-for dialogue and cooperative action following the 1972 Report? *What if...?* games are always treacherous, especially if several variables come into play at the same time (Muller 1973; Kahn et al. 1977). One must beware of errors like projecting backwards from the present day attitudes and climates of opinion that scarcely found expression twenty years ago – such as, in this context, the current acceptance of sustainable use and the espousal by government of such sentiments as 'We see even stronger arguments against wasting...this country's natural resources and bequeathing a burden of environmental debts tomorrow' (UK Government 1990). It is equally dangerous to ignore or underrate the significance of external forces or events quite outwith the power of the actors in the scenario to control or even influence, such as Britain's successful application for EC membership in 1973. The presence of factors like these means that the assumptions made in any speculation about outcomes must be very conservative – as must be the findings themselves.

Without question the 'Rural' section of the 1972 Report was correct in two respects. The first was in demarcating an important field of Scottish land use in which the interests of the four 'heavyweight' institutions (DAFS, the FC, CCS and NC/NCC) intersected, namely the uplands. This did not constitute by any means the whole of the field of interest of any one of the institutions, but it was still highly significant. It remains so today. Second, the Report pinpointed certain priorities for the institutions in terms of survey, research, policy development, and coordinated experiment and action: these too are still relevant today (Usher and Thompson 1988, Mather 1992, Mutch 1992, Coppock 1994).

The modest scenario based on the above is that, if any of the agencies had taken up the challenge presented by the Select Committee (and generally endorsed by government), then – even in the face of DAFS resistance or torpor – results could have followed, especially in the uplands. Survey and scientific research could have been better directed and further advanced. Afforestation would almost certainly have been more environmentally friendly, and multiple use would have been a practical possibility much earlier. The deer research carried out on Rum over many years under NCC auspices might have been put to more practical use in showing how the red deer population could be kept under better control. Advances could have been made in sheep management on heather moor and rough grazing generally. The Department of Agriculture might even have been persuaded not to spearhead the EC sheepmeat regime, which has not been in the long-term interests of the Scottish uplands (Mowle and Bell 1988).

Perhaps most valuable of all, there might be the beginnings of an understanding of the way in which the decisions of individual land users in the uplands are arrived at – to parallel the multi-disciplinary work of Munton et al. on the lowlands (1987 onwards). It is unlikely that, even with all these desirable outcomes, the Scottish uplands would look much different from what they do now, but a start would have been made on enhancing their condition, rather than merely limiting damage.

The trouble with this hypothesis – tentative though it is – is that it is still predicated on a highly debatable premise: that one or other of the agencies could at the critical period (the early 1970s) have taken the kind of initiative that would have been necessary. Clearly none of them actually did take up the challenge. The question then is: Were they capable of doing so, and prevented merely by force of circumstances, or by not happening to have the right kind of personalities at the helm? Or were they structurally incapable of doing so?

This brings us back full circle to the character of the agencies as institutions. The contention of this study is that the agencies were incapable in principle of acting in a consistently cooperative mode in relation to the custodial aspects of Scottish land use problems – of which the uplands is a clear example.

NOTES

1. 'Stewardship' is however rejected by the deep ecologists. 'The arrogance of stewardship consists in the idea of superiority which underlies the thought that we exist to watch over nature like a highly respected middleman between the Creator and the creation' (Naess 1989, p187).

2. A new device for reinforcing accountability (not of course limited to agencies) is represented by the Government's Citizen's Charter. This requires organisations to offer the public certain standards of service, and also appropriate remedies if the standards are not met. This amounts to transferring measures of output efficiency from the internal management domain to the public domain. Unfortunately, because it touches only efficiency and not effectiveness, which is not easily quantified, the 'charter' approach has little relevance to the work of land use agencies.

3. The World Charter for Nature was ratified in October 1982 by resolution 37/7 of the UN General Assembly. It includes the following principles:

> Every form of life is unique, warranting respect regardless of its worth to man, and to accord other organisms such recognition, man must be guided by a moral code of action.

> Nature shall be respected and its essential processes shall not be impaired.

The UN resolution attracted support from the great majority of member states, including UK (presumably because the terms of the Charter were considered to be quite unenforceable). The US abstained.

4. It is not easy to summarise the findings of Usher and Thompson (U & T) or of Dargie and Briggs (D & B), but what follows is a statement of the main points they make with regard to the uplands. There is said to be clear evidence of intensification in sheep husbandry, with a corresponding decline in cattle: but information on the environmental impact is lacking (D & B *pp* 17-18). Mowle and Bell (U & T *p* 177) assert that the wildlife and landscape of the uplands have suffered, and continue to suffer, serious losses as an accidental result of rural subsidy policies; and that conservationists agree on what the ecological requirements of policy are (eg a halt to the losses of semi-natural vegetation)

Third, professionals in senior positions find it difficult to accept being overruled by an administrative superior or even a governing board, believing that their professional integrity is being infringed. (Again, this was a problem for NCC in its final years.)

All these are real dangers, and they have had distorting effects on the discharge of the three agencies' functions in Scotland. But the basic problem about specialism in an agency's remit is that it makes it too single-minded in its pursuit of its own objectives and intolerant both of the objectives of other agencies and of the viewpoint of the general public. This lies behind most of the tragic failures in cooperation and the alienation of Scottish sympathies for NCC. It is inevitable, too, that a limited-purpose agency will have a constant tendency to put disproportionate effort into its specialised executive functions at the expense of its more generalised custodial role. This has been apparent throughout the history of FC, in which the overriding objective until the late 1980s was the fulfilment of planting or financial targets.[1] In the case of NC/NCC the preoccupation was with designated sites as against the wider countryside. With CCS, always less specialised, this tendency was not so marked, but as we have seen the Commission virtually lost sight of general land use for nearly a decade.

The creation of SNH as an amalgam of the nature conservation and countryside agencies is, among other things, a deliberate attempt to dilute the risk of over-specialisation. Similarly, the steps taken to constitute the Forestry Authority as something nearer an entity in its own right are no doubt intended partly to place the specialist Forest Enterprise under a measure of supervision. This separation parallels the trend in most European countries (Hummel and Hilmi 1989). Although it remains the case that countries throughout the world have found it necessary to set up a specialist forest enterprise, most of them are under the jurisdiction of a Ministry responsible for another function, usually agriculture. Denmark has a combined Nature and Forest Service.

Appointed status: Members of Great Britain agencies are invariably appointed rather than elected. Some have castigated this feature as a scandalous exercise of Ministerial patronage, but Pliatzky (1980) saw it rather as 'an onerous responsibility for securing scarce talent and ability'. Either way, there is the minimum of guidance, in the statutes governing each of the three agencies under review, as to the kinds of people to be appointed to the controlling board of the agency; nor is there any Parliamentary or other approval (on the lines of the US Senate's 'advice and consent') over the individuals appointed.

It is not surprising that in the literature surrounding the three agencies there is a fair volume of complaint over the Ministers' choice of Commissioners or Council members. Allegations of bias in NCC appointments have already been mentioned. In 1988 the Scottish Countryside Activities Council analysed the sources of nominations for appointment to CCS and concluded that, while the Commission itself as well as local authority, farming/landowning and Departmental (including FC) interests were generally successful in getting their nominees appointed, the voluntary recreation and amenity sector might as well never have submitted any names (R Aitken pers. com.).

It is not the intention here to comment on the way in which patronage has been exercised over the years, or on the balance in the membership of the three agencies.[2] The approach in this study is institutional: while the effects of imbalance in the membership from time to time are not discounted, the structural factors are regarded as more significant. In that context the question to be addressed is: what consequences necessarily arise from the fact that the governing boards of the agencies are appointed, and are neither democratically elected nor readily called to account to the public?

There is of course no magic in democracy as a means of ensuring the successful working of an organisation. As Churchill is reputed to have said, as a system of government it has little to commend it except in comparison with every other system that has been tried. And it is important not to exaggerate the democratic sensitivity of alternatives to appointed boards (Johnson 1982). But it remains true that an agency is very far removed from scrutiny by or answerability to the general public. It tends to see its lines of responsibility in terms merely of its sponsor department and its client group.

So long as an agency is engaged in what is viewed as a technocratic exercise, such as identifying patches of interesting habitat or creating plantations in remote places, there is no problem. Sooner or later, however, the custodial aspect comes to the fore, and it is then that agencies tend to be caught out. They may be too late in realising that their concerns have deviated widely from those of the population as a whole, or of local communities. The Forestry Commission found this, for example, in relation to afforestation in Dumfries and Galloway, NCC to SSSIs in Islay and Orkney, and CCS to the Mountain Areas exercise. What is more, the agencies may be unable to find the way back. It is all very well to seek to mend fences by intensive public relations, but what is needed is to take the public into confidence in drawing up the agenda in the first place. And that the three land use agencies never learned, although CCS did try hard at the beginning. It looks as though their lack of democratic accountability was a fatal obstacle to their doing so.

GB orientation: The fact that the FC and the NC were given remits covering the whole of Great Britain was no accident, and it was acceded to by Scottish interests. This happened because the remits were seen as basically technocratic and executive in character, and not in any important sense custodial. All the same, built-in safeguards were demanded in respect of Scottish concerns – and these were not merely political and nationalistic but had regard also to administrative, geographical and ecological factors. What was principally insisted upon in the agency was a strong Scottish presence, in terms of delegated functions and decentralised administration.

In the case of the NC, both sides of this condition were fairly well met at first, with delegated functions and a strong Scottish headquarters. Later, however – partly by accident and partly by deliberate policy – NCC delegation was weakened and the administration was brought under ever tighter central control, right up to the end of the Council's life. With the FC there was administrative devolution, of a diminishing kind, until 1965, when the Directorates for the three countries were abolished following the Murrie report, at which time the national committees were also declared redundant.

It is reported that, when the decision was taken in 1971 to transfer the FC national headquarters to Edinburgh, the moving spirit was the then Permanent Secretary at the Scottish Office, Sir Douglas Haddow; and that he had opted for the FC after having been offered the choice of the FC or NC/NCC, but not both (J Balfour, pers.com.). If this is correct, then from a Scottish point of view Haddow may be considered to have made the wrong choice. The reason is that, especially since 1965, the FC had become a thoroughly integrated Great Britain 'monolith', in which staff structures and so on had been perfectly unified and there were no distinctive national elements left. All that happened, therefore, was that a Great Britain headquarters, with a consistently Great Britain viewpoint, operated from Corstorphine Road instead of from Savile Row. With the NC/NCC there was far less complete integration of personnel, and each 'country' headquarters retained a measure of distinctiveness. In 1984/85 NCC became strongly centralised at Peterborough, which also became the headquarters for England. From then on especially the English perspective on nature conservation was dominant, with its emphasis on species protection, designated areas, preservation of wetlands and so on. Had NCC headquarters moved to Edinburgh instead of Peterborough – so it can be argued – the perspective would have been different, and the Scottish viewpoint on land use could have been more effectively articulated.

Whatever the differences between the FC and NCC, it can hardly be disputed that in both the distinctive Scottish voice was suppressed, Scotland being viewed as a resource for Great Britain (or England) rather than as an entity in its own right. This probably played a part in the resistance which both agencies offered to the devolution of their functions to Scotland in the 1970s. Forestry policy in Scotland has long been, and remains, different from forestry policy in England – but not so much because of objective differences or Scottish preferences as because it has been thought possible to get away with less attention to amenity in Scotland. Nature conservation has been deemed pre-eminent in parts of Scotland, overriding the interests of local communities, because they are the last refuges in Great Britain of certain species or certain kinds of natural habitat (see eg NCC 1986-87 Annual Report; *Birds, Bogs and Forestry* [1987]). In either case, the agency has fallen down on its custodial responsibilities, which require it to be sensitive to its resource in its local as well as its national context.

It would be over-simplistic to see the constitutional changes of the 1990s as a straightforward judgment on the handling by the Great Britain agencies of their regional custodial duties. However, the Government announcement of the break-up of NCC did refer to 'inefficiency and insensitivity'; and the FC reorganisation, which reconstituted the Forestry Authority in three separate national offices, was aimed at 'improving the effectiveness of the Authority'.[3] It is hardly possible to use CCS as a control in this context, because it was itself totally reorganised at the same time. Nevertheless, as an agency operating wholly within Scotland, it improved its custodial performance throughout the 1980s, and it attracted no Government criticism in connection with the plans for reform.

Summing-up

It has been asserted here that the three agencies fell short of a satisfactory performance chiefly for structural reasons. This may appear to beg the question: What of the other possible reasons? How can one be certain that factors such as the personalities in charge of the agencies, the degree of interference or constraint applied by the sponsor Departments, or the tide of affairs or of public opinion during formative periods of the agencies' histories, were not equally or more critical?

It is very difficult to disprove a negative, but the following considerations may be relevant:

Personalities – whether at Board member or chief officer level – may have a significant influence on the policies and performance of an agency. The contributions made by several individuals, notably Robinson, Nicholson and Ratcliffe, have been referred to in the course of this investigation.

However, it is perhaps not a coincidence that the influence of each of these characters was on the side of professionalism. In other words, their strength of character was exerted in such a way as to entrench the agencies in the over-specialist path on which they were already launched. There appears to have been no case in which a forceful individual stood in the breach against harmful structural tendencies to which an agency was subject, and thus significantly changed the course of its history.

The other side of the coin is the potential effect of weak personalities, or of individuals only weakly committed to the objectives of the agency. This study has not explored the make-up of the governing boards of the agencies or the extent of their individual or corporate contribution. It is likely that at any particular time a governing board would contain its share of 'passengers', and this of course is a matter for regret. But it is unlikely that such people would exercise a marked drag on the discharge of the agency's custodial functions.

The influence of sponsor Departments has been noted previously at various points – usually in a restrictive mode. What was at issue, almost invariably, was the exercise of the agency's executive function, not of its custodial role. Admittedly, the Government's response in 1973 to the HC Select Committee Report was on the whole negative and potentially disheartening to a land use agency that was alive to its custodial responsibilities. But there is no evidence that any of the three agencies was disheartened by it. It can also be argued that in the late 1970s, when CCS restated its concern over the control of development in scenic areas, the Department responded with half-measures. While this is true, it is also the case that CCS professed itself perfectly satisfied with the half-measures. Generally speaking, governments exercise less pressure on agencies than some commentators believe. In the words of Munton et al. (1992): '...the institutional structure of Government is complex and fragmented...an endemically fractured bureaucracy exhibiting overlapping functions, internal disagreements over policy, and different links with producer and consumer interests'. It is a scenario in which an agency can very often do what it likes, subject only to budgetary constraints.[4]

The tide of affairs: It would certainly be unjust to criticise an agency for failing to take up a custodial posture, at a given point in time, which was not politically feasible until much later. Without wishing to labour the point, however, it has to be said that from the early 1970s onwards any or all of the agencies could have swum with the tide of opinion, articulated by the HC Select Committee's Report, in favour of a coherent strategy for land use in Scotland. In that way many desirable initiatives which are only now beginning to get off the ground might have been advanced by a decade or more. The agencies failed to respond to the challenge, not through the pressure of external events, but mainly because of structural considerations.

Into the future

This study is not concerned with the destiny of SNH or of the Forestry Commission. It is a look back and not a look forward. All the same, if it is correct to say that the agencies under review fell short (mainly for the reasons summarised on page 209), it may be pertinent to consider how far these structural deficiencies have now been addressed. The answer must be – only very partially. The FC and SNH still have appointed status, and limited-purpose remits; the FC still has a Great Britain orientation.

Any solution which fully met these criticisms would, it seems to the author, have to proceed by absorbing the functions of the agencies into either central government (ie the Scottish Office) or local government. Whichever route was taken, there would be new problems, but they would not be as intractable as those which had been overcome.

The local authority option is not quite as far-fetched as it might seem. Countryside functions were considered a candidate for assignation to Scottish local government, even before the 1975 reorganisation: and the 1972 HC Land Resource Use Report saw a significant role for multi-purpose countryside committees of local authorities. Local government plays a significant part in nature conservation in Germany, France and Spain (Cloke 1988, Dickinson 1991), and in forestry in Germany, Austria, Switzerland and Scandinavia (Hummel and Hilmi 1989). However, it has to be conceded that the constitutional position of local authorities in all these countries allows much more flexibility in the discharge of functions than occurs in UK.

The option of assigning the various agency functions to a Department of Rural Affairs within the Scottish Office was commended to the HC Select Committee by Mutch (1972 51-xviii) but rejected on the ground that this would mean 'settling all major questions of land use behind closed doors'. The Committee saw separateness of the different interests 'up to a point as a necessary safeguard for the general interest': the four heavyweights (DAFS and the three agencies) should therefore continue to flourish 'in constructive tension' under the fairly loose aegis of a Land Use Council.

Even if one accepts the justice of the Select Committee's critique of Mutch's proposal, it is still possible to envisage a halfway house based upon the proposal. This would use as a model (though by no means as a pattern) the 'agency' described in *Improving Management in Government: The Next Steps* (1988).

(For the purpose of the next few paragraphs this kind of institution will be called an Agency. It is defined as being 'part of government' but is given considerable freedom within policy and resources guidelines to carry out tasks which are most commonly executive though they can be advisory or custodial. Historic Scotland and the Agricultural Scientific Services are examples of such Agencies within the Scottish Office at present.)

On this scenario most of SOAFD would become an Agency (or perhaps a series of Agencies), as would each of the existing institutions SNH and the Scottish end of the Forestry Authority and Forest Enterprise, shorn of board members and Commissioners. Other self-standing agencies like RDC and the Macaulay Institute (MLURI) might be brought within the Agency net. These would all form part of a Rural Affairs Department headed by a junior Minister, with a broad policy and supervisory role.

Hays S P (1987). *Beauty, health and permanence: environmental politics in the United States 1955-1985.* Cambridge University Press.

Heinen J T and Low R S (1992). 'Human behavioural ecology and environmental conservation'. *Environmental Conservation* 19 2, pp 105-116.

Hogwood B (1979). *The tartan fringe: quangos and other assorted animals in Scotland.* University of Strathclyde, Glasgow.

Hogwood B (1982). 'Quasi-government in Scotland: Scottish forms within a British setting', in: Barker A (ed.) *Quangos in Britain*, Macmillan, Basingstoke, Hants., pp 69-87.

Holland P (1979). *Quango quango quango.* Adam Smith Institute, London.

Holmes G (1979). 'An introduction to forestry in upland Britain', in: Ford E D, Malcolm D C & Atterson J (eds.) *The ecology of even-aged forestry plantations*, ITE, Cambridge :7-19.

Hood C C (1982). 'Governmental bodies and government growth', in: Barker A (ed.), *Quangos in Britain*, Macmillan, Basingstoke, Hants, pp 44-68.

Hood C C (1988). 'PGOs in the United Kingdom', in: Hood C C & Schuppert G F (eds.) (1988) pp75-93.

Hood C C and Dunsire A (1981). *Bureaumetrics.* Gower, Farnborough, Hants.

Hood C C and Schuppert G F (eds.)(1988). *Delivering public services in Western Europe: sharing Western European experience of para-government organisations.* Sage, London.

Hummel F C and Hilmi H A (1989). *Forestry policies in Europe: an analysis.* FAO Forestry Paper 92, Rome.

James N D G (1981). *A history of English forestry.* Blackwell, Oxford.

Johnson L E (1991). *A morally deep world.* Cambridge University Press.

Johnson N (1982). 'Accountability, control and complexity: moving beyond Ministerial responsibility' in: Barker A (ed.), *Quangos in Britain*, Macmillan, Basingstoke, Hants., pp 206-218.

Kahn H, Brown W and Martel L (1977). *The next 200 years: a scenario for America and the world.* Associated Business Programmes, London.

Kanowski P J and Potter S M (1993). 'Making British forest policy work'. *Forestry* 66 3, pp 233-247.

Keating M (1981). *The Scottish Office in the United Kingdom policy network.* University of Strathclyde, Glasgow.

Kennedy J J (1985). 'Concerning forest management as providing for current and future social value'. *Forest Ecology and Management* 13, pp 121-132.

Lindley F (1935). *Lord Lovat [1871-1933]: a biography.* Hutchinson, London.

Lipset M (ed.) (1969). *Politics and the social sciences.* Oxford University Press, New York.

Long A P (1953). in: *Forestry* XXVI, pp 1-3.

Lowe P (1983). 'Values and institutions in the history of British nature conservation', in Warren A & Goldsmith F B (eds.) *Conservation in perspective.* Wiley, Chichester, pp 329-352.

Lowe P and Goyder J (1983). *Environmental groups in politics.* Allen and Unwin, London.

Lowe P, Cox G, O'Riordan T and Winter M (1986). *Countryside conflicts: the politics of farming, forestry and conservation.* Gower/Temple Smith, Aldershot, Hants.

Lowe P, Ward N and Munton R J C (1992). 'Social analysis of land use change: the role of the farmer', in: Whitby M C (ed.), *Land use changes: the causes and consequences* (ITE Symposium No 27). HMSO London, pp 42-51.

Mackay D G (1990). 'Rural land use in Scotland: a review of the 1980s'. *Scottish Geographical Magazine* 106, pp 12-19.

Malcolm D C (1991). 'Afforestation in Britain - a commentary'. *Scottish Forestry* 45 4, pp 267-273.

Manion T and Flowerdew R (1982). 'Institutional approaches in geography', in: Flowerdew R (ed.) *Institutions and geographical patterns,* Croom Helm, London, pp 1-50.

Marren P (1993).'The siege of the NCC', in: Warren A & Goldsmith F B (eds.) *Conservation in progress.* Wiley, Chichester, pp 283-299.

Mason C (1989). *Pining for profit.* Adam Smith Institute, London.

Mather A S (1986). *Land use.* Longman, London.

Mather A S (1991a). 'Pressures on British forest policy: prologue to the post-industrial forest', in: *Area* 23 3, pp 245-253.

Mather A S (1991b). 'The changing role of planning in rural land use: the example of afforestation in Scotland'. *Journal of Rural Studies* 7 3, pp 299-309.

Mather A S (1992).'Land use, physical sustainability and conservation in Highland Scotland'. *Land Use Policy* April 1992, pp 99-110.

Mather A S (ed.) (1993). *Afforestation: policies, planning and progress.* Belhaven, London.

Mather A S and Thomson K J (1993). *The effects of forestry planting on agricultural structure.* University of Aberdeen report for SOAFD, unpublished.

Mattingly A (1992).'An environmentalist's view', in: *New forests for the 21st century: the scale, nature and location of forestry expansion in Britain* (FC conference 26-27.3.92). FC, unpublished.

McNicoll I, McGregor P and Mutch W (1991). 'Development of the British wood processing industries'. Paper No 5 in *Forestry expansion: a study of technical, economic and ecological factors.* FC, Edinburgh.

McVean D N and Ratcliffe D A (1962). *Plant communities of the Scottish Highlands: a study of Scottish mountain, moorland and forest vegetation.* HMSO, London.

McVean D N and Lockie J D (1969). *Ecology and land use in upland Scotland.* Edinburgh University Press.

Miles J (1987). 'The effects of man on upland vegetation', in: Bell M & Bunce R G H (eds.) *Agriculture and conservation in the hills and uplands* (ITE Symposium No 23), ITE, Grange-over-Sands, Cumbria, pp 7-18.

Miller H G (1991). 'British forestry in 1990'. Paper No 1 in *Forestry expansion: a study of technical, economic and ecological factors.* FC, Edinburgh.

Moore N W (1987). *The bird of time: the science and politics of nature conservation.* Cambridge University Press.

Mowle A and Bell M (1988). 'Rural policy factors in land use change', in: M B Usher M B & Thomson D B A (eds.) *Ecological change in the uplands*, Blackwell, Oxford, pp 165-182.

Muller H J (1973). 'Possible advances of the next hundred years: a biologist's view', in: Carlson E A (ed.) *Man's future birthright: essays on science and humanity by H J Muller*, State University of New York Press, Albany, pp3-7.

Munton R, Marsden T and Eldon J (1987). *Occupancy change and the farmed landscape.* Report to CCEW, Cheltenham, unpublished.

Munton R and Marsden T (1991). 'Occupancy changes and the farmed landscape: an analysis of farm level trends 1970-1985'. *Environment and Planning A* 23, pp 499-510.

Munton R, Lowe P and Marsden T (1992). 'The social, economic and political context', in: Whitby M C (ed.) *Land use change: the causes and consequences* (ITE Symposium No 27). HMSO, London, pp 15-27.

Mutch W E S (1992). 'Priorities for research in land use change', in Whitby M C (ed.) *Land use change: the causes and consequences* (ITE Symposium No 27). HMSO, London, pp 187-190.

Naess A (1984). 'A defence of the deep ecology movement'. *Environmental Ethics* 6, pp 265-270.

Naess A (1989). *Ecology, community and lifestyle.* Cambridge University Press.

NCGB (1984). *Nature conservation in Great Britain.* NCC, Peterborough.

Newbould P (1958). in: *The biological productivity of Britain, Institute of Biology* (Symposium No 7), p112.

Newby H (1985). *Green and pleasant land.* Wildwood, Hounslow, Middlesex.

Nicholson E M (1987). *The new environmental age.* Cambridge University Press.

O'Riordan T (1982). 'Institutions affecting environmental policy', in: Flowerdew R (ed.) *Institutions and geographical patterns,* Croom Helm, London, pp 103-139.

O'Riordan T (1983). *Environmentalism.* Pion, London.

O'Riordan T and Turner R K (eds.) (1983). *An annotated reader in environmental planning and management.* Pergamon, Oxford.

Paterson D (1992). *The West Highland Way.* Canongate, Edinburgh.

Pearce D W, Markandya A and Barbier E B (1989). *Blueprint for a green economy: a report.* Earthscan, London.

Peterken G F (1993). *Woodland conservation and management* (2nd edition). Chapman and Hall, London.

Pliatzky L (1980). *Report on non-departmental public bodies.* Cmnd 7797, HMSO.

Poore M E D (1987). 'Changing attitudes in nature conservation: the Nature Conservancy and

Nature Conservancy Council'. *Biological Journal of the Linnean Society* 32, pp 179-187.

Post-war forest policy (1943). Report by HM Forestry Commissioners. Cmd 6447, HMSO, London.

Pye-Smith C and Hall C (eds.) (1987). *The countryside we want: a manifesto for the year 2000.* Green Books, Bideford, Devon.

Ramsay P (1993). 'Land-owners and conservation', in: Warren A & Goldsmith F B (eds.) *Conservation in progress.* Wiley, Chichester, pp 255-269.

Reed M G and Slaymaker O (1993). 'Ethics and sustainability: a preliminary perspective'. *Environment and Planning A* 25, pp 723-739.

Rose C and Pye-Smith C (1984). *Crisis and conservation: conflict in the British countryside.* Penguin, Harmondsworth, Middlesex.

RSPB (1984). *Hill farming and birds: a survival plan.* RSPB, Sandy, Bedfordshire.

Ryle G (1969). *Forest Service: the first forty-five years of the Forestry Commission of Great Britain.* David and Charles, Newton Abbot, Devon.

Sayer A (1984). *Method in social science: a realist approach.* Hutchinson, London.

Schuppert G F (1988). 'PGOs in the Federal Republic of Germany', in: C C Hood C C & G F Schuppert (eds.) (1988), pp134-150.

Scott W G (1967). *Organizational theory: a behavioral analysis for management.* R D Irwin Inc, Illinois.

Scottish Council (Development and Industry) (1961). *Natural resources in Scotland* (symposium at Royal Society of Edinburgh). S C (D & I), Edinburgh.

Scottish Office (1981). Letter from Earl of Mansfield to Rt Hon Lord Ross dated 29.5.81.

Scottish Office (1991). *Factsheet 19: Scotland: land use and physical features.* Scottish Office Information Directorate, Edinburgh.

Sheail J (1976). *Nature in trust: the history of nature conservation in Britain.* Blackie, Edinburgh.

Sheail J (1981). *Rural conservation in inter-war Britain.* Clarendon Press, Oxford.

Sheail J (1984). 'Nature reserves, national parks and post-war reconstruction in Britain'. *Environmental Conservation* 11 No 1, pp 29-34.

Sheail J (1992). *The Natural Environment Research Council: a history.* NERC, Swindon.

Simon H A (1957). *Administrative behavior* (2nd edn.), Macmillan, New York.

Simmons I G (1981). *The ecology of natural resources* (2nd edn.). Edward Arnold, London.

Smout T C (1990). 'The Highlands and the roots of green consciousness, 1750-1990'. *Proceedings of the British Academy* 76, pp 237-263.

SNH (1992). *Enjoying the outdoors: a consultation paper on access to the countryside for enjoyment and understanding.* SNH, Edinburgh.

Stamp L D (1969). *Nature conservation in Britain.* Collins, London.

Stephenson T (1989). *Forbidden land: the struggle for access to mountain and moorland.* Manchester University Press.

Steven H M and Carlisle A (1959). *The native pinewoods of Scotland.* Oliver and Boyd, Edinburgh.

Stewart P J (1987). *Growing against the grain: United Kingdom forestry policy.* Council for the Protection of Rural England, London.

Stone C D (1972). 'Should trees have standing?: toward legal rights for natural objects'. *S California Law Review* 45 2, pp 450-501.

Symon J A (1959). *Scottish farming past and present.* Oliver and Boyd, Edinburgh.

Tompkins S C (1986). *The theft of the hills: afforestation in Scotland.* Ramblers Association, London.

Tompkins S C (1989). *Forestry in crisis.* Christopher Helm, London.

Tracy M (1989). *Government and agriculture in western Europe 1880-1988* (3rd edn.). Harvester Wheatsheaf, New York.

Turner R K, Pearce D W and Bateman I (1994). *Environmental economics: an elementary introduction.* Harvester Wheatsheaf, London.

UK Government (1990). *This common inheritance.* Cm 1200, HMSO, London.

Usher M B (1986). *Wildlife conservation evaluation.* Chapman and Hall, London.

Usher M B and Thompson D B A (eds.) (1988). *Ecological change in the uplands.* Blackwell, Oxford.

Warren L (1991). 'Conservation - a secondary environmental consideration', in: Churchill R,

Warren L, & Gibson J (eds.) *Law, policy and the environment*, Blackwell, Oxford, pp 64-80.

Westoby J C (1989). *The purpose of forests*. Blackwell, Oxford.

Wigan M (1991). *The Scottish highland estate*. Swan Hill Press, Shrewsbury, Shropshire.

Wilding R (1982). 'A triangular affair: quangos, Ministers and MPs', in: Barker A (ed.) *Quangos in Britain*. Macmillan, Basingstoke, Hants., pp 34-43.

Williams A and Anderson R (1975). *Efficiency in the social services*. Blackwell, Oxford.

Wonders W C (1990). 'Forestry villages in the Scottish Highlands'. *Scottish Geographical Magazine* 106, pp 156-166.

Wood R F (1974). *Fifty years of forestry research (1919-1969)*. HMSO, London.

Woodruffe B J (1989). 'Rural land use planning in West Germany', in: Cloke P J (ed.) *Rural land use in developed nations*. Unwin Hyman, London, pp 104-129.

Wright P (1992). 'The disenchanted forest'. *Weekend Guardian* 7.11.92, pp 6-9, 52.

Young O R (1982). *Resource regimes: natural resources and social institutions*. University of California Press, Berkeley.